MONEY MAGNET

Steve McKnight's

MONEY MAGNET

HOW TO ATTRACT AND KEEP A FORTUNE THAT COUNTS

WILEY

First published in 2023 by John Wiley & Sons Australia, Ltd

Level 1, 155 Cremorne St, Richmond Vic 3121

Typeset in Adobe Garamond Pro 12/15pt

ISBN: 978-0-730-38380-2

NATIONAL LIBRARY OF AUSTRALIA

A catalogue record for this book is available from the National Library of Australia

Cover design by Steve McKnight and Wiley
Cover and internal page image: Magnets: © ilyast/Getty Images
Cover image: Gold Foil: © janniwet/Shutterstock
P276: Army man image: © Morrowind/Shutterstock

Disclaimer

The material in this publication is of the nature of general comment only, and does not represent professional advice. It is not intended to provide specific guidance for particular circumstances and it should not be relied on as the basis for any decision to take action or not take action on any matter which it covers. Readers should obtain professional advice where appropriate, before making any such decision. To the maximum extent permitted by law, the author and publisher disclaim all responsibility and liability to any person, arising directly or indirectly from any person taking or not taking action based on the information in this publication.

This book contains factual information for educational purposes only. Nothing in this book constitutes the provision of financial product advice and no statements made in this book are intended to imply a recommendation or opinion about a financial product.

CONTENTS

ACKNOWLEDGEMENTS

Thank you to everyone who played a part in making *Money Magnet* happen.

In particular, thanks to:

- My book buddy team: Sharon & Oliver, Shehan & Lisa, Kat & AJ, Benny, Ralph and the team at Wiley, especially Lucy and Chris, who went on the journey with me on this one;
- Jules, Cassie & Alyssa — for their unwavering support and for making me feel significant; and
- My Lord and Saviour Jesus Christ — from whom I hope to hear the words 'Well done, good and faithful servant'.

Faith

I drifted off the faith path in my adolescent years before returning to following Jesus as an adult after I became financially rich, but felt spiritually poor.

While that's a story for chapter 24, my Christian faith adds an important context for the way I think and act around money and you'll note I make references to it and the Bible from time to time. While I do this unashamedly, I also respectfully acknowledge other beliefs, faiths and religions.

Royalties

One hundred per cent of the royalties received from this book will be applied to supporting environmental revegetation endeavours, including my carbon sequestration project at Carriage Range in north-east Victoria where 300 000 trees have been planted to establish a new permanent native forest. To find out more please visit: **www.TreeChange.com**.

Steveisms

You'll note that each chapter begins with a quote. I had initially included a variety of sayings and phrases that I found interesting or pertinent, but due to copyright and permission issues it became too difficult to include them. So, although it might outwardly appear a little indulgent, I have instead self-quoted short comments and sayings that I'm renowned for and that others have affectionately coined 'Steveisms'. I hope you find them interesting and helpful.

ABOUT THE AUTHOR

Steve McKnight holds a Bachelor of Business (Accounting) from RMIT University and is a qualified Chartered Accountant. He also has a Diploma of Financial Services. After a decade-long career in accounting he became a professional investor where he used his accounting and investing knowledge to purchase 130 properties in 3.5 years. In 2012 he established a managed investment fund that went on to purchase more than $100 million worth of commercial property. Through his books, training programs and websites McKnight has positively impacted the lives of millions of people. Steve recently turned his attention to land conservation and ecosystems management endeavours. He and his team have now planted more than 300 000 trees on previously cleared land with the goal of establishing a new permanent carbon sink native forest. Steve is married and when not in Melbourne can usually be found walking among nature at Bindi.

PREFACE

HOW THIS BOOK CAME TO BE

Dear Reader,

Something very strange happened on the 13th of July 2006 — something that hadn't happened before, and hasn't happened since: I woke up from a dream sobbing, with tears streaming down my face.

In that dream I believe I encountered God. There was no booming or thunderous voice; He did not speak in words, but rather in thought. There was no burning bush; rather God appeared as an intense, swirling cloud of light, with shining stars in it, and radiant colours of dark blue, and purple, with flecks of gold and silver.

Word-for-word, here's what I wrote in my journal on what I experienced:

> *I woke up in awe, overwhelmed and excited to the point of tears. I could not speak nor move. It was the most intense feeling I have ever felt. I had an incredible sense that God wanted me to run a learning based program teaching people how to use their money effectively. Three times did this thought come into my mind; each time stronger.*

Which brings us to today: to the here, and to the now.

I've had an unpleasant encounter with skin cancer, and it's reminded me that time is finite and that I needed to get busy doing what God asked me to do — to write this book.

In it I've shared many important lessons and insights gleaned from the front line of personal wealth creation: from the things I've witnessed being a chartered accountant and advising a variety of clients spanning mums and dads, to multi-millionaire business owners, to my personal experience building a family fortune buying and selling hundreds of properties, and even professional funds management where I've looked after more than $100 000 000 of other people's money.

I don't know where you are on your faith journey, and I'm not sure how or why this book has crossed your path, but I do know this: *it's no fluke*. The same God that gave me that prophetic dream back in 2006 wants to use the knowledge and experience I have about how to make and attract a fortune that counts to reveal something deeply personal and important about the way you think, or act, around money.

What might that be? Let's find out.

Steve McKnight

PART ONE
INTRODUCTION

A better and brighter financial future is yours for the taking, and there's not a moment to lose!

By the time you've finished Part 1 you'll have cast a monetary vision for the rest of your life. All going well, that plan will empower you to live a life of financial freedom and a self-funded retirement where you won't have to rely on government handouts for survival.

As you work through the four options in chapter 5, ask 'Is the model I'm following (perhaps even without knowing it) going to deliver a wealth-creation outcome I'm happy with, and if not, which model will?'

Make sure you attempt all the exercises as the answers you give and the insights you gain will provide an important platform upon which the rest of this book builds.

CHAPTER ONE

A SHORT INTRODUCTION TO WHAT'S AHEAD

The more you do of what you've done, the more you'll get of what you've got.

It stands to reason that the more you do of what you've done, the more you'll get of what you've got.

That is, if you're flush with cash, are debt free, have investments that are performing and have a life rich in meaning, then well done and keep it up!

On the other hand, you can't expect to change and yet stay the same.

If you're feeling financially overwhelmed, find yourself bogged down in debt, want a retirement that's not reliant on welfare, or have money but lack passion and purpose, then keep reading.

My hope in writing this book extends well beyond helping the wealthy get wealthier. The pursuit of more, when you already have more than enough, might feed your ego, but could come at the cost of a withered soul. What's the point of having a lot that only means a little? My goal is to help you make, manage and multiply your money to become financially empowered, and then to make your money count by using it to live a life rich in happiness.

Some people believe money is evil. It's not. As my good friend Brendan Nichols once told me, 'It's just a tool that can be used to *get a life* (let's call that *survival*) and to *give a life* (let's call that *significance*)'. That is, it is our attitude towards money, rather than money itself, that will determine whether it's a blessing or a burden in our lives, and the lives of others.

Survival means 'making bank'—having enough income to pay for your desired lifestyle, plus stashing some extra aside for rainy-day reserves.

Significance refers to 'largesse'—the pursuit of using your money in an altruistic manner to give your life meaning, by using it to fund a legacy for which you'll be remembered long after you're gone. How you use your money is how you'll be known and remembered.

How you use your money is how you'll be known and remembered.

Will that be for the materialism you amassed, or your magnetism attracting admiration for the way you made your life and money count by touching, moving and inspiring others?

A common belief I've encountered is 'I'll start working on significance once I've got survival sorted'. Such thinking is flawed though, as survival and significance are not mutually exclusive, but rather complementary: one spurs the other on. If you want your money to multiply, invest in survival. If you want your money to count, invest in significance. Want both? Do both! It's more than possible … it's recommended!

To be clear, don't work on survival *then* significance, work on survival *and* significance. What you do that matters will give meaning to your money and motivate you to keep making the sacrifices needed to attract and keep a fortune. This is critical because borrowing from tomorrow and spending it today is surely a recipe for a lifetime of financial disempowerment. Friend, here's the principle: *if you want to attract more, **first** become more attractive.*

If you want to attract more, first become more attractive.

I can't explain how it works, just that it does. When you invest a little from your survival into your significance, you become more 'magnetic', with your magnetism attracting more opportunity while also 'levelling up' the calibre of the people who are drawn into your sphere of influence. No, not in some modern-day ATM kind of way: you can't 'game' the principle of sowing and reaping. The law of attraction only works if you give from the heart (what's in it for others), rather than giving from the head (what's in it for me).

So, what's ahead in the book? Put simply, I'm going to do what I can to help you count your money, and to make your money count.

We're going to explore and unpack two concepts in detail: your Financial IQ and your Financial EQ. The former relates to how you think and act financially, and the latter to how you recognise, understand and manage your financial feelings and emotions.

As you'd expect, they're related, and if you want to become and remain wealthy, you need to master both. Thinking poor and acting rich will result in the appearance of wealth, but the substance of poverty: a flash-looking car with no engine. Thinking rich and acting poor will lead to great ideas, few of which will come to pass because you're not financially empowered to make them happen: a flash engine with no car.

The goal is to think rich, and act rich. But hang on and make no mistake! I am not talking about materialism here. Materialism amounts to lots of toys and babies prone to tantrums: spoiled people spoiled by possessions without purpose.

A better interpretation of what I mean by 'rich' is 'empowered', so if there's something disempowering about the way you think or act financially then we need to find and fix it. Otherwise you'll be building wealth on shaky foundations, meaning any wealth you manage to attract might not stick.

Chapter highlights

- If you're happy with your current wealth situation, then you don't need to change. Keep doing what you're doing.
- It is not possible to change and stay the same. If you aspire to a better and brighter financial future, then you have to do something different, to get something different.
- For many, wealth creation is a struggle to meet and maintain their version of survival – having enough to keep the home fires burning, and ideally a little extra for emergencies. Beyond survival is significance, which is an awareness and desire to use your money to add meaning to your life by positively impacting others.
- Most people concentrate on survival *then* significance. The better approach is survival *and* significance.
- Materialism reflects the external appearance of wealth. Magnetism reflects the people and opportunities that are attracted to you. What good is it to be financially rich, but socially and spiritually poor with fake friends and a lonely soul?
- The law of sowing and reaping mandates that any investment you make in significance will increase your attractiveness. Being more attractive will help you to attract more opportunities and 'level up' the calibre of people drawn into your sphere of influence.
- No-one is born a money magnet. It is a learned skill that can be improved over time with effort and diligence.
- If you want to make, manage and multiply more money, then you'll need to strengthen the way you think and act financially (your financial IQ) and also the way you feel financially (your financial EQ).

CHAPTER TWO
NOW AND THEN

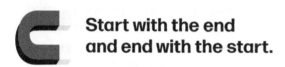

Start with the end and end with the start.

Is it possible to get rich, quick? Some say no, but I say yes, depending on your definition of *rich* and *quick*, of course!

Take, for example, people who win the lotto jackpot and become instant multi-millionaires, or the enterprising folks who sell their businesses for billions in their twenties or thirties. In my case, I achieved financial freedom — no longer having to swap my time for money — in less than five years. Compared to working 50 years, that was quick! Don't be mistaken though, I've never owned a boat, nor a Ferrari; I define rich in terms of minutes (i.e. time), not materialism. More on that later.

Time for another question. 'Can *you* get rich, quick?'

That depends on whether you're inclined to try, and whether you're willing and able to pay the price.

Inclined to try

10

Out of 10, with 1 being the least important, and 10 being the most important, how big a priority is it for you to start working on securing a better and brighter financial future? Don't just think it, write your answer in the box, and note the date under it.

If you answered, say, 5 or below, then you're probably facing bigger challenges, perhaps struggling with the hustle and bustle of life and making ends meet. Alternatively, you may be young and believe you have time on your side to sort out your finances in the years to come.

If you answered 6 or above, then you're probably thinking it's time to make your financial future a bigger priority. Hmmmm ... what to do, though? Pump some more money into superannuation? Dabble in the stockmarket, or maybe try your hand at real estate? Perhaps crypto? Buy a franchise or start a business?

There are lots of options, but instead of making the common mistake of letting the strategy determine the outcome, you'd be much better off starting with the end, and ending with the start. Or, in other words, don't let any available shoe determine your foot size—have the financial strategy fit you, not the other way around. That is, cast a vision for your financial future, make a plan and then work with the strategies that will see you make the most money, in the quickest time, for the least risk and lowest aggravation.

Paying the price

Financial freedom: the name is certainly deceptive, because there's nothing free about financial freedom. It's bloody hard work, unless you want to cheat.

There's nothing free about financial freedom.

'Cheat! Cheat?' I hear you ask. 'How do people cheat?' By trying to get-rich-instant or get-rich-easy and hacking an outcome without putting in the work.

Take lotto, for instance. According to Oz Lotteries (2021), 76 per cent of Aussies like to go out on a date with lady luck, but it's not easy to win her favour. You're 3750 times more likely to be hit by lightning than win the Oz Lotto jackpot[1]. A more-proven and less-risky (that's a good combination, by the way!) idea would be to take the $50 per week spent buying lotto tickets and invest it. The following table gives you an idea of what the balance of doing this would be, depending on the return achieved and the period of time.

Future values of $50 per week, invested for different time periods and annual before-tax returns				
Time	6%	8%	10%	12%
10 years	$31,954	$39,786	$44,607	$50,170
20 years	$79,616	$128,276	$165,747	$216,509
30 years	$150,708	$325,093	$494,722	$768,013
40 years	$256,749	$762,849	$1,388,110	$2,596,540
50 years	$414,920	$1,736,494	$3,814,259	$8,659,077

If you don't think in numbers, the following graph reveals that the combination of return and time are certain to make you wealthy. Why rely on luck, when you can depend on skill?

[1]The chances of winning OzLotto are about 1 in 45 000 000 compared to a 1 in 12 000 chance of being hit by lightning in Australia.

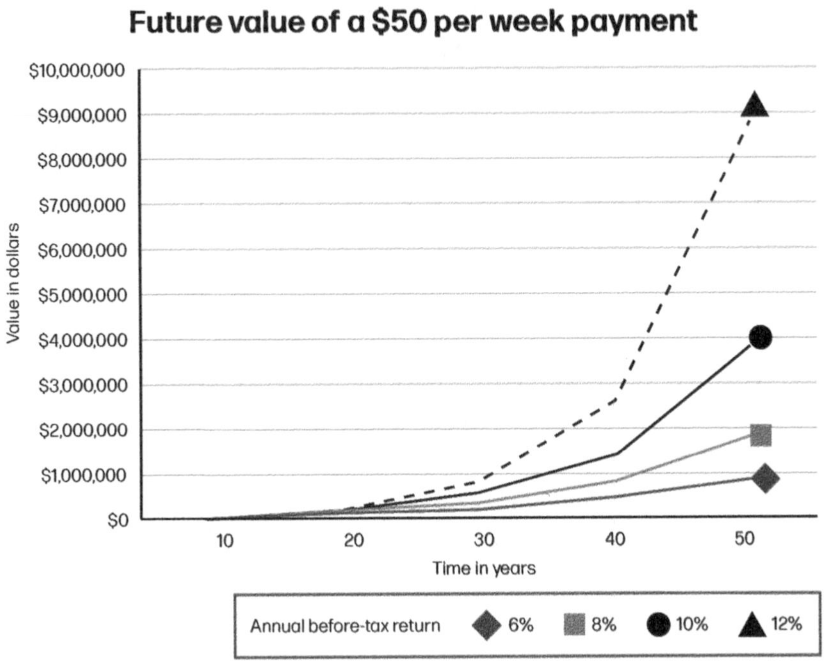

You don't have to invest in hare-brained schemes either. For reference, according to Vanguard (2021), the 30-year return for listed Australian shares is 9.7 per cent per annum. That's pretty close to the 10 per cent column in the table above, which has a 50-year 'jackpot' of $3 814 259.

It's your choice: rely on a 1 in 45 million chance (by the way, you're eight times more likely to be killed by an elephant in captivity[2]) or the 100 per cent mathematically proven millionaire method?

But hang on a moment, 30+ years doesn't sound quick, does it? Well, that's the get-rich-slow option. If you want to speed things up, then there's a price you have to pay. Not a physical price such as buying a litre of milk, but more so an ongoing combination of sacrifice (choosing not to have something ever) and delayed gratification (choosing not to have something now).

[2] A one in 45 000 000 compared to a one in 6 243 604 chance of being killed by an elephant in captivity (US data).

For instance, rather than indulging and living above your means, resulting in stuff and debt, the price of a better and brighter financial future is living below your means to accumulate savings, which you can use to purchase investments.

Or, as I like to put it, work now so you don't have to work later.

Sounds simple enough, right? It's definitely not. The combination of powerful materialistic marketing messages, coupled with easy-to-access debt, means you have to fight against so-called 'normal' all the way.

True financial empowerment means not being casual with your money, lest you become a financial casualty. It's having the capacity, but electing not to purchase something because you don't want to be defined by your material possessions. This is not to say you need to live in a sackcloth, but rather that you spend from what you have (rather than what you don't have), and what you can afford.

True financial empowerment means not being casual with your money, lest you become a financial casualty.

There are two ways you can approach your financial future: chance or choice.

If you're happy to rely on chance, then you don't need a plan because you don't have a destination. You'll get what you get, and you don't get upset.

If you want to rely on choice, then you need to decide between slow and steady — where you let time and trend be your friend — or fast and furious — where you put on the afterburners and accelerate your wealth building. Or maybe a combination of the two.

Whatever you do, stay away from get-rich-instant or get-rich-easy, where the odds of failure are astronomically high. Just ask any elephant.

Chapter highlights

- It's possible to get rich—quick or slow. It's just not realistic to get rich instantly or easily, because schemes that promise maximum returns for minimum effort are almost certainly too good to be true.
- There is nothing free about financial freedom. It takes considerable effort and comes at the cost of sacrifice and delayed gratification.
- Beware trying to find an easy solution to a complicated problem, like trying to overcome a financial problem that has taken years to eventuate by using quick-fix or hare-brained schemes that rely heavily on luck or good fortune.
- Winning lotto really is a dream that will statistically almost never come true.
- Don't rely on chance when you can depend on maths. A small amount regularly saved and invested at a reasonable return over a long period of time is a sure bet.
- No-one will care more about your money than you will (or should). If you're casual with your finances, then you run the risk of being a financial casualty.

CHAPTER THREE
SEEING IS BELIEVING

Compelling vision is the secret to turning small ideas into world-changing action.

I've been short-sighted since I was 13 years old. I remember going to the optometrist for the first time and having my eyes tested, and being amazed at just how clear and sharp the letters became as different lenses were trialled. Upon getting my specs, the world jumped into focus. Who knew trees had leaves that weren't blurry blobs?

A lot of people I've met are short-sighted with their finances, meaning that without assistance money is a fuzzy mess. Try as they might, they just can't see straight; their vision is skew-whiff, resulting in a lack of clarity and perception.

Consider budgets, for example. Budgets are like diets: we all know we'd benefit by being on one, but who can be bothered sticking with it once the need for being on it has passed? I put it to you that one reason why people go on a diet is so, after they've lost the weight, they can eat whatever they like guilt free. The consequence of that is that they'll pile on the kilos when they go off the diet, resulting in them needing to go back on the diet soon thereafter. On. Off. On. Off. And so it goes — like trying to drive in a straight line by veering right and left.

Are budgets a waste of time then? Yes, they are, unless …

'Unless what?'

Unless you have a compelling reason to make one and stick to it; otherwise, whatever benefit you gain from budgeting can be easily blown by some errant binge spending.

Finding a compelling long-term vision

I've been teaching wealth creation now for more than two decades. That makes me an 'old timer' in the industry. There aren't too many 'old timers' around because of the tendency for people to sell their reputations and fade into ignominy, and because some methods taught don't stand the test of time and are proven ineffective — promising much, but delivering little.

A while back I was chatting with a fellow old-timer, Brendan Nichols, about why it might be that so many people seem interested in improving, but so few people seem to stick with it and achieve their full wealth potential — perhaps as few as 5 in 100.

We canvassed various possible reasons why people make a start and experience some degree of success, but don't stick with it to achieve their full wealth potential: difficulty of the subject matter, inability to apply the strategy, unrealistic expectations, changing market conditions, and so on.

I had heard Brendan say previously that the enemy of a great life is a good life, meaning that people give up on great because they get comfortable with (and don't want to risk) good. I think there's something profound in that.

'Bren, I think I have it.'

'What?' he replied with a note of curiosity in his voice.

'I believe people give up when the pain of going forwards becomes greater than the pain of going backwards.'

Said differently, if you lack a compelling reason that drives you to make, and keep making, the effort and sacrifices required for sustained success, then you'll plateau out.

Here's the principle: you're likely to spend if you lack a compelling reason to save.

You're likely to spend if you lack a compelling reason to save.

That is, you need to create and maintain personally convincing reasons to make, and keep making, the effort to sacrifice and delay gratification so that the outcome you're working towards tomorrow (by choosing not to spend) remains greater than the reward you'd receive by spending today.

How do you do this? How do you make something compelling to the point of it becoming motivating enough to delay gratification?

First, you need to *think it* — to give birth to an idea — and then you need to *want it* in a powerfully irresistible way: to build enough desire so that your idea becomes a must, rather than a maybe.

What's your reason? What makes it compelling?

One option is pleasure: you want the reward of the achievement. The other is pain: you want to avoid the consequences of not changing.

Consider quitting smoking. Some find the motivation they need to quit because they want the benefits of improved health. Others can only quit when they get to the point of receiving the unpleasant ultimatum that they'll die if they don't.

Let's apply this to money and how you can find the motivation to save rather than spend. Two ideas come to mind: things and time.

Things

The first is to set your mind on something you want — a thing — that gives you a reason to go without.

My daughter, Cassie, has a car. To drive it, she needs insurance — and that's expensive. The freedom and flexibility she gets from having the car is the motivator she needs to save rather than consume her cash by purchasing $28 cocktails on Chapel Street in Melbourne. She wants her car more than the cocktails.

Other examples of things people save for include their kids' education, a house, a holiday, and so on.

Time

The problem with saving for things is that you're consuming rather than compounding your money. You may never have thought about it, but money can also be used to 'buy back' the time you'd otherwise have to spend working in a job.

For instance, let's say you get paid the average amount an Australian receives by swapping a year of their adult life for money: $60 000 per annum, a little over $28 per hour. It just so happens that that's the price of a Chapel Street cocktail, so you could say that 1 cocktail = 1 hour of work. Another way you could look at it is that every $224 you save = 8 hours (i.e. $224 ÷ $28) = 1 day you don't have to work.

An even more advanced way to look at the time–money relationship is that if you could save (rather than spend) enough money to buy an investment that provided $224 of weekly recurrent income, then you'd be able to enjoy a permanent long weekend for the rest of your working life without impacting your living standards.

Here's a carrot to contemplate: one sensible property deal can make enough money for you to permanently buy back one day a week that you'd otherwise have to spend working.[3]

[3] On the basis that you reinvested the profit into income-producing assets.

Josh and Shehan

Josh and Shehan are joint-venture partners. They purchased a 1970's-style four-unit site (4 × two-bedroom, one-bathroom units) in regional Victoria. Their strategy was to undertake a cosmetic renovation. Once complete, and including purchase costs, the project 'owed them' $928 550. Soon after they were finished they received an offer of $1 260 000, but they declined that and decided to rent the units out for positive cashflow.

Had they accepted the offer, they would have made a before-tax profit of a little over $300 000 in only six months.

What will it be: things or time? Would you rather have more stuff but have to work for the rest of your life? Or less stuff and the freedom to work when, where, how and however long you want? Maybe you want both? That's fine, but you have to choose which you want first.

Let's return to the question I asked in the previous chapter about how much of a priority a better and brighter financial future is for you right now (on a scale of 1 to 10). The following graph illustrates the relationship between your motivation and your interest in changing.

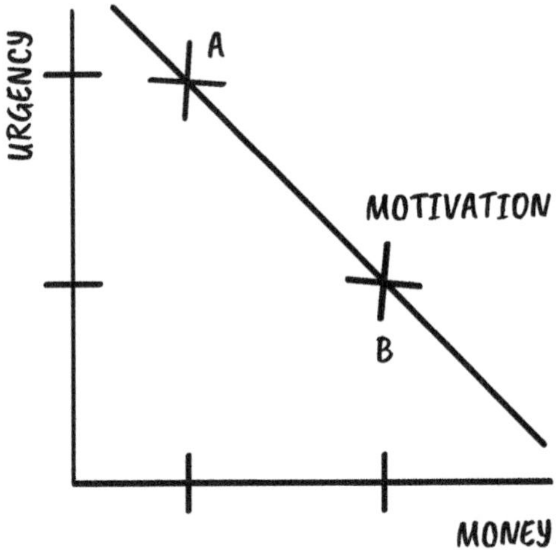

You'll see that urgency is measured on the vertical axis, and money on the horizontal axis. The scale increases as you go further up, and further left. Motivation is being measured.

Two points are charted:

- Point A indicates a little bit of money and a lot of urgency to act — something has arisen that means you need money in a hurry — and so you are highly motivated to act.
- Point B is where you have more money and less urgency, so your motivation is much lower.

It makes sense, doesn't it? If you're hungry, you're motivated to hunt, but if you're feeling full, why go to the effort?

The shape of the motivation line as shown in the diagram is linear, but in real life it's more likely to be inverse, as drawn in the following diagram.

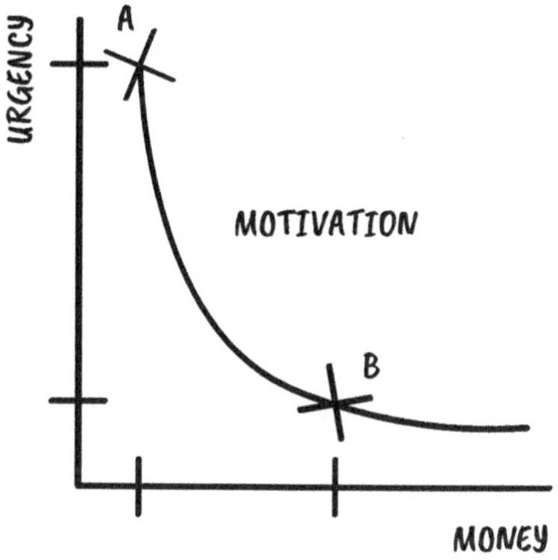

Point A is being in a highly motivated state, spurred on by an urgent need that you can't resolve with your current resources. Motivation drops off quickly though as you move from uncomfortable to comfortable, which is represented by Point B. It's where Brendan's comment about the enemy of a great life is a good life becomes apparent.

Here's the point: how do you stay motivated after the circumstance(s) that motivated you to act to begin with have eased? That is, how do you stay hungry, even if you're not? How do you keep pushing forward when the pain of doing so is greater than the pain of stopping?

The answer is … a compelling long-term vision. Having a compelling vision will keep you hungry for making progress.

Having a compelling vision will keep you hungry for making progress.

Everyone is different, but in my case, I *had* to get out of accounting. The severe stress I was experiencing from feeling trapped in an unrewarding job was affecting my health, resulting in ulcers on, ahem, unusual body parts. The prognosis was an early grave if I persisted.

What about after achieving financial freedom though? How have I *stayed* motivated? I needed a vision bigger than myself, which in my case was faith. What drives me today is pursuing causes that add significance and meaning to my life, rather than more money simply for more money's sake.

Compelling vision is the secret to turning small ideas into world-changing action. With it, you have a reason for making, and continuing to make, the effort needed to bring vision to fruition. Without it, you're left to battle out each day according to what spot fire needs your attention to ensure it doesn't burn the house down.

Back to budgets

If you try to do a budget without a vision, then in my opinion you're almost certain to fail to achieve lasting success. Why? It's not that budgets aren't useful or helpful; it's just that the effort associated with doing one, and persisting to track and measure and report, will soon escalate to the point where the pain of going forward will be greater than the pain of going back. The more difficult a budget is, the more pain will be associated with trying to persist with it. The tipping point will be when the pain becomes greater than the urgency (probably because the circumstance for the urgency has eased).

Your budget is only as strong as your reason for budgeting. For example, say you have a strong desire to save for an overseas holiday. You're motivated to do what it takes, and the chatter in your head has changed so that not spending is a thing because every dollar saved is a dollar more for your holiday. You've even gone so far as to start budgeting to propel your progress. Success! You go on the holiday, have a great time and return with happy memories. With nothing else to save for, the need for a budget becomes redundant and without it, there is no system for spending restraint.

Your budget is only as strong as your reason for budgeting.

Have you ever made a budget but failed to stick with it? Don't feel bad, because most people sign up believing it's only for a short time to solve a temporary problem. Like a diet, the reason for doing one is so you don't have to do one. Here's the secret to sticking to a budget: instead of making it restrictive, make it empowering.

Restrictive means you want to spend but your nasty budget says you can't. Empowering means measuring and appreciating your progress, which confirms you're on the right track. What's the missing ingredient between restrictive and empowering? Vision: having a reason for saving that's more compelling than the reason for spending.

If you can't see a reason to sacrifice or delay gratification, why bother with consumption restraint? This conundrum plays out every day when people buy stuff they don't need because they don't see how spending now can lead to financial disempowerment later.

Have a vision for your money

If you don't have a vision for your money, then rest assured someone else does because they'd rather have your dollars in their bank account than leave them in your pocket. In fact, I've found that money is attracted to people who have financial foresight, and repelled from people who don't.

What if you don't have a vision for your money? Sadly, as outlined in the next chapter, the consequences are likely to be most unpleasant.

Chapter highlights

- It's hard for the body to achieve what the mind can't see, so before starting a budget, cast a vision.
- Money is attracted to people with financial foresight, and repelled from people who spend today because they lack a vision for tomorrow.
- Your budget is only as strong as your reason for budgeting.
- You can't expect a temporary fix to result in permanent improvement. A short-term budget can't overcome long-term financial mismanagement.
- Budgets are best used as an empowering tool to propel progress (i.e. a carrot), and worst used as a restrictive or punitive measure to force fiscal compliance (i.e. a stick).
- Motivation to start sacrificing and delay gratification is triggered by urgency and a lack of financial resources. Motivation to keep sacrificing comes from a compelling vision that puts a high price on failure. What's your vision and what makes it compelling?
- You'll give up when the pain of going forwards becomes greater than the pain of going backwards.
- If you want to attract and keep a fortune, cast a bigger vision and make the reasons for achieving it more compelling.

CHAPTER FOUR
THE FORMULA FOR FINANCIAL FREEDOM

If you do what everyone else does, then you'll get what everyone else has.

Do you have a plan to retire poor? Do you have a plan not to?

In the previous chapter I canvassed the carrot of achieving financial freedom to motivate you to save (and invest) rather than spend. That's the pleasure angle. The pain angle, sadly, is living until you have no more time of any value to swap for money, and then retiring reliant on welfare and in poverty.

Here's a disturbing statistic: 76.5 per cent of retired men and 78.7 per cent of retired women in Australia receive the age pension (Wilkins et al., 2019). Furthermore, another report (The Treasury—Australian Government, 2020) estimated that 60 per cent of those on the age pension were on the maximum rate, making it their main source of income.

Surely that's a shocking statistic: more than three quarters of retirees need government welfare (with the majority of them having the age pension as their major source of income) and only 2 or so in 10 are self-sufficient.

Another way to interpret those stats is that unless you approach your finances in a different way from the masses, there's an 8 in 10 likelihood that you'll need to lean on the government for survival when you cease full-time employment.

The age pension

In case you don't know, the age pension is (emphasis added in italics) ...

> ... *designed to provide income support to older Australians who need it*
>
> (Department of Social Services, n.d.).

The age pension isn't given to everyone — only those who have so little assets or income that they wouldn't survive without it. Some authors and wealth advisers believe you should do what you can to qualify for a pension because if the government's handing out money, then you should get in line. *I couldn't disagree more.* Your goal should be to not qualify for the pension because you're independently wealthy enough to retire when you want, with the means to self-sufficiently afford the lifestyle you desire.

Sustenance, not supplement

Perhaps you expect the government to look after you in your retirement — that after paying a lifetime of taxes, you're entitled to receive some of it back in the golden years of your life? If so, then what's outlined below might shock you.

The old-age pension (aka age pension) was never designed to be free money in retirement. A more accurate way to view it is as a survival payment for those no longer employable: retirees who have reached career obsolescence but are unable to financially sustain themselves.

This is certainly not written to be a put-down to those who need or rely upon the age pension. However, today's concept of an age pension as an *entitlement* is very much at odds with what was envisaged when it was created: a meagre form of income survival, not an income supplement.

> **The pension was envisaged as a form of income survival, not as an income supplement.**

Beginning in Australia in 1909, the age pension was difficult to qualify for. To receive it, you had to be 65 years old—not an easy feat given the life expectancy of someone born in circa 1844 was 40 or so years (O'Neill, 2020). Who needs retirement savings when you won't live to retire?

Today, the eligibility age for the age pension is somewhere between 65 and 67 years (see the following table) and given we're all living longer (as outlined in the next chapter), it's reasonable to expect that either the amount paid will fall and/or the eligibility age will increase in years to come to match the number of people who can be supported to what's available in the federal government's coffers.

Age pension eligibility age	
Date of birth	**Eligibility age**
Before 1 July 1952	65 years
From 1 July 1952 to 31 December 1953	65 years and 6 months
From 1 January 1954 to 30 June 1955	66 years
From 1 July 1955 to 31 December 1956	66 years and 6 months
From 1 January 1957 onwards	67 years

Source: Department of Social Services, n.d.

Aside from an age limitation, the age pension was (and still is) means tested, limiting those who receive it to people who can prove they have insufficient income and assets to be self-sufficient. The limits in 1909 were not generous by any means, ensuring that only the very poor were eligible. The pension was a flat £26 per annum, and equated to about one-sixth of what a full-time, low-skilled worker earned. Imagine trying to survive on that!

Any wealth creation plan that lists receiving the pension as a long-term goal is surely a poor plan leading to a poor outcome—both metaphorically and literally. How so? Well, today's age pension is a little over one-quarter of what the average person in full-time employment earns, which means it's more generous than in 1909, but it's below the Australian poverty line (Melbourne Institute: Applied Economic & Social Research, 2021).

Any wealth creation plan that lists receiving the pension as a long-term goal is a poor plan leading to a poor outcome.

How does working your whole life to end up living in poverty sound? No thank you. I appreciate the age pension as an emergency backstop, but I'd rather chart a different course. How about you?

A miscalculation of time

I doubt anyone deliberately sets out wanting to live below the poverty line by relying on the age pension for survival in retirement. It just kind of happens. But how? One reason is a miscalculation of available time, a distraction caused by the hubbub and busy-ness of life.

In our younger years we tend to earn less because we're at the beginning of our careers, and pay is low at the bottom of the totem pole. It doesn't matter; with time on our side, we can spend what little we earn in the happy knowledge that we can pay more attention to wealth creation ... *tomorrow*.

As our expertise and experience improves, so does our income-earning ability. That's awesome, but we're also starting to spread our wings and flex our independence. It's time to move out of home, so while our pay packets might be bigger, so too are our expenses. That's okay, because we can use debt to buy stuff, and there's still plenty of time to worry about repaying it and creating wealth ... *tomorrow*.

Before we know it, our age has a 3 at the front of it and our 20s have come and gone in a flash. With the pace of life seeming to get faster and faster, it's now time to 'grow up', 'settle down' and establish some more permanency in our lives. The three Ms beckon: marriage, mortgage and menagerie (i.e. the pitter-patter of little feet). Heck! How did life get so ex-pen-sive?! Two incomes are helpful, but everything earned, and more besides, goes to keeping the home fires burning. Today's priorities are survival, and sleep! Wealth creation? That can wait until ... *tomorrow.*

Oh dear. Our 40th birthday has come and gone, and with the family growing, we need more space. The value of our home has gone up, and lucky for us, our friendly lender is willing to increase our credit limit so we can renovate, extend or trade up to a bigger abode. Then there are the school fees, music and tennis lessons, the annual trip to the in-laws, and so on, and so on. Yep, you guessed it, putting money aside for retirement is a problem we'll tackle ... *tomorrow.*

And so it goes, through our 50s and into our 60s when there's always something that seems to get in the way of giving us a clear run at increasing the rate at which we can save and multiply our money. Maybe it's an unexpected redundancy, a dud investment or failed business, an illness or a market downturn. Whatever it is (or was), it wasn't expected and it made the going harder than anticipated, which resulted in less progress than hoped.

Finally the big 'Double-R' day arrives: retirement and reality. As we shake the dust from our shoes and say goodbye to full-time work, we also say farewell to a full-time income. If we're like the majority of retirees, we won't be able to self-fund our desired retirement, and instead will need the support of welfare in the form of an age pension to survive.

The takeaway from this chapter is: if you do what everyone else does, then you'll get what everyone else has, and statistically, that's not enough income or assets to live independently when you stop full-time work. Instead, you'll need government support to help soften the unpleasant reality of permanent financial hardship.

If you don't like the sound of that, then make a new plan while you can and before it's too late.

How much will you need in retirement?

A reason why people don't get around to planning for their retirement is because they don't know how much they'll need. Let's solve that problem, keeping in mind that how much you may *want* and how much you may *need* are two entirely different numbers. In this section you'll find five suggestions. All of them assume you own your home outright.

1. Rule of thumb

A simple guideline for the amount of income you'll need when you stop full-time work is 80 per cent of what you earned before you retired. This assumes that your living standard equals what you used to earn, scaled back a little because you won't have work expenses. The problem with this approach is that you don't know what your pre-retirement income will be, so it's a bit of a fuzzy number. Still, the following table might help you.

Average working-life taxable income by income percentile			
Income group	**Percentile**	**Gross income**	**80% gross income**
Low-income earners	10	$22,100	$17,680
	20	$36,300	$29,040
	30	$48,000	$38,400
Middle-income earners	40	$58,100	$46,480
	50	$68,400	$54,720
	60	$80,200	$64,160
	70	$94,500	$75,600
High-income earners	80	$112,900	$90,320
	90	$144,900	$115,920

Source: The Treasury – Australian Government, 2020; McKnight.

2. ASFA Standard

The Association of Superannuation Funds of Australia's (ASFA) Retirement Standard is an often-quoted benchmark. It distinguishes between two levels: comfortable and modest. Assuming you want to aim for the more desirable *comfortable*[4] level, ASFA's numbers (for June quarter 2022) are as shown in the diagram and table below, and compared (in the table) to the maximum basic rate of the age pension (Services Australia, 2022).

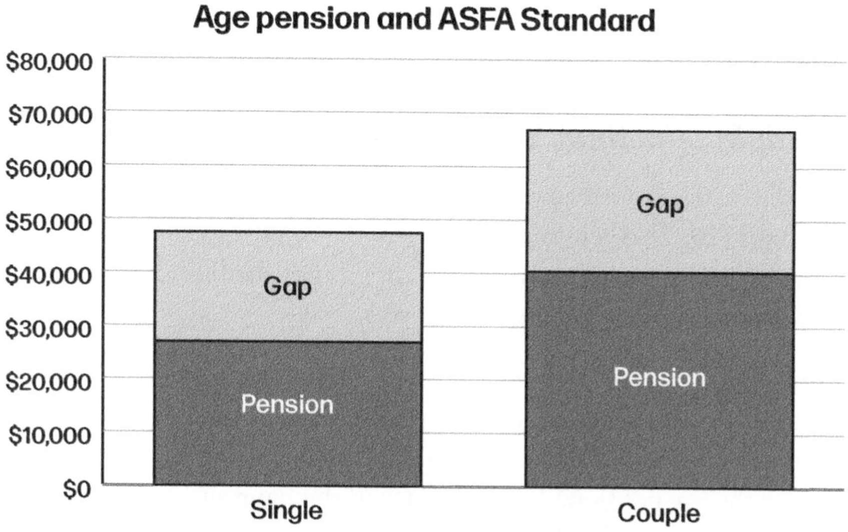

	ASFA	Age pension	Gap
Single	$47,383	$26,689	$20,694
Couple	$66,725	$40,238	$26,487

A simple explanation of the diagram is that the age pension won't provide enough money for you to live a comfortable life in retirement.

[4] Defined as 'accounts for daily essentials, such as groceries, transport and home repairs, as well as private health insurance, a range of exercise and leisure activities and the occasional restaurant meal … an annual domestic trip and an international trip once every seven years'.

And speaking frankly, the ASFA Standard for comfortable—an occasional restaurant meal and international travel every seven years—sounds rather miserly too. It means you'll likely retire with a lower standard of living than you enjoyed while you were employed, and who wants that?

The value of this measure is also questionable, with the Productivity Commission's comprehensive report (Australian Government, 2018) on the state of the superannuation system referring to this standard as '... no more than an arbitrary benchmark that should be ignored in policy making'. Ouch!

3. Super Consumers Australia

I prefer to lean on the work done by the folks at Super Consumers Australia (2022). Their findings contemplate a savings target to support an annual spending at three standards: high, medium and low, and separate the data for singles and couples.

Their numbers, reported in July 2022 and summarised in the tables that follow, assume you will own your own home outright when you retire, or otherwise won't pay rent or a mortgage, and that you will receive the age pension. The difference in the figures is due to expected inflation, among other factors.

Savings targets for pre-retirees (aged 55-59)				
Living Status	**Living Standard**	**Fortnightly Spending**	**Annual Spending**	**Savings target (at age 65)**
Living Alone (By yourself)	Low	$1,308	$34,000	$88,000
	Medium	$1,692	$44,000	$301,000
	High	$2,115	$55,000	$745,000
Living Together (In a couple)	Low	$1,846	$48,000	$111,000
	Medium	$2,462	$64,000	$402,000
	High	$3,115	$81,000	$1,003,000

Savings targets for retirees (aged 65-69)				
Living Status	**Living Standard**	**Fortnightly Spending**	**Annual Spending**	**Savings target**
Living Alone (By yourself)	Low	$1,115	$29,000	$73,000
	Medium	$1,462	$38,000	$258,000
	High	$1,962	$51,000	$743,000
Living Together (In a couple)	Low	$1,615	$42,000	$95,000
	Medium	$2,154	$56,000	$352,000
	High	$2,885	$75,000	$1,021,000

The two age groups are pre-retirees (currently aged 55–59) who are expecting to retire in ten or so year's time, and those on the cusp of retiring now (aged 65–69).

Assuming you want to 'go for gold', you'll want to aim for a high standard of living, which I've highlighted in the table. What's particularly helpful about this data is that it provides savings targets, which will become the amount of income-earning assets you need.

For instance, if you're presently single, aged 57 and were planning on retiring in about 10 years' time, then your fortnightly spending (based on a high standard of living) is estimated to be $2115, your annual spending is $55 000 and you'll need to have saved $745 000, plus you own your home or are otherwise living rent-free.

4. Choose your own adventure

You don't need to be constrained by what others say. Here's a three-step process for coming up with your own number:

1. Nominate your desired annual income, then
2. Divide it by your expected return, to
3. Derive the amount of investment capital you'll need.

Have a go at filling in the following boxes.

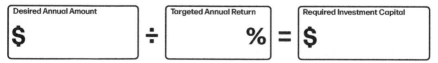

Desired Annual Amount		Targeted Annual Return		Required Investment Capital
$	÷	%	=	$

For example, if you wanted an annual income of $60 000 and believed you could achieve an 8 per cent annual return, then you'd need $750 000 ($60 000 ÷ 0.08) of investment capital. That is, $750 000 of investment capital, invested at 8 per cent per annum, will deliver $60 000 per annum in investment income.

Desired Annual Amount		Targeted Annual Return		Required Investment Capital
$60,000	÷	8%	=	$750,000

How much annual income do you need?

Naturally, that's up to you, but assuming you are about to retire then here's a summary of how much income ASFA and Super Consumers Australia believe you'll need to afford a comfortable / high standard of living:

Living Status	ASFA Retirement Standard	Super Consumers Australia
Living Alone	$47,383	$51,000
Living Together	$66,725	$75,000

What investment return do you need?

What return do you think you can get based on your risk tolerance? At one end of the safety scale you have bank term deposits, and at the other end any number of different high-return, high-risk schemes.

The table that follows might be helpful. The values are based on $10 000 invested in 1991.

Asset class	Investment value in 2021	Per annum returns
US Shares	$217,642	10.8%
Australian Shares	$160,498	9.7%
Australian Listed Property	$118,013	8.6%
International Shares	$107,939	8.3%
Australian Bonds	$75,807	7.0%
Cash	$38,938	4.6%

Source: Vanguard 2021; McKnight.

It's up to you if you want to use before-tax or after-tax rates. I suggest matching them with whether you're using before-tax or after-tax annual income.

Remember that risk and return are related, so that the higher the return, the higher the inherent risk. We'll return to this topic later in the book when I outline how to dial up returns while also dialling down risk.

Remember that risk and return are related, so that the higher the return, the higher the inherent risk.

What investment capital do you need?

The amount of capital you need is the result of your annual income divided by your estimated return. The relationship of the equation means:

- The higher the annual income, the larger your required investment capital.
- The lower the investment return, the larger your required investment capital.
- The larger the required investment capital, the harder it will be.

If you're feeling that the required amount is simply not achievable, then you have these options:

1. Lower your targeted income.
2. Increase your targeted investment return.
3. Conclude that you may not know how to do it right now, but you're open to learning new ideas that could open new doors that turn improbable into entirely possible.

I tend to be a #3 kind of person. I had no idea how I'd buy 130 properties in 3.5 years, but not knowing didn't stop me from setting the target. You're going to have to acquire and apply new knowledge if you want to surpass the results you're capable of achieving based on what you know now.

At the other end of the spectrum there might be a few readers who are surprised to learn that they already have the required amount, but still feel anything other than financially free because their wealth is largely on paper and not deployed in the way needed to release them from their full-time jobs. If that's you, then keep reading: all will be revealed.

Shuffling the boxes

You can also mix up the boxes to calculate the following:

- *Annual income* based on available investment capital and targeted annual return

Available Investment Capital		Targeted Annual Return		Annual Income
$	×	%	=	$

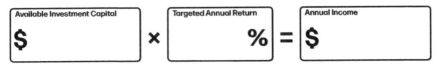

- *Required annual return* based on desired annual income and available investment capital.

Desired Annual Income		Available Investment Capital		Required Annual Return
$	÷	$	=	%

5. Steve's magic number

Finally, we have my number, which is a nice round $100 000 per annum, regardless of whether you're a single or a couple.

Where does this number come from? It's the result of asking 'how much per annum would you like to retire on?' at many seminars, at many venues, in many countries, over many years. It's also a step up on what the other standards recommend, so if you aim for the $100k grand prize and fall a little short, you'll still be in the top bracket of the other benchmarks.

I should point out that $100k is an ambitious target and would place you among the wealthiest retirees based on income. But why not aim high?

Next, because I like to keep things simple, let's assume an 8 per cent after-tax return on your investments. This is a middle-of-the-road, long-term return that you should be able to source with your own research or by engaging the services of a competent financial planner.

The amount of capital you need is calculated using the same formula as outlined in point 4:

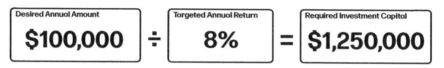

Desired Annual Amount		Targeted Annual Return		Required Investment Capital
$100,000	÷	8%	=	$1,250,000

And there it is ... in black and white. Something to aim for: $1 250 000, invested at an average 8 per cent after-tax return, will deliver $100 000 per annum, which will place you among the richest retirees in the country.

$1 250 000, invested at an average 8 per cent after-tax return, will deliver an annual income of $100 000 for the rest of your life.

Game over. Book down. Let's go eat ice-cream.

Phew! We've covered a fair bit, haven't we? Completing this small step is a giant leap for your retirement planning. You might now be wondering whether or not you'll be able to accumulate enough superannuation to achieve your investment capital target, and if not, what you can do about it. They're good questions, and when you're ready, we'll tackle them in the next chapter.

Chapter highlights

- Do you have a plan to be poor? Do you have a plan not to be?
- The hubbub and busy-ness of life forces us to focus more on today than tomorrow. This is causing the majority of people to leave it too late to accumulate enough wealth to afford their pre-retirement lifestyles when their full-time incomes end.
- If you're hoping for a better and brighter financial future than what the majority of retired Aussies experience, then you'll need to chart a different path while you can – and before it's too late.
- The age pension is not an income supplement; it's income sustenance: the equivalent of a permanent old-age dole.
- If the age pension is your only source of retirement income, then you'll be living below the poverty line and are likely to experience extreme financial hardship.
- Because it's means tested, to qualify for the age pension you'll need below average income and/or assets. If that's your long-term plan, it's time to make a better one.
- One of the reasons why people don't plan for retirement is because they don't know how much they'll need.
- The act of setting a goal and engaging your mind to figuring out how it could be achieved is an important step to becoming more financially attractive.
- An ambitious retirement income target to aim for is $100 000 per annum. That's possible if you can save $1 250 000 and invest it at an average return of 8 per cent per annum.

CHAPTER FIVE

ARE YOU SUPER SUFFICIENT?

You can't do the minimum and expect the maximum.

What does retirement mean? You might be interested to learn that the origin of the word comes from the French *retirer*, which means 'to remove or withdraw'—for example, to retire (i.e. remove yourself) from full-time employment.

It used to be that the upper-class gentry retired (from society) and lived off the pensions provided by their estates, and the well-to-do middle class retired because they were able to save for retirement. The working class, however, almost never retired, and instead worked until their bodies broke, after which time their families looked after them as invalids, or they begged.

Things are different today. The following graph (Macrotrends, 2021) illustrates that Australians born after 1956 are expected to live past age 70, increasing to 83.79 years for those born in 2022, and a projected 92.79 years for those born at the turn of the 21st century.

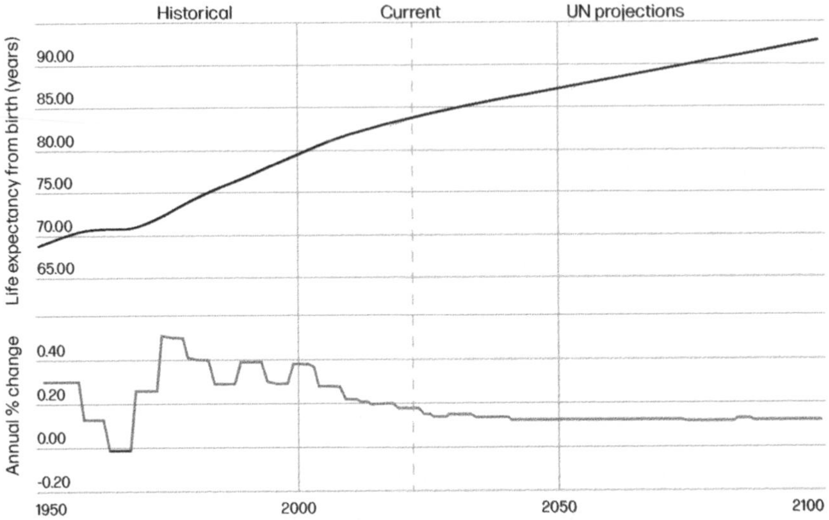

Source: Macrotrends. (2021). Australia Life Expectancy 1950-2020. www.macrotrends.net. https://www.macrotrends.net/countries/AUS/australia/life-expectancy

Whereas it was once likely that you'd die before retiring, it's now highly probable that there will be a gap of several to many years between when you permanently leave the workforce and when you die. How are you going to survive when you're no longer willing or able to swap your time for money? Let's consider four options.

Option 1: Welfare

We've already seen that the age pension isn't an option you'll want to rely on because it's a subsistence payment that's barely enough—indeed many say not nearly enough—to survive on. Even when used as a supplement to other income, the age pension is still welfare—a government handout—not an entitlement or return of taxes paid, and is only available to those with insufficient income or assets to look after themselves.

The age pension is still welfare not an entitlement or return of taxes paid.

In the following diagram, the 'Welfare' and 'Employment Income' boxes represent the money received from social security benefits and small amounts of employment income paid as cash, or otherwise too small to attract compulsory superannuation. In this pre-retirement example, all the money received is spent on living costs, illustrated by the lines pointing to 'Tax & Living Expenses'.

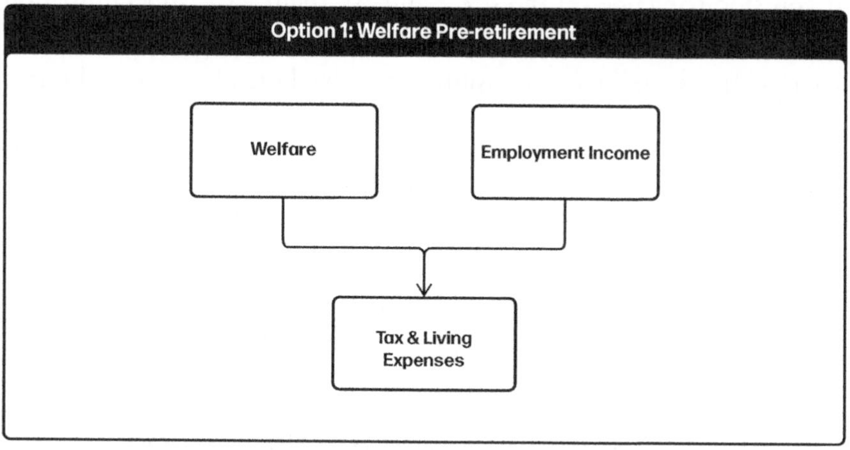

As shown in the following diagram, after retirement the only source of income is the age pension, which is used to pay for living expenses. If extra money is needed, savings and home equity (if any) are drawn down, illustrated by the 'Savings & Home Equity' box pointing up to 'Tax & Living Expenses'.

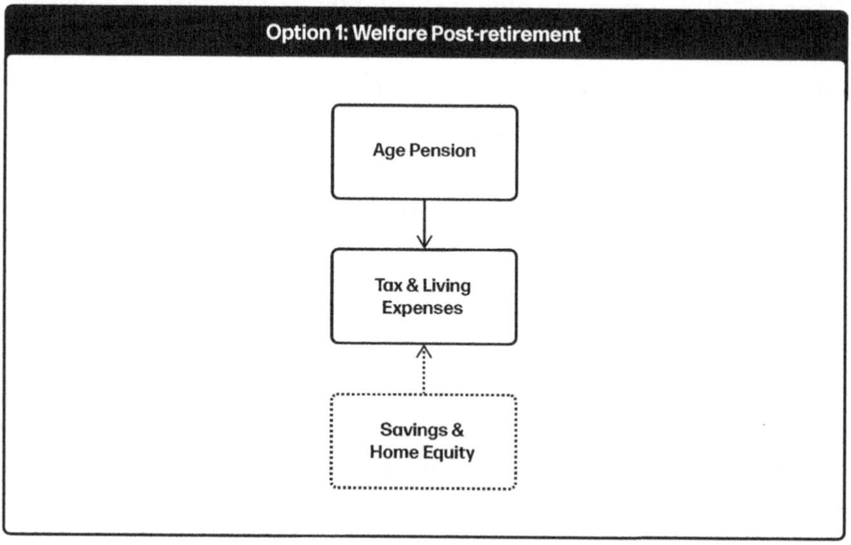

The age pension is best seen as your fallback position if all else fails, not your go-to plan to aspire to.

Option 2: Compulsory super

If you stop someone on the street and ask them what superannuation means, they'll almost certainly say something to do with retirement savings. That's a modern extension and evolved use of the word though.

A little research reveals superannuation is the noun of *superannuate*, which means 'to be rendered obsolete'. Further study indicates that superannuate is borrowed from the Latin *superannuri*, which means 'to be too old'. With this knowledge, we can piece together the modern and historical use of superannuation to mean 'money to live off when you reach employment obsolescence'. Pretty brutal, eh?

Superannuation is the noun of *superannuate*, which means 'to be rendered obsolete'.

Prior to 1992, superannuation was voluntary rather than compulsory. This changed when the federal Labor government of the day, faced with an ageing population and a booming welfare obligation, mandated that employers deduct money from their employees' pay and send it directly to their employees' nominated superannuation (i.e. retirement) fund. This money was to be locked away (i.e. preserved) until the mandated retirement age. Today, an estimated 90 per cent of all workers are paid superannuation, compared to 51.3 per cent in 1988 (Parliament of Australia, 2010).

From the following pre-retirement diagram we can see that Option 2 begins with Employment Income, which is earned by swapping time for money, and from which compulsory superannuation is deducted by the employer and sent to the employee's superannuation fund. This is illustrated by the curved line below and to the left of Employment Income. Tax & Living Expenses consume all of what's left, leaving nothing to buy financial assets with.

The money invested in superannuation earns a return (see the line from Superannuation to Investment Income), which cannot be accessed until after retirement so it is reinvested back into superannuation (see the line from Investment Income to Superannuation).

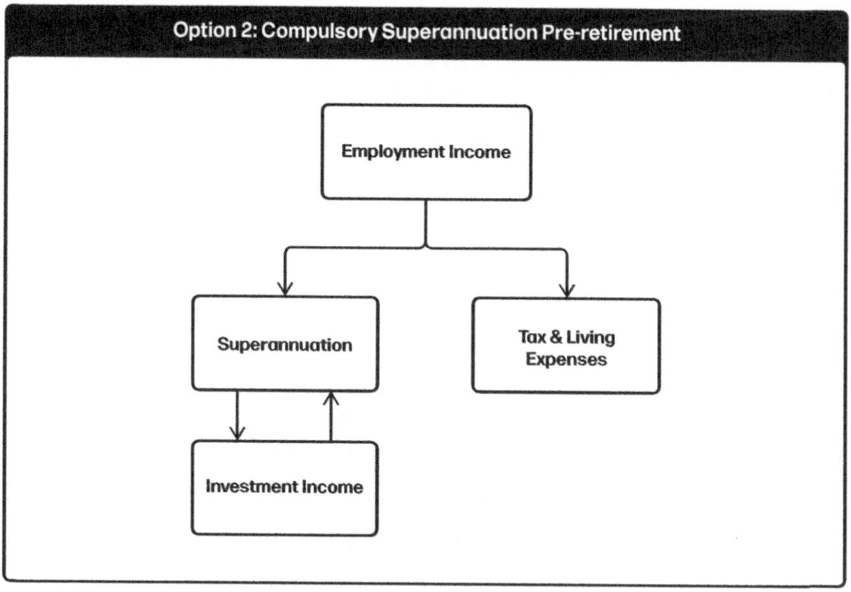

In the following post-retirement diagram we can see that employment income ceases on retirement and in the diagram is replaced by Superannuation, which is the source of Investment Income that you can use to pay your Tax & Living Expenses (solid lines from Superannuation to Investment Income to Tax & Living Expenses).

Additional money may be available via the Age Pension, if you're eligible (as illustrated by the dotted box and line to the left), and money may be drawn down from Savings & Home Equity and Superannuation to fund any shortfall (all shown by dotted lines to the right).

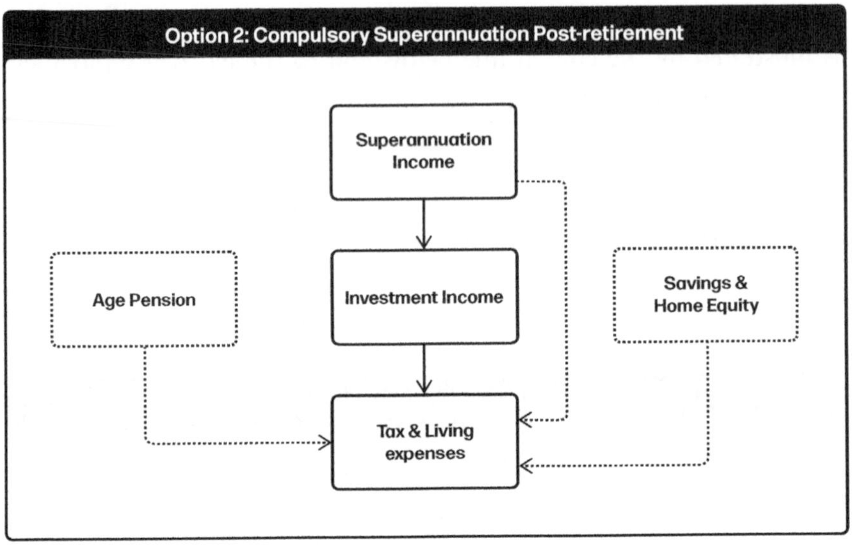

A question you may be asking is this: will those superannuation contributions that my boss deducts from my pay be enough to allow me to live a comfortable, self-sufficient life in retirement?

Will my employer's superannuation contributions be enough to allow me to live a comfortable, self-sufficient life in retirement? The answer is no.

The answer is no.

The latest government report into retirement, *Retirement Income Review* (The Treasury—Australian Government, 2020) is a daunting 648 pages long and makes for good bedtime reading for insomniacs. It says a lot, but here's the relevant bit for this discussion (p. 19):

> *If they [retirees] only draw down their superannuation at the legislated minimum rates, which many people currently do, those in the upper half of the income distribution will not achieve the 65–75 per cent replacement rates.*

Let me interpret this for you: expect to draw down your savings and home equity to fund the gap between your cost of living and the income you receive from your investments and the age pension.

In other words, if you don't want to rely on the age pension, or don't want to have to sell assets or tap into your superannuation balance or home equity, *then compulsory superannuation alone won't get the job done.*

In fact, that's a key takeaway from this chapter: you can't do the minimum (compulsory superannuation) and expect to get the maximum (a wealthy retirement). If you want more, you'll have to do more.

If you want more, you'll have to do more.

Cracks in the system

The *Retirement Income Review* also made the insightful observation that the current superannuation and pension system favours retirees who own their own home. However, with home affordability and home ownership diminishing, when Millennials and those who come after them reach their 60s, an increasing number of them will be renting in retirement, meaning housing costs will gobble up a significant portion of their available income. This will cause them to have to sell assets to fund the shortfall, resulting in less income from investments, and leading to more asset sales, to the point of having less and less wealth and ultimately needing to downsize living standards to what can be supported based on living off the age pension.

The authors of the *Retirement Income Review* (p. 36) make the point that:

> *... people misunderstand the purpose of superannuation, believing that in retirement they should only draw on the return from the investment of their retirement savings and not touch the capital amount. Yet the system is designed on the basis that people should draw down their savings to support them in retirement.*

and

> *Importantly, and in line with the policy intent of the retirement income system, it was assumed that retirees will run down their superannuation assets by age 92... [and] will not leave bequests and will purchase a longevity product at retirement that provides them with income from age 92.*

Reading this might come as a shock, especially if you're counting on an inheritance injection to your retirement plans. With the population living longer, more and more wealth will be distributed to health and aged care providers, with less and less passed on to future generations. Another thought to throw out there... with Baby Boomers and Gen Xs expected to live longer, more and more of their retirement nest egg will be needed to pay for their aged care and healthcare requirements. This will have the effect of locking up and dwindling down the inheritance that their beneficiaries may be relying on to help them get into the property market or pay down their massive mortgages.

Option 3: Voluntary super

What about supplementing the compulsory amount that is automatically deducted and sent off to your super fund by voluntarily topping up from your savings from time to time?

That sounds like a good idea, and indeed it is for those who are not too far off retirement—say 10 years or less. However, for others, locking up extra money for decades that can't be accessed in an emergency may result in a severe loss of flexibility, making this option quite unattractive.

There are also limits on how much can be voluntarily contributed on tax-effective terms.

As shown in the following diagram, Option 3 begins with Income, which may be from employment (and from which the dotted curved line down and to the left represents the compulsory superannuation that must be deducted as per Option 2) or from other sources from which superannuation does not have to be automatically deducted, such as business profits.

As for other options, tax and living expenses are deducted from the income, but in Option 3 there is a surplus that is sent off to your superannuation fund as a voluntary contribution (see the dotted line from Income to Superannuation).

The money invested in superannuation earns a return (solid line from Superannuation to Investment Income), which cannot be accessed until after retirement so it is reinvested back into superannuation (solid line from (Investment Income to Superannuation).

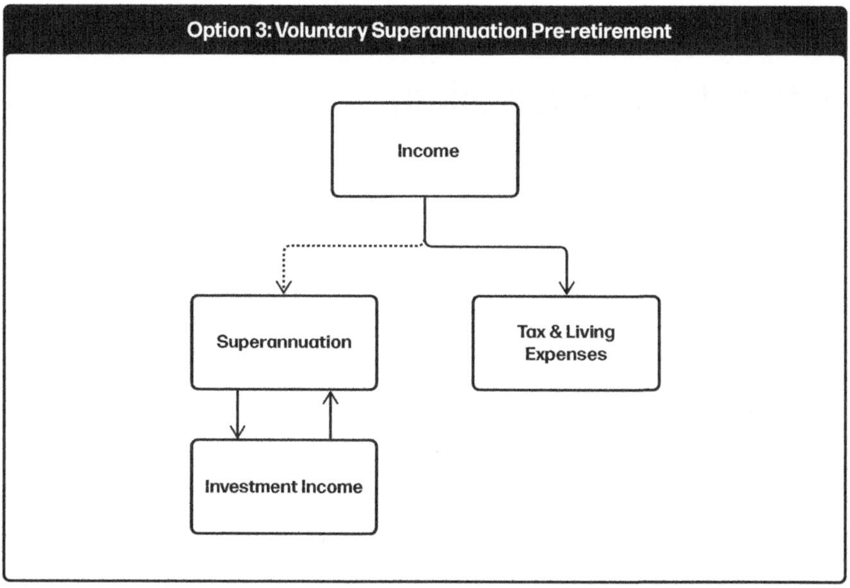

Post-retirement (as shown in the following diagram) is the same as what was described in the post-retirement diagram for Option 2, only the balances in Superannuation and Investment Income will be higher because voluntary contributions were made over and above the compulsory contributions.

Option 3: Voluntary Superannuation Post-retirement

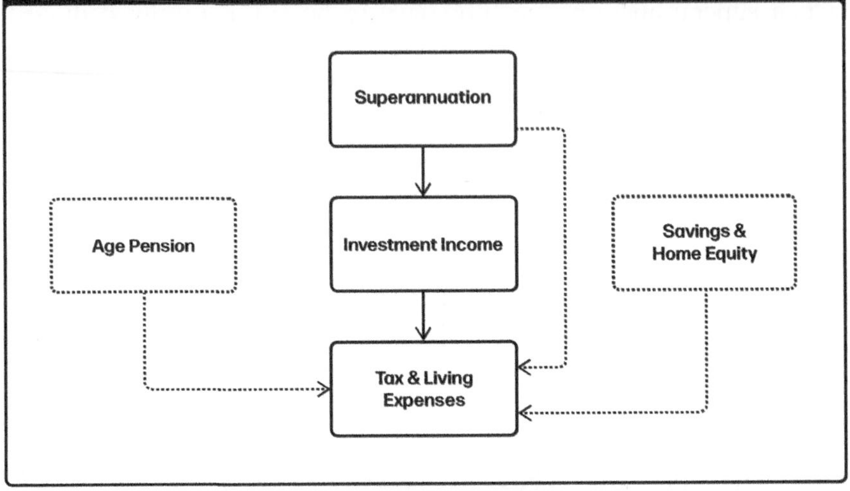

Option 4: Super sufficient

You can, of course, save and invest outside the superannuation regime, in your own name or using an entity such as a company or a trust (e.g. family trust, unit trust).

At first glance you might feel overwhelmed by the following pre-retirement diagram, but after we've chunked it down it'll make more sense.

Like Option 2 and Option 3, we begin with the Income box. If that income comes from employment, then compulsory superannuation will need to be deducted—represented by the dotted line and boxes under and to the left of the Income box. How those lines and boxes work is the same as was outlined earlier on pages 44–45.

However, under Option 4 we're seeking to build wealth outside superannuation, and that is represented by the solid lines under and to the right of the Income box.

First of all, the line from Tax & Living Expenses to Assets implies there is a surplus left over from Income less Tax & Living Expenses, which is used to purchase (non-superannuation) assets.

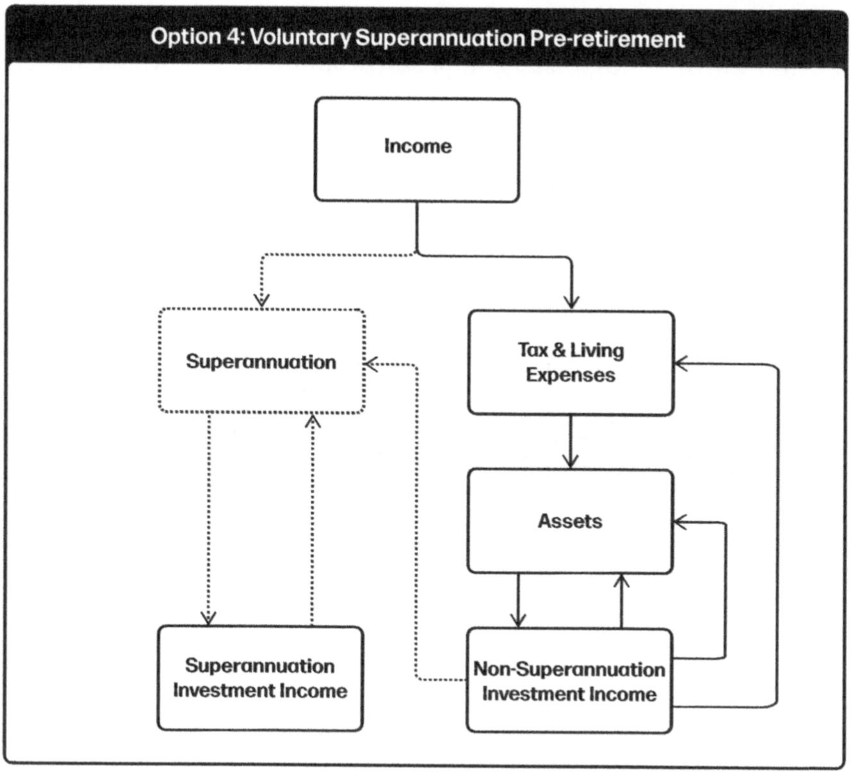

Those assets generate Non-Superannuation Investment Income, which can be reinvested to buy more of the asset-generating income (the vertical line back up to Assets), used to purchase different non-superannuation assets (curved line to the right and up pointing to Assets), pay for Tax & Living Expenses (curved line to the right and up pointing to living expenses) or even pay for voluntary contributions to your superannuation fund (dotted curved line to the left and up to Superannuation).

Do you see how this model can grow bigger and bigger over time as you reinvest the income from your investments, while also hopefully benefitting from an increase in your assets' values?

The downside to Option 4 is that your non-superannuation investment income won't qualify for the tax breaks available inside the super system, but the upside is you'll have unrestricted access to your money. It's also worth noting that a competent accountant will be able to help you plan so the tax you'll pay on your non-superannuation income is the lowest legally possible, which in many cases, isn't that much more than what you'd pay inside superannuation.

The following post-retirement diagram shows that once you reach retirement, the assets you have in super (if any, so a dotted line is used) and non-super will provide investment income (i.e. the lines from Superannuation and Non-Super Assets to Investment Income).

Option 4: Voluntary Superannuation Post-retirement

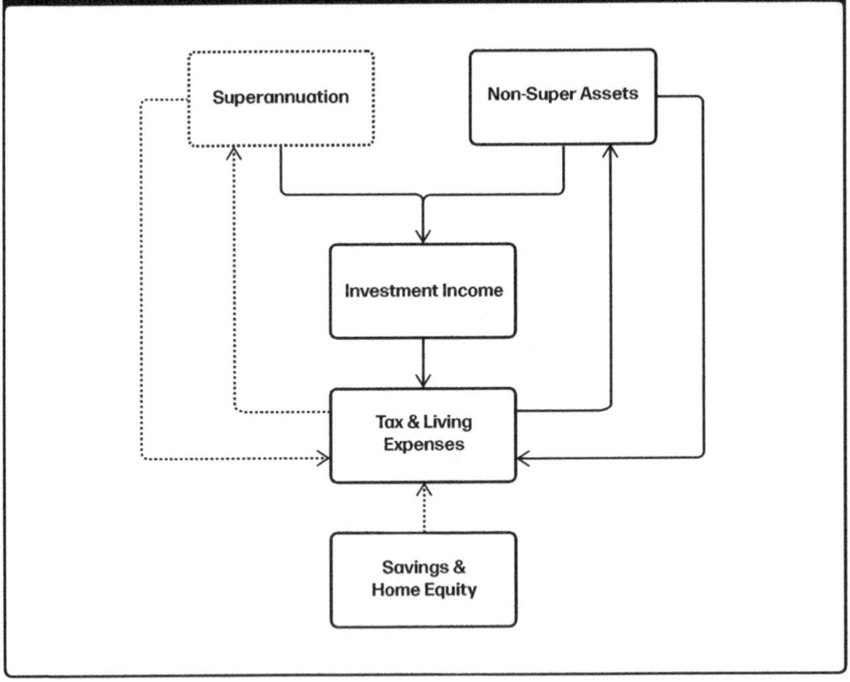

Your investment income can be used to pay your Tax & Living Expenses. All going well, you'll have the 'problem' that the income generated by your assets will far exceed your tax and living expenses, leaving a surplus that can be reinvested back into super or non-super assets (curved lines pointing up from Tax & Living Expenses).

If you happen to need more money than your income provides, you can cash in some of your super or non-super assets (lines from those boxes to Tax & Living Expenses) or even your savings or home equity (although the latter is highly unlikely because you've set yourself up to never need to sell your home).

This model provides for complete self-sufficiency, and given the number of assets and amount of income you're likely to accumulate, you won't qualify for the age pension (so there's no Age Pension box needed).

• • •

Is your head spinning? That's understandable, especially if you've never seen or read anything like this before.

Perhaps you're wishing someone had sat you down and explained this to you earlier in life? There's not much I can do about that, but you can certainly sit down with someone you know or love and use the diagrams included in this chapter to make sure they can take full advantage.

Which option is best?

The answer is that it depends on your circumstances, choices and chances.

Circumstances

Time is the biggest consideration you face. The less of it you have, the fewer options are available to you.

Time is the biggest consideration you face.

I wish I had better news, but the cold hard truth is that if you're in your 60s or older and don't have much investment income or capital, then your choices are limited. Your risk profile will be very low, because any losses incurred will be devastating, thus restricting you to the shallow end of the risk pool, and therefore to investments with lower returns.

For you, the age pension is a benefit you're likely going to have to rely upon, supplemented by income from part-time work, if you can find it, low-risk investments and converting assets to cash when the need arises. Hopefully though, the lessons you've learned over a lifetime of earning and spending can be passed down to younger generations with ears open to listening. One thought that comes to mind is 'Time is your friend, until it's your enemy'.

Choices

The more time you have, the more 'runway' is available for your investments to take off. This relates to the ability to benefit from compounding and also recover from losses.

Rather than limit yourself to one option, you'd be smart to keep your options open and consider all the options in some sort of combination: the age pension (to the extent you qualify for it), money inside superannuation (topped up when your circumstances say it is sensible to do so) and also wealth outside of superannuation that you can access as needed before you retire.

For example, if you're already in your 60s or older and haven't been able to accumulate enough wealth to live self-sufficiently in retirement, then Option 1 (Welfare) will be a blessing. Hopefully you can supplement the age pension with investment income from the assets you've accumulated in Option 2 and Option 4, as well as drawing down on those assets as the need arises.

If you're in your early 50s or older and plan to keep working for the foreseeable future, then a combination of Option 2 (compulsory super) and Option 3 (voluntary super) is worth exploring. It would be wise for you to make an appointment with a qualified accountant or financial planner to see what tax advantages are on offer as you approach retirement age.

If you're in your 40s or younger, then you can leave Option 2 (compulsory super) to tick away in the background (out of sight, but not forgotten—you still need to manage your money), while also pursuing Option 4 (super sufficient) to build wealth that you can access before retirement, if needed. Option 3 is less attractive because of the inability to access your money if you need it before retirement.

Chances

You might be lucky some of the time, but you can't be lucky *all* of the time. I've found that while luck does have a role to play, investing skill is a far bigger determinant of an investor's long-term success.

You might be lucky *some* of the time, but you can't be lucky *all* of the time.

I remember a story my dad told me about how he was playing chess one day against a much younger player. After my dad comprehensively beat him several times, the younger player sulked and remarked, 'I've got all the brains, but you've got all the luck'.

Professional golfer Arnold Palmer is quoted as saying, 'It's a funny thing, the more I practice, the luckier I get', and I've found the same applies to investing. That is, luck is attracted to skill, and repelled by ignorance.

Luck is attracted to skill, and repelled by ignorance.

If you want to improve your chances, to improve your choices, to improve your circumstances, then invest inwards (by improving your financial IQ and financial EQ—see Part 2) before investing outwards (and acquiring investments). It's hard to be an A-grade student with a D-grade study ethic.

What I did

Unsurprisingly, my father is one of the biggest role models in my life. Graham McKnight was known by some of his work colleagues as Graham McTight, and I've certainly inherited his tendency to be, ahem, thrifty.

Growing up, I watched Dad regularly head off to work at 7 am, and not come home until 7 pm. He worked long, and he worked hard, finally retiring at age 60 after 40 years' faithful service to one employer. While I greatly admire my father, I didn't want to have to work 12-hour days, and I didn't want to have to work until I was 60.

If you're saying 'Amen!' to that, then you are where I was back in 1999, aged 27 and staring down the prospect of 40 more years of work as an accountant. A good life was certainly on offer, but a great life?

Given my age, choosing superannuation as my preferred wealth-creation vehicle made little sense because I wanted to retire well before I turned 60. Furthermore, superannuation is more for people of an employee mindset, whereas I was more of an entrepreneur and wanted the flexibility to make my own fortune.

This pushed me down the road of Option 4: building wealth outside superannuation with the goal of acquiring enough assets that generated enough income to replace the salary my wife and I earned in our jobs. If I could do that, then I wouldn't have to work anymore.

Sadly, books like this were few and far between when I started, so I had to mainly figure things out for myself. That's when I sat down and mapped out the Option 4 model, which was an assimilation of what I'd learned in accounting school, what I'd read in books and what I'd figured out on my own. I've been following this model for more than 20 years and today I have:

- a seven-figure property portfolio that generates a six-figure annual investment income. This pays all our living expenses, with extra for philanthropy and reinvestment
- a six-figure superannuation balance generating a four-figure annual investment income that is on reinvestment auto-pilot. That money is locked away for at least another 10 years.

I don't say this to impress you, but rather to impress upon you that if you want to be wealthy, you have to aspire to, and do more than, the minimum. Making a goal is important, but settling on the system and structure for achieving it is critical. That is, it's one thing to say you want to drive to Darwin (i.e. set a goal), but you won't make any progress until you've planned the route you want to take, obtained a roadworthy vehicle that will take you there and started driving (i.e. settled on the system and strategy, and begun implementing it).

Chapter highlights

- Superannuation has a two-fold meaning: a stage in life when you become obsolete for full-time work, and the retirement savings available for survival once you retire.
- The government knows that most people can't be trusted to put enough away for their retirement, so they invented a system where your employer has to deduct money from your pay and send it off to fund your retirement survival.
- Relying on compulsory superannuation alone is unlikely to result in you being able to live a better life post-retirement than you did pre-retirement. Instead you'll need to reduce your living costs, draw down your savings, sell assets and tap into your home equity.

(*continued*)

Chapter highlights (cont'd)

- There are tax benefits to building wealth inside the superannuation regime, but your money will be locked away until you retire. You'll need to weigh up whether the financial upside of some tax benefits is worth the downside of a lack of flexibility.
- My preferred model is a combination of Options 2, 3 and 4, where you leave your super money to tick away in the background (being careful to still manage and monitor it and top up when age and circumstances warrant), while actively building wealth outside of superannuation in the foreground.
- If you want to achieve financial freedom and retire early, then you'll need to build wealth outside of superannuation, because money inside the super regime is locked away until at least age 60.
- What model are you following? Will it provide the system and structure you need to arrive at the outcome you desire? If not, will you change while there's still time?
- If you never start saving, you'll never stop worrying.

CHAPTER SIX
THE DEFINITION OF FINANCIAL FREEDOM

Slavery is swapping your time for money. Freedom is swapping your money for time.

Let's keep talking about financial freedom—also known as financial independence—a concept that's gaining popularity among people who want more flexibility and choice. They've seen their parents work their knuckles to the bone, and decided they don't want bony knuckles too.

The *freedom* relates to control over time. That is, the *choice* of working rather than the *obligation* of having to work. The *independence* stems from having sources of income independent of what's earned from employment.

The problem with financial freedom is that it sounds like a nice goal, but it's very much at odds with the massive marketing machine that popularises the myth that you need to spend to be happy. Also, financial freedom isn't free. It comes at a hefty price of having to sacrifice and delay gratification—that is, to go without now so you can have something better later.

Financial freedom isn't free.

Born free

We're all born free. We come into the world owing nothing to anyone. We're a blank canvas of opportunity and optimism. Our childhoods are, hopefully, sheltered from the adult burden of financial responsibility—that is, having to find a way to pay the bills to keep a roof over our heads, and food on the table.

As we grow up though, the financial responsibilities of being an adult can put our dreams and ideals on the backburner. That's what happened to my father, Graham. He left school before completing Matriculation and went to study at an agricultural college, where he graduated dux of his class. His dream was to own a farm, but to do so he needed a sizeable down payment and a bank loan for the balance. Without any savings or family members who could assist, he had no option but to get work where he could and save, so he took an entry-level job selling tractors and farm equipment.

Dad's dream of owning a farm never materialised. How so? To begin with, he was a victim of his own success. The gentrification of the outer eastern suburbs of Melbourne in the 1960s caused a decrease in interest in farm equipment, but a boom in demand for new and used trucks. Dad moved over to truck sales and never looked back, winning sales competitions and banking large commission cheques that dwarfed what could be earned living off the land.

His higher pay, supplemented by credit, afforded a middle-class lifestyle. Land was purchased, and a new house built upon it, happily financed by the National Bank. A first child arrived. Then a second. Then a third. A larger house was needed, and an extension was added, with debt added to the mortgage. As the kids grew, so did the costs: food, clothes, family holidays, and so on.

Without knowing it, Dad's dreams of owning a farm died the day he and Mum bought the land and built the house. On that day they wandered into a debt trap, an obligation to swap his time for money for the next 20 years to repay the mortgage. The only way out of the trap was to sell the house and compromise the lifestyle they were accustomed to, or increase the mortgage and take on extra risk.

'Don't forget we were a single income family,' Dad told me recently. 'I had to work to earn the money to pay the bills. From time to time I thought about taking a risk, perhaps even starting my own business, but I was too chicken. I never managed to save enough money to feel confident enough to leave my job, and I didn't want to go into debt and risk losing the family home.'

Have you ever had a chat with your parents about the dreams they sacrificed on the altar of raising a family?

Financial slavery

The precursor to financial slavery is obtaining a secure job. Once you have a reliable income, a new world of opportunity opens before you, enabling you to use debt to fund a lifestyle above and beyond what you could have afforded without it: the ability to borrow and use someone else's money to pay for things you haven't been able to save for yourself.

It starts with little things, especially today with the proliferation of easy-to-access buy-now-pay-later options. Maybe some new clothes or other fashion accessory, the latest gaming console or hot game, or a mobile phone on a 24-month plan. Then the middle-sized things: tertiary education, cars, holidays and the like. Then the big one: a home.

The bonds of financial slavery are weak to begin with, and people fool themselves into believing that they'll only use a little bit of debt to get set up. However, the ability to consume today and repay tomorrow quickly becomes a lifelong habit — one that provides the appearance of wealth but the substance of slavery. The combination of paying today's bills and servicing yesterday's debts means there's little to none left over to invest for tomorrow. Pay increases aren't diverted to savings, they're spent on stuff — or worse, used to justify more debt.

Consuming today and repaying tomorrow quickly becomes a life-long habit – one that provides the appearance of wealth but the substance of slavery.

Those bonds become iron clad once you need your job more than your job needs you. This is a risky position to be in, because your financial future hinges on the assumption that your job status is secure. What happens if your employer goes bust, you're made redundant or you suffer a health crisis and can't work?

The job security walls you erect to protect yourself from financial shock can become a prison that traps you within. Around middle age a crisis builds, fed by unfulfilled ambitions, the grind of constant financial hardship associated with making ends meet, and feeling trapped into having to work in a job that you find less and less enjoyable. Instead of living to work, you're working to live. Physical and mental health issues may appear, as well as alcoholism or other self-destructive behaviour. Family breakdown is a real danger, with more than one in three marriages ending in divorce.

Financial freedom

The opposite of financial slavery (i.e. having to work) is financial freedom (i.e. choosing to work). It's a liberating experience because you're able to buy back the time you'd otherwise have to swap for your salary or wage.

You can achieve financial freedom at any age, provided you can access enough non-employment income to fund your desired survival and significant living expenses. The money to do that can come from drawing down your savings or selling assets (i.e. capital) or it can come from the profits your savings and investments generate (i.e. income).

You can achieve financial freedom at any age, provided you can access enough non-employment income to fund your desired survival and significant living expenses.

Consider the example of the goose that laid the golden egg. You only get to eat the goose once, which is what you're doing when you use capital to fund your retirement. Or you can keep the goose alive and eat the eggs it lays each morning, which is what happens when you preserve your assets and 'eat your profits'.

If you want to achieve full financial freedom, your goal is to acquire a flock of golden geese that lay enough eggs to feed you, your loved ones and others too (i.e. the causes you want to pursue or support). Plus, if you decide to splurge beyond what your income can afford and eat the occasional goose, you can without risking the whole gaggle.

Examples of recurrent non-employment income include rent, dividends, interest and royalties. I do not include capital gains, as this type of profit can only be made once, and remains unreal until the asset is sold, in which case you're killing the goose. Borrowing against unreal capital gains to fund financial freedom increases your debt, thus increasing your non-deductible interest and risk, which is an unwise source of money to fund your financial freedom.

Rent from real estate is my preferred source of recurrent income, but I also receive interest (from savings) and dividends (from shares). I also receive royalty income from book sales, but all that money is allocated to causes and charities I support.

Up until the point where your investment income matches your employment income, you're going to need to keep swapping your time for money as you'll need the cash to pay for living expenses and to buy assets. You may decide to keep working after you reach financial freedom, in which case any money you earn is gravy on top of the meat (or tofu if you're a vego) and potatoes provided by your investment income.

So, what will it be? Financial slavery—where you get sucked into the cycle of swapping your time for money until you have no more time to give? Or financial freedom—where you sacrifice and delay gratification today, so you don't have to work tomorrow?

Chapter highlights

- We're all born free, but many sell themselves into financial slavery when they use debt to access tomorrow's income and consume it today. The more you live beyond your means, the more debt you'll need, and the more time you'll owe.
- Financial slavery has nothing to do with how little or much you earn, just how bonded you are to having to sell your time for money. If anything, higher income earners are more likely to be financial slaves because they can borrow so much more money.
- The opposite of financial slavery is financial freedom: the choice to work, rather than the obligation to work. In order to be financially free you'll need capital to draw down on (eating the goose) or non-employment income (eating the eggs) to fund your lifestyle.
- If you want the ability to work less, or not at all, without suffering a fall in living standards, then you'll need to save and invest, rather than spend and borrow. Choosing to do this will put you at odds with the prevailing materialism mindset of 'I don't care. I want it (now)'. You'll need to reprogram your mindset to 'I do care, which is why I say "no"'.
- Financial freedom is not free. The cost is sacrifice and delayed gratification over many years. Is it a price you're willing to pay?

CHAPTER SEVEN
IT'S ABOUT TIME

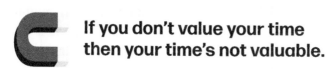

If you don't value your time then your time's not valuable.

What value do you put on your time? Trying to answer this question is how I found the courage to leave my safe, secure and high-paying career as an accountant, to chase the foggy dream of financial freedom. Allow me to explain …

Time accountability

My accounting degree was a four-year course, with the third year being paid work experience.

So it was that in December 1991, in the middle of the recession we had to have, a fresh-faced, newly suited Steve McKnight turned up to his first day of work as a 'professional' at a two-partner firm of chartered accountants located at the far end of Melbourne's St Kilda Road.

My pay was \$20 000 per annum. That's \$1666.67 a month, or about \$9.61 an hour, before tax. Not much, eh? Wrong! For a 19 year old used to running up and down the basketball court umpiring for \$16 a night, \$1000+ in the hand each month was a king's ransom.

Almost immediately as I walked in the door on my first day I was introduced to a new friend that I'd grow to love to hate. No, not a work colleague, but rather a 'special' A4 pad of paper, pre-printed with four columns on it. Columns 1 and 3 were the entire day, starting at 8 am and ending at 6 pm, split into six-minute intervals: 8:00 am, 8:06 am, 8:12 am, 8:18 am, and so on. Columns 2 and 4 were wider and allowed room to write down the name of the client you were working on, and the sort of work you were doing.

I was instructed to put a line through the time I started working on a job, and another line through the time I finished the job. Then I had to count the 'units' I had worked—the number of six-minute intervals—with the requirement that I work at least 75 units a day (i.e. seven and a half hours), with at least 75 per cent of that time being 'chargeable'—that is, work that could billed to a client.

The structure of time accountability via timesheets is mechanical and unforgiving. You couldn't just doodle a day away, and if you spent too much time on something that wasn't productive—either not billable, or not recoverable—then you knew your supervisor would be razzing you up for it. If it sounds anal, it was. Your time was either productive, or it was unproductive. There was no middle ground.

No-one I've ever met likes doing timesheets, yet there's no doubt that the structure of being ultra accountable instilled and ingrained the habit of valuing time—literally, as most accountants bill via an hourly charge-out rate. How do you count your time, and make your time count?

How you count your time is how you make your time count.

A waste of time

Fast forward to 1998. I'd left big accounting, was engaged to be married, and had taken a position as a manager in a small accounting firm. Kennett was Premier of Victoria and had decided to sell the state's silverware by privatising its power network. One of the last utility companies to be sold was Ecogen. It ran the gas-fired power station in Newport, which is the massive chimney you see as you drive over the West Gate Bridge.

Ecogen rarely produced electricity, except on the hottest of hot days, because gas-fired electricity was heaps more expensive to produce than coal-fired power. However, it was very active in the energy futures market. So long as it could write future contracts for energy supply above its cost of production, it always had the option of generating its own power if it couldn't otherwise trade out its position profitably. Heads it wins. Tails it wins.

Kennett had set aside a substantial sum of money for getting Ecogen ready for sale and it turned out that Ecogen's head honcho was good mates with one of the partners of the firm where I worked. That's how Dave (another high-billing staff member) and I came to set up camp for an extended period in Ecogen's boardroom, writing a report on how the Australian taxation system might apply for a non-Australian buyer of Ecogen's business.

You already know that accountants bill by the hour; now imagine our job of sitting in Ecogen's boardroom and writing a report that we were pretty sure no-one was ever going to read. The weeks came and went until, thankfully and finally, the generous budget allocated for the work ran out.

This was the equivalent of being asked to dig a hole, only to know that at the end we'd have to fill it in. It was a soul-sucking experience—a genuine waste of time.

Cleaning toilets

One day, while sitting in Ecogen's boardroom, my mind drifted to another client I'd once worked on in my big accounting days: the City of Melbourne. It had asked us to perform a quality review on one of its internal audit programs. Nothing unusual in that, except this one was for cleaning toilets in the public parks in and around the city.

I'm not sure what captured my interest in that, other than I remember being quite impressed by the level of detail in the program, a literal A to Z of how to efficiently and accurately clean a public toilet, including the use of chemicals that complied with Australian standards.

Perhaps it was the pointless and crappy nature of the Ecogen engagement, but I started wondering how much someone got paid to execute that program and scrub those toilets until they shined, and whether someone who did that would be happier than I was writing ghost words destined to be shredded.

Turning to my colleague in time wasting, I said, 'Dave, how much would you have to get paid to clean toilets for the City of Melbourne?'

'Huh?' he said. 'What do you mean?'

'Well, it seems to me that cleaning toilets might be a crappy job, but it's stress-free and doesn't follow you home at the end of the day or on weekends.'

'I tell you what,' I said. 'The City of Melbourne really wants you to do the job. They'll offer you $100 000 per annum for a nine-day fortnight, with eight weeks' annual leave, plus they'll give you a ute and all the equipment you need to do the job. They only stipulate you have to do the job. You can't sub-contract it. Are you in?'

Chewing his lip and pausing for thought, Dave said, 'Nah, I don't think so'.

'Okay,' I replied. 'They really want you Dave. How about 250 grand a year?'

'No thanks,' Dave said. 'That's still not enough. Maybe for $1 000 000 a year.'

'Okay! Done deal! A million it is,' I said, 'Now let's say one month into the gig you come home with a strange red rash. You go to the doctor and she says that, unfortunately, it's incurable and you only have six months to live. What do you do with your high-paying job?'

'I'd chuck it in for sure,' Dave said.

'Exactly!' I replied. 'The short amount of time you have left is worth much more than the money you might earn.'

We went back to typing on our laptops in thoughtful reflection. A few minutes passed before Dave broke the silence: 'Steve-o, why did you ask?'

'Well,' I said. 'It seems to me that we're more or less doing the accounting equivalent of cleaning toilets for the City of Melbourne. We're trading our time for money, doing a job we don't enjoy that stinks.'

Continuing on, I said, 'The only reason we're doing it is because we believe that the money is worth more than our time. And that's only the case because we assume there'll be lots more tomorrows'.

In my case, I was unhappy at work, but I kept turning up day after day for the paycheque. The unhappiness was temporarily softened when I received a pay increase, but sooner rather than later, I'd go back to feeling unfulfilled and empty—like I was using money to bribe my conscience.

I wonder, what's going through your mind as you read this? Does the situation I've described resonate? What are you going to do about it?

Best- and worst-case scenarios

How did I find the courage to finally leave accounting? It was the realisation that I was living my worst-case scenario as if it was my only-case scenario. That is, if I quit and followed a different pathway that didn't work out, I could always go back to working as an accountant, so what did I really have to lose?

Are you living your worst-case scenario as if it is your only-case scenario?

On 1 January 1999 Dave and I started our own accounting firm. Out on our own, we worked fewer hours and got paid more money than what we did as employees. This improved my health, but my soul remained discontented, and I started researching ways to build wealth fast. You can read what happened in my book, *From 0 to 130 Properties in 3.5 Years.* In short, within three and a half years of starting, Dave and I bought 130 properties and no longer had to sell our time for money because the income from our real estate investments surpassed our accounting fees.

As an aside, you might like to know that to this day I chunk the property profits I make into $20 000 lots—the amount I was paid for a year of my life. That is, if I make $100 000, then I equate that to five years of blood, sweat and timesheets. I find equating the money you make with a time context helps give it meaning beyond dollars and cents.

I'm sometimes asked how I've been able to do so much: write books, run a fund, teach millions of people, buy and sell hundreds of properties, run a charity, oversee the planting of 300 000+ trees to establish a native forest, be a dad and husband, all without blowing a head gasket. The answer is time accountability. I don't waste time because I don't have time to waste.

My mindset is this: how can I invest a minute to save an hour, an hour to save a day, a day to save a week, a week to save a month and a month to save a year?

How much of what you do today is an investment in tomorrow? Acting with a sense of purpose and urgency will increase your attractiveness. Your ability to invest time today and do what others won't, so that tomorrow you'll be able to do what others can't, is what will attract opportunity to your door. Things will start to happen because you're driving outcomes rather than being a passenger in life.

How much of what you do today is an investment in tomorrow?

The takeaway from this chapter is two-fold. First, if you don't value your time, then your time's not valuable, and second, in order to make your time count, you have to count your time.

Chapter highlights

- Time is only valuable to the extent you value time.
- Time accountability builds discipline and forces you to count your time, and to make your time count.
- A time trap exists when you live a lifestyle that locks you into your worst-case scenario as if it was your only-case scenario. The inability and inflexibility to choose how you spend your time will unsettle your soul.
- It's easy to waste time that you're not accountable for. However urgency – the ability to prioritise and act on what's most important before what's most fun – attracts opportunity.
- Time, like money, can be spent, or it can be invested. How much are you spending? How much are you investing?
- The return on time is time. If you want more free time tomorrow, you have to invest some of your free time today.

CHAPTER EIGHT

THE TIMESHEET OF LIFE

Time is your friend until it is your enemy.

Let's put the theory covered in the last chapter into action by completing a revealing exercise: a timesheet of your life. 'Mercy!' I hear you say. Pleasingly, I'm not going to ask you to do the unpleasant six-minute variety I had to endure. Instead we'll lengthen the timeframe to one-year intervals with the goal of being able to fit your entire life on one page.

Seven steps for creating a life timesheet

I've created a grid ('My Life Timesheet') for you on page 71 that contains the numbers 1 to 100 in a 10-column, 10-row format. Each square represents one year of your life. Your task is to complete the following seven steps. It won't take long—only a few minutes at most—but the results will be quite revealing, a little scary, but hopefully empowering.

Free template download

Note: If you prefer not to write in your book, or you need another copy of the table, then a replacement is available for download at **www.moneymagnet.au**

Step 1: Age now

Turn to the next page and locate the box in the life timesheet corresponding to your current age. Draw a circle around the number inside that box. For instance, if you are 40 years old, put a circle around 40.

Next, write down that number in the circle at the bottom of the life timesheet under the heading 'Age Now'.

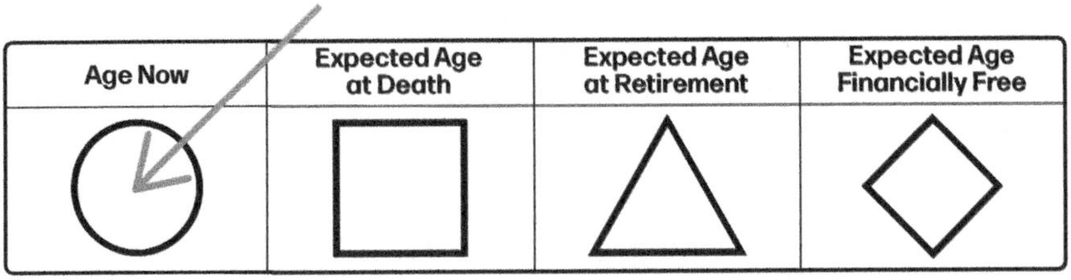

Step 2: Time gone

In the life timesheet, draw a line through all the years that you've lived, from 1 to the year before your current age. For example, if you're 35 years old, draw a line through years 1 to 10, 11 to 20, 21 to 30 and 31 to 34.

Step 3: Expected age at death

Referring to the information in the table overleaf, draw a square in the life timesheet around the age you're expected to live to, based on the year closest to your year of birth[5]. For instance, if you were born in 1971, you would reference 1975, which is age 73 for males, and age 79 for females. Hopefully you'll live longer, but let's go with what the statistics say for this exercise.

Write the answer in the square at the bottom of the life timesheet (to the right of the circle) under the heading 'Expected Age at Death'.

[5] The data in this chapter is sourced from data supplied by the ABS (2019), modified so that your expected age of death is referenced to the year closest to the year you were born, and the age you would be now based on that year.

My Life Timesheet

Name: ______________________________ **Date:** ___/___/_____

1	2	3	4	5	6	7	8	9	10
11	12	13	14	15	16	17	18	19	20
21	22	23	24	25	26	27	28	29	30
31	32	33	34	35	36	37	38	39	40
41	42	43	44	45	46	47	48	49	50
51	52	53	54	55	56	57	58	59	60
61	62	63	64	65	66	67	68	69	70
71	72	73	74	75	76	77	78	79	80
81	82	83	84	85	86	87	88	89	90
91	92	93	94	95	96	97	98	99	100

Age Now	Expected Age at Death	Expected Age at Retirement	Expected Age Financially Free
○	□	△	◇

Years of Life Left	Years of Work Left	Years Retired	Years Until Financial Freedom	Years of Financial Freedom
□ - ○	△ - ○	□ - △	◇ - ○	□ - ◇

	Year closest to year of birth							
	1946	1953	1965	1975	1985	1995	2005	2015
Male	89	77	77	73	76	77	80	81
Female	89	80	81	79	81	81	84	85

Source: ABS, 2019; McKnight

Note that the ages in the table have been adjusted to reflect your current age. That is, you'll see the lifespan of someone born in 1946 is 89 years, higher than any other year. This is not because of some elixir given to those born in that year; rather they would already be 76 years old (at the time of writing this book) and so are expected to live longer still.

Step 4: Time not applicable

Draw a line through all the years from your expected age at death through to age 100. Regrettably, this is time not expected to be available to you.

Step 5: Time left

Grab a highlighter (colour of your choice) and highlight the time left, which is represented by the boxes between the age you circled in Step 1 and the age you put a square around in Step 3.

I've found this to be quite a confronting task. Being 50, and only expected to live until I'm 73, there are only 23 years left on my 'life clock', which is less than 50 per cent of the life I've lived so far. I hope to prove the statistics wrong, but this exercise sure puts things in perspective.

Step 6: Expected age at retirement

Next, draw a triangle on the life timesheet around the *latest* age you want to retire from full-time work. For most people, this will be some time after you've turned 60, since you can't access your superannuation before then. As a reference, the average age people expect to retire is 65 (ABS, 2019).

Write the answer in the triangle at the bottom of the life timesheet under the heading 'Expected Age at Retirement'.

Step 7: Years of financial freedom

Finally, if you're planning to retire from the need to have to work before age 60, then draw a diamond around the age you hope to make that happen. Remember that in order to be financially free you'll need enough non-employment non-superannuation assets and income to cover your living expenses.

Write the answer in the diamond at the bottom of the life timesheet under the heading 'Years of Financial Freedom'.

All done! Now let's analyse your answers.

Analysing your time parameters

We now need to do five simple calculations to work out your time parameters.

Transfer the numbers you wrote down earlier (in Steps 1, 3, 6 and 7) into the shapes in the box at the bottom of the life timesheet page. I've used different shapes so you can match these up easily. Write the answer for each equation in the box under the shapes. Let's have a go at each calculation.

Calculation 1: Years of life left

Years of Life Left	Years of Work Left	Years Retired	Years Until Financial Freedom	Years of Financial Freedom
□ - ○	△ - ○	□ - △	◇ - ○	□ - ◇

This is the age at which you're expected to die (square), less your current age (circle). The difference is your expected remaining lifespan in years.

If you don't like the answer and would like more life than what the statisticians say, then be sure to prioritise healthy living!

Calculation 2: Years to work

Years of Life Left	Years of Work Left	Years Retired	Years Until Financial Freedom	Years of Financial Freedom
□ - ○	△ - ○	□ - △	◇ - ○	□ - ◇

This is the age at which you expect to retire (triangle), less your current age (circle). The answer is how many years you expect to keep having to work (i.e. remaining in full-time employment) before you retire.

Calculation 3: Years retired

Years of Life Left	Years of Work Left	Years Retired	Years Until Financial Freedom	Years of Financial Freedom
□ - ○	△ - ○	□ - △	◇ - ○	□ - ◇

This is the age at which you expect to die (square), less the age at which you expect to retire (triangle). The answer is how many years of life you expect to live in retirement.

Calculation 4: Years until financial freedom

Years of Life Left	Years of Work Left	Years Retired	Years Until Financial Freedom	Years of Financial Freedom
□ - ○	△ - ○	□ - △	◇ - ○	□ - ◇

This is how many years you have left to accumulate the required non-employment, non-superannuation assets and income to support your financial freedom. Calculate this by deducting your current age (circle) from your expected age of financial freedom (diamond).

Time compression

To demonstrate just how hard achieving financial freedom is likely to be, compare your answers for 'Years of Work Left' and 'Years Until Financial Freedom'. By achieving financial freedom you are essentially seeking to cram or compress all the years you expect to work down into the number of years until financial freedom. For example, say you're 35 years old. You would normally expect to work until 65, but you want to aim to be financially free by 50. In this case you'd be seeking to compress 30 years of work (i.e. 65–35) into 15 years (i.e. 50–35). If this is so, you couldn't afford to loll around for the next few years. Rather, your expectation should be to do in one year what normally takes two.

Calculation 5: Years of financial freedom

Years of Life Left	Years of Work Left	Years Retired	Years Until Financial Freedom	Years of Financial Freedom
□ - ○	△ - ○	□ - △	◇ - ○	□ - ◇

The final calculation is the age at which you expect to die (square), less the age at which you expect to achieve financial freedom (diamond). This is how many years you plan to live financially free.

• • •

That's it. Task over! Take a deep breath and give yourself a high-five. In my experience, by completing this exercise you've elevated yourself into the top 1 per cent of people who plan their life. The telling question is . . . what are you going to do to improve the answers, and do you have enough motivation to act urgently and change immediately?

Chapter highlights

- It might be an uncomfortable topic, but part of planning to live is planning to die.
- What makes your time valuable is an appreciation that you only have a finite amount of it remaining, and that the quality of what's left usually diminishes as your age increases and your health deteriorates.
- If you don't make an alternative plan, then it's likely you'll have to work until you're 65, and then live approximately a decade before dying. The quality and comfort of the final years of your life will be influenced by your available financial resources.
- If you want a different outcome than what your life timesheet reveals – to live longer and / or better – then you need to plan for it, and align your thinking and actions with it.
- Time is ticking. Make every minute count.

CHAPTER NINE

A BLUEPRINT FOR FINANCIAL FREEDOM

If you don't know where you're going you won't know how to get there.

To attract and keep more money, you need to draft a financial blueprint—a picture of what you want your finances to look like—and then follow it.

Imagine trying to build a house without printed plans. Instead, you just organically cobble together something on the fly as best you can, using what's available at the time. My daughter's prep teacher, Ms Boucher, had a great saying for this sort of approach: 'You get what you get, and you don't get upset'. Not planning might result in a 'workable' situation, but it certainly won't be organised, nor will its construction be as efficient or as cost-effective as making a master plan before beginning, and following it.

The financial freedom blueprint

I've found people generally lack an effective financial blueprint because they either don't know how to draft one (i.e. a lack of knowledge) or they have one but they're not following it (i.e. a lack of intent). Do either of these apply to you?

Lack of knowledge

How are you supposed to know, if you don't know? It's unreasonable to expect you to be able to do something that you've never been shown or taught how to do. If you want to, and are ready to, learn how to draft a financial blueprint, then my one-page template as outlined in this chapter is an excellent starting point.

It's unreasonable to expect you to be able to do something that you've never been shown or taught.

Lack of intent

If you have a blueprint but you're not following it, why aren't you? Do you not understand it? Do you not believe that it is workable or the results are attainable? Perhaps you've failed to implement it, and rather than face up to reasons why, you've stashed it out of sight where it's gathering dust. Or you may have prepared one at some stage, but it's now more in your mind than in your face.

The point I'm trying to make is that it's unrealistic to expect your financial situation to improve on its own. Whatever's been holding you back will keep holding you back until you've identified and fixed it once and for all. Truly, a failure to plan is a plan to fail.

A failure to plan is a plan to fail.

Completing the blueprint

Your Financial Freedom Blueprint assumes you want to be financially free, plus own your own home, with absolutely no debt. It attempts to quantify where you are now, where you want to be and the gap you'll need to bridge to achieve your goal.

The blueprint is a one-pager. The calculations aren't difficult and completing it won't take long, provided you've prepared beforehand, beginning by gathering the information you need, especially data on how much you earn and spend, and the value of your assets and debts.

The less distractions the better. Allocate quality time to complete it, rather than jamming it in between moments of busy-ness. My recommendation is to set aside time when you won't be exhausted after work, ideally an afternoon or evening on the weekend. If you have kids, arrange for them to be looked after by family or friends (unless they're old enough to be included in your discussions). Arrange takeaway to remove the stress of cooking and clear the kitchen table of clutter so you have somewhere tidy to work.

Once you're ready, turn the page to reveal my template for your Financial Freedom Blueprint template.

My Financial Freedom Blueprint

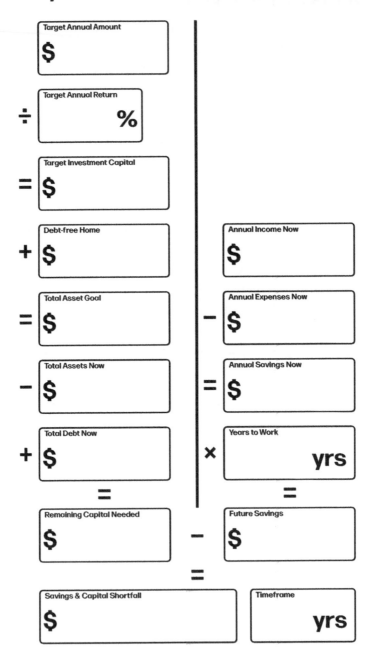

	Target Annual Amount $		
÷	Target Annual Return %		
=	Target Investment Capital $		
+	Debt-free Home $		Annual Income Now $
=	Total Asset Goal $	−	Annual Expenses Now $
−	Total Assets Now $	=	Annual Savings Now $
+	Total Debt Now $	×	Years to Work yrs
	=		=
	Remaining Capital Needed $	−	Future Savings $

=

Savings & Capital Shortfall $

Timeframe yrs

How does it work?

Your job is to fill in the blueprint boxes and perform the calculations as indicated by the maths symbols. Here's how:

- Start from the top of the left column and work down it until you've calculated Remaining Capital Needed.
- Switch over to the right column and work down from top to bottom until you've calculated Future Savings.
- Finally, complete the bottom boxes: Savings & Capital Shortfall and Timeframe.

Don't make this mistake

Some readers might be tempted to skip completing this template and just read on regardless. This would be a huge mistake. The content of this book builds upon itself, so if you miss this step then you'll be self-sabotaging the benefits on offer from reading and studying it.

Let's begin.

Preparation

The more accurate the data you use, the more precise and insightful your blueprint will be. To prevent unnecessary running around and ensure you are able to complete the template in the quickest possible time, gather the following information before starting:

The more accurate the data you use, the more precise and insightful your blueprint will be.

- Payslips evidencing how much you earn, and how much tax and superannuation is deducted from your pay
- Evidence you need to calculate how much investment income you received over the past 12 months, such as bank statements for interest, dividend statements, rent reports, and so on
- Documentation that will help you determine how much it costs you to live each year (i.e. your annual expenses).

  It would be handy if you were one of those extremely organised sorts of people who track their spending down to the last dollar. If that's you, then well done because your diligence will make your job quite straightforward. For everyone else, you have two options:

  1. *The best-guess approach.* Jump online and search for 'Monthly Household Budget Template'. Select one of the results that you like the look of, print it out and fill it in based on your 'best guess' of what you spend each month for each category listed. Multiply the result by 12 to get an annual number.
  2. *The savings approach.* Work out how much you have saved over the past six months and deduct the result from how much you've earned. You can do this by looking up your bank balance today, deducting what it was six months ago, and adjusting for any significant ins or outs that were not related to living expenses, such as purchase of investments, repayment of principal debt balances, and so on. If that sounds a little complicated, the diagram in appendix 1 walks you through what to do

- An estimate of the current market value of your assets. You don't need to engage a third-party valuer—your own conservative opinion is enough.
- A list of all your debts: who you owe money to, how much you owe and the percentage of interest payable.

When you have all the information you need, keep reading and fill in your blueprint as you go. Each of the following headings relates to one box in the blueprint.

Target annual income

Your target annual income is the amount of investment (i.e. non-employment and non-welfare) income you estimate you'll need to afford the lifestyle you desire once you leave full-time work and no longer receive employment income[6].

If you'd like guidance on how much annual income you might need in retirement, flick back to chapter 4.

Target annual return

This is the average total return your investments will need to deliver to generate your target annual income, expressed as a percentage per annum.

Not every asset in your portfolio will deliver the same return, so the number you write down needs to be the average annual percentage return across all your assets, expressed as a decimal. For example, 10 per cent = 0.1, 8 per cent = 0.08, 6 per cent = 0.06.

Remember to *divide* the annual income by the decimal equivalent of the average return percentage.

[6] Some authors call this passive income, but I think this term is misleading because there's nothing passive about the hard work needed to find, buy and manage good investments.

Why divide?

If you're confused about why you're dividing, then start with this formula:

Investment Capital × Return = Income

For instance, \$100 000 × 10% = \$10 000

Next, instead of solving for Income, we can solve for Investment Capital by re-expressing the formula as follows:

Income ÷ Return = Investment Capital

For instance, \$10 000 ÷ 10% = \$100 000

The maths of this formula reveals that the *higher* the average return is, the *lower* your Investment Capital needs to be. This is because you're dividing by a larger decimal. For instance, 1 divided by 0.10 (i.e. 10%) is 10, whereas 1 divided by 0.08 (i.e. 8%) is 12.5.

You'll find more information about what's a reasonable percentage for a target annual return in chapter 4.

Target investment capital

[*Target Annual Income ÷ Target Annual Return*]

This is the amount of investment capital, deployed at your target annual return, you need to accumulate your target annual income.

Debt-free Home

If owning a home is part of your long-term plan, then its estimated cost must be added to your Target Investment Capital. You'll want it to be ultimately debt free (i.e. no mortgage owing on it at retirement) so it's never at risk and you don't have to pay interest.

If you'd like to own multiple homes, such as a main residence and a holiday home, or homes in multiple locations, then include the total value of all your homes without any debt. You may like to add on a little extra for your furniture and other household items.

Target asset goal

[Target Investment Capital + Debt-free Home]

This is a calculation of the total value of the assets you need to accumulate to achieve financial freedom and own your home(s) debt free.

Total assets now

Your total assets are the estimated market (i.e. cash resale) value of all the assets you own now. Include your home, personal items and effects, property and share portfolios, savings and personal effects, and so on. Use a conservative rather than best-case value: the cash you'd receive if you had to sell everything in a hurry.

It's your choice whether or not to include your superannuation. If you're planning to achieve financial freedom before age 60, then I recommend leaving it out because you won't be able to access it.

Total debt now

This is how much money you currently owe. Include all personal or investment debts, such as the home mortgage, credit cards, store credit, buy-now-pay-later balances, car loans, IOUs, investment loans, and so on.

Remaining capital needed

[Target Asset Goal – Total Assets + Total Debt]

This is the amount of capital you need to accumulate to reach financial freedom and own your home(s) debt-free. It's the 'gap' you'll need to bridge using future savings, profits and money from other sources (such as an inheritance).

Is your remaining capital needed negative?

If your result for Remaining Capital Needed is negative, then pull out the streamers and put on a party hat because congratulations ... you're financially free! That is, you've accumulated enough assets to achieve financial freedom.

'Hang on Steve,' you might be saying. 'I don't feel financially free!'

If that's the case, then it's probably because the returns your assets are providing are currently lower than your targeted return, and / or your returns are unrealised (i.e. are on paper, so are unreal), rather than cash returns that reach your bank account.

Growth assets are appropriate to build wealth, but income assets are needed for financial freedom. Rarely is an asset good for both growth and income, so it's likely you'll need to sell and redeploy some or all of your assets (from growth to income) once you're ready to cross over into financial freedom. More on this topic is available in chapter 22.

Growth assets are appropriate to build wealth, but income assets are needed for financial freedom.

Let's move on to the right-hand side of the blueprint.

Annual income now

Include the amount of your annual recurrent income from *all* sources: employment, welfare, investment, and so on. For your investment income, include realised (i.e. paid in cash) and unrealised (i.e. exists on paper only, such as capital appreciation) returns, provided those profits are recurrent.

If you have income from sources that are difficult to measure, such as commission or tips, include a conservative amount that you believe you'll receive because it's better to under-promise and over-deliver than to be caught short.

Annual expenses now

Estimate your annual cost of living. Include taxes, all household costs and interest—everything except:

- principal debt repayments (i.e. repaying the balance owed) as that amount will be captured in the 'Total Debt Now' box
- compulsory or voluntary superannuation contributions sent off to your superannuation fund; let them flow through to savings.

Remember to catch what you spend from your bank account, and what you've bought using credit.

Annual savings now

[Annual Income – Annual Expenses]

Enter the amount you expect to save each year.

Is your annual savings now negative?

If it is, then we have a problem because you're currently living above your means (i.e. spending more than you earn) and are not in a position to save money to use to buy assets. Your options are to earn more or spend less (or both!) and / or to invest your way out of your financial woes.

Years to work

This is how many years you plan to keep working in full-time employment.

You calculated this number back in chapter 8: the result of subtracting your current age (circle) from your latest expected retirement age (triangle).

Future savings

[Annual Savings × Years Until Retirement]

Calculate how much you expect to save (i.e. income exceeding spending) over your remaining working life.

Savings & capital shortfall

[Remaining Capital Needed – Future Savings]

This is the shortfall to be made up from future investment profits, and from other sources not yet determined.

Is your savings & capital shortfall negative?

A negative Savings & Capital Shortfall is an amazing result because it means you are forecasting a Savings & Capital Surplus! This is extra money above and beyond what you expect to need to fund your financial freedom that you can use to build a legacy by supporting people and causes you're passionate about helping (or, as I like to do, invest that capital and donate the income it receives so I can make a gift into perpetuity).

Timeframe

This is the number of years you have given yourself to achieve your Savings & Capital Shortfall. This could be the same as your Years to Work, or it could be less if you want to achieve financial freedom before retiring from full-time work.

The results

High five! You've done it and are now the proud owner of your very own blueprint for achieving financial freedom! How do you feel?

One possibility is that you're feeling dejected believing the task at hand is impossible. If that's the case, then I recommend revisiting the variables to see if any changes could be made to achieve a more palatable result, such as reducing the annual income target, reducing the value of the debt-free home (or removing it all together) or increasing the years until retirement.

At the other end of the spectrum, you've completed this exercise and discovered you're actually financially free now, perhaps even without knowing it. Well, that's a nice surprise, isn't it? You might still have some work to do to turn your theoretical position into an actual one (e.g. asset redeployment) while also exploring ways to make your money count by using it to touch, move and inspire others.

However, most people who have done this exercise report that they find the results very interesting but that they're not sure how they'll bridge the savings and capital shortfall. That is, you now know *what*, but are not yet sure *how*. If that's you, then don't stress: we've got the rest of the book to sort that out.

Chapter highlights

1. Identifying the reasons why you haven't made or successfully implemented a financial blueprint will be critical to finally overcoming that obstacle.
2. Drafting a blueprint for financial freedom clarifies *what*, but it doesn't explain *how*. You still need to make and implement a plan for achieving your outcome.
3. Having done this template once, you can do it again as often as you like to 'check measure' your progress.

Free bonus chapter

If you'd like to see what a real-life Blueprint for Financial Freedom looks like, then head to **www.moneymagnet.au** and follow the links to download chapter 9A – a free bonus chapter.

CHAPTER TEN

ACHIEVING A SEEMINGLY IMPOSSIBLE MISSION

You can't change and stay the same.

One of the most ambitious adventures that humanity has ever undertaken was the Apollo 11 mission to the moon. US President John F Kennedy launched the idea on 25 May 1961. The mission was accomplished only eight years later: at 12:56 pm (AEST) on 21 July 1969.

Achieving the financial destination you plotted in the previous chapter might seem about as possible as a mission to the moon did on 24 May 1961. However, the success of Apollo 11 reminds me that the impossible becomes possible when a compelling vision is properly nourished (i.e. resourced) and nurtured (i.e. supported).

Having given birth to the idea of financial freedom, will you now allow it to remain as an unfulfilled dream—something that *might* happen in the future if some undetermined series of random events somehow conspires to bring it to fruition? Or is the idea worthy enough for you to want to nourish and nurture it so it grows and succeeds?

How do you eat an elephant?

Big goals are notoriously difficult to accomplish. If your vision for financial freedom seems too big to achieve, then the metaphor for how to eat an elephant may help: one bite at a time.

The way to eat an elephant is one bite at a time.

Imagine sitting down at a table faced with eating an adult elephant. How do you do that, knowing that you'll almost certainly be too full before you've completed the task? The answer is to make a start and get as far as you can, and then come back for more when you're ready.

How did I buy 130 properties in 3.5 years? One deal at a time.

A ladder with two rungs

If eating elephants isn't your thing, here's another illustration. Imagine you're standing on the ground looking up at the roof of a two-storey house. You want to climb onto the roof, but you can't do it without help. Leaning against the house is the perfect tool for the job: a tall ladder. Great! All you need to do is climb it, except there's a problem. The ladder only has two rungs, one at the bottom and one at the top, and nothing but open space in between. Now what do you do?

This situation well describes your dream of financial freedom. There is a bottom step representing where you are now, a top step representing the finishing line and a gap that needs to be bridged so you can scramble up in safety. You bridge the gap by adding in new rungs a certain width apart that are within your risk tolerance to climb. Such steps can sometimes be added before you start climbing; others only once you're already on the ladder.

Bridging gaps

Here are two ideas for how to bridge the gap on your ladder to financial freedom.

The linear approach

The first is to adopt a linear, or equal, method to accomplishing your goal. This approach, which you can follow by filling in the following boxes, assumes that your steps are an equal distance apart: the first just as easy or hard as the last.

Savings & Capital Shortfall		Timeframe		Annual Savings & Capital Goal
$	÷	yrs	=	$

For example, as illustrated in the following filled-in boxes, if your goal was to accumulate $1 000 000 to plug your required savings and capital shortfall, and you had a 10-year timeframe, the linear target would be $100 000 per annum (i.e. $1 000 000 ÷ 10 years).

Savings & Capital Shortfall		Timeframe		Annual Savings & Capital Goal
$1,000,000	÷	10 yrs	=	$100,000

The graph that follows illustrates this outcome.

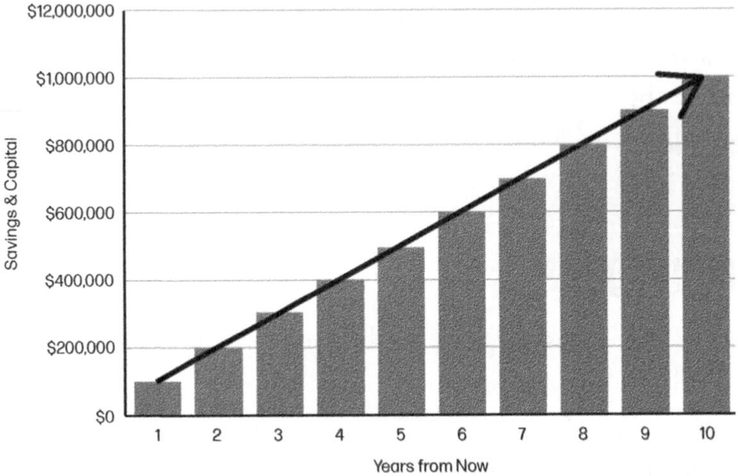

The linear approach appears simple and logical, but it assumes that your progress will be constant and consistent. That is, you will make the same progress from years 0 to 1, as in years 9 to 10. In the ladder metaphor, each rung is an equal distance apart.

Regretfully, I have rarely seen this sort of predictable progress. Rather, it takes time for new skills to be acquired and for old habits to change, resulting in less progress in earlier years, but more progress in later years.

It takes time for new skills to be acquired and for old habits to change.

The 'half-life, third-value' model

Another approach was pioneered by Brendan Kelly, a coach I employed in the mentoring program I used to offer. Brendan was a school teacher prior to working for me, and he borrowed from his maths and science knowledge to devise an approach that better mirrored the improvement we saw our mentorees making over time.

Using this method you apply a 'half-life' to the number of years, while also dividing the total required savings and capital base by three. The reason for dividing by three is that it reflects the notion that you will likely increase your wealth-creation capacity in the latter years when you have more time, experience and capital behind you.

You don't need to be a maths teacher to apply the 'half-life, third-value' model, just continue to divide your timeframe by two, and your savings and capital shortfall by three, until you get to 12 months remaining (or thereabouts).

Using the same $1 000 000 in 10 years example, the half-life, third-value would look like this:

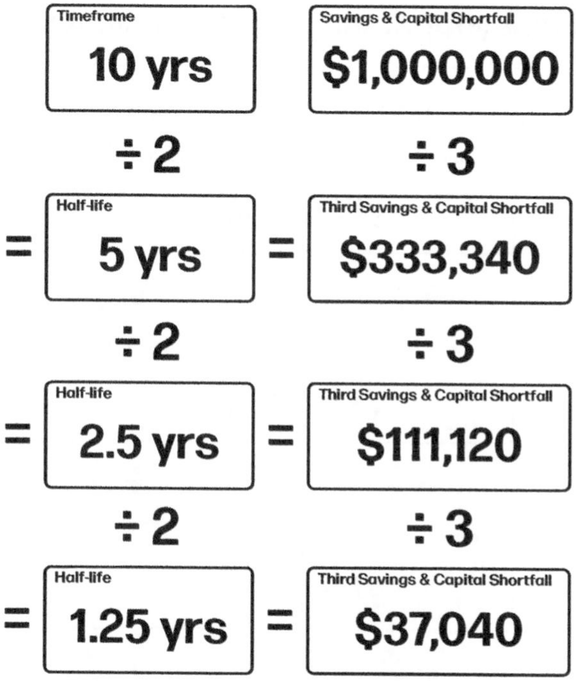

We need to divide a total of three times to get the timeframe to approximately 1 year: 10, 5, 2.5 and 1.25. You could argue the merits of dividing a fifth time to 0.625, but 1.25 is closer to 1 than 0.625, so I didn't bother.

We also divide the savings and capital shortfall by one-third each time, and round up to the nearest $10 for easy maths: $1 000 000; $333 340; $111 120; $37 040.

Each time period represents a rung in your ladder. They aren't evenly spaced, as was the case in the linear model, but they do better reflect that it will be easier at the start as the distance between the rungs will be shorter.

In summary, the half-life, third-value approach would require you to save or accumulate $37 040 in year one whereas the linear method would require $100 000 in savings or accumulated profit. Don't forget the concept here is not to just save money to accomplish your goal, but rather to save, invest and compound your profits to achieve the required target.

The concept here is not just to save, but to invest your savings and re-invest your profits.

Have a go at filling in the boxes for yourself and your situation.

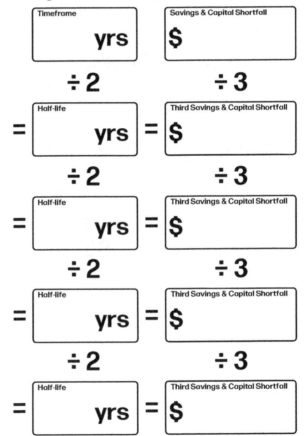

Timeframe: yrs	Savings & Capital Shortfall: $
÷ 2	÷ 3
= Half-life: yrs	= Third Savings & Capital Shortfall: $
÷ 2	÷ 3
= Half-life: yrs	= Third Savings & Capital Shortfall: $
÷ 2	÷ 3
= Half-life: yrs	= Third Savings & Capital Shortfall: $
÷ 2	÷ 3
= Half-life: yrs	= Third Savings & Capital Shortfall: $

Here's a graph of what the example of the half-life, third-value model looks like.

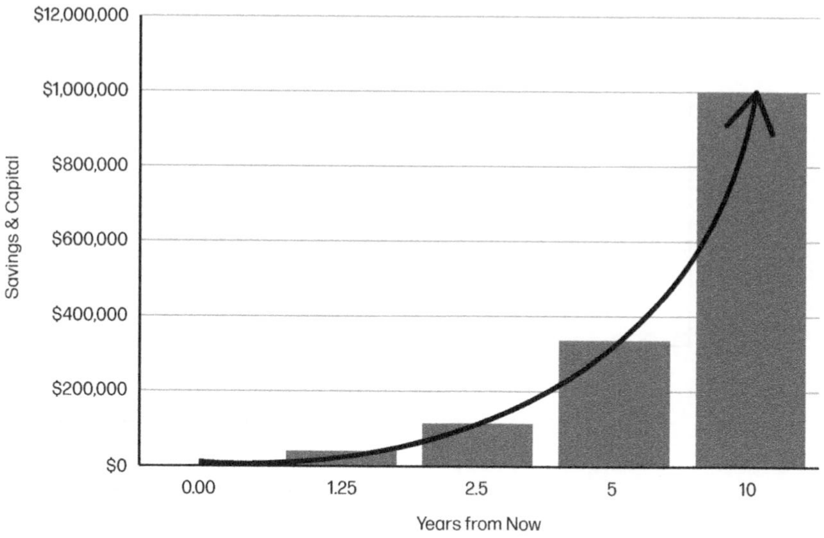

The following table gives a comparison of the values at various points in time for both methods. You'll see that the half-life target is easier in the earlier years and harder in the latter years.

At year	Linear target savings & capital	Half-life target savings & capital
0.00	$-	$-
1.25	$125,000	$37,040
2.50	$250,000	$111,120
5.00	$500,000	$333,340
10.00	$1,000,000	$1,000,000

The following graph shows a comparison of both methods over time.

To illustrate that progress is neither even nor steady, it took many months for Dave and me to go from one to two investment properties. A couple of years later we bought 30 or so in an afternoon.

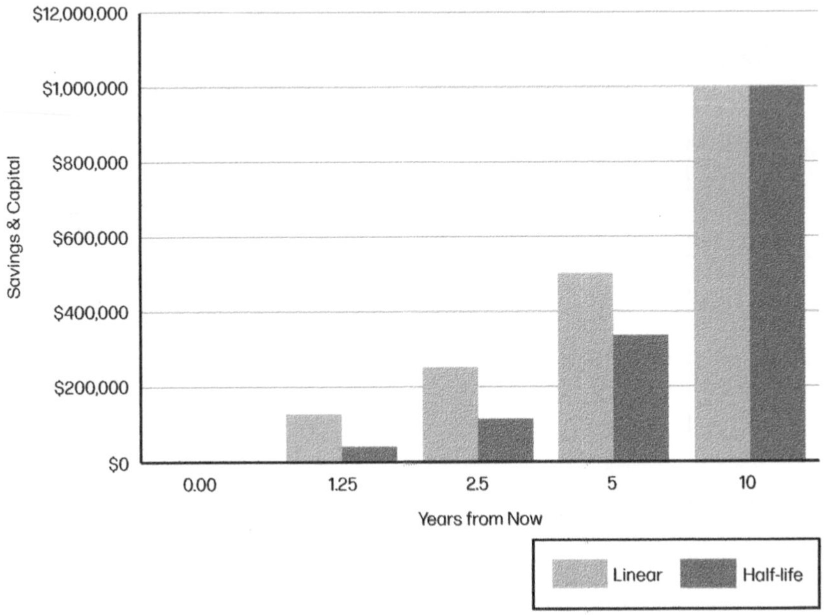

Feeling overwhelmed?

The example used — to accumulate $1 000 000 in savings and capital in 10 years — is an extremely, *extremely* ambitious target by any standard. If you're feeling like the required milestones, especially the first one, are beyond impossible to achieve, then reduce the required savings and capital amount and / or increase the timeframe.

For example, assuming you're following the half-life approach, the following table indicates the $1 000 000 goal over four time periods: 10 years, 20 years, 30 years and 40 years.

10 years		20 years		30 years		40 years	
½ life	⅓ value	½ life	⅓ value	½ life	⅓ value	½ life	⅓ value
				15	$333,340	20	$333,340
		10	$333,340	7.5	$111,120	10	$111,120
5	$333,340	5	$111,120	3.75	$37,040	5	$37,040
2.5	$111,120	2.5	$37,040	1.88	$12,350	2.5	$12,350
1.25	$37,040	1.25	$12,350	0.94	$4,120	1.25	$4,120

Pay attention to the last row. Do you see that the amount needed is smaller the longer the amount of time you have available (i.e. $37 040 for 10 years as opposed to $4 120 for 40 years)? No doubt 10 years sounds better, but 40 years is more feasible, unless you don't have 40 years left to live or work, of course.

Helpful hint

There is a series of online calculators available at **www.moneymagnet.au** you can use to help you complete the calculations outlined in this chapter.

If you want a different outcome then you'll need to chart a different course.

Expect a stretch

Remember that there's nothing free or easy about financial freedom; you'll have to extend yourself by improving your financial IQ and your financial EQ (I'll talk about these in Part 2 of the book). Without changing old habits, and making new ones, you'll remain on your present financial trajectory. If you want a different outcome then you'll need to chart a different course.

Course corrections

Small course corrections are barely noticeable over long distances.

For example, Rus—a pilot mate of mine—tells me that if you were flying from Perth to Sydney, the course direction would be 112°. Flying from Perth to Melbourne would be 104°. The conclusion: an 8° change in direction—something Rus tells me is a relatively small adjustment in the cockpit—will result in approximately 700 kilometres of difference in destination over the length of the Australian continent. Moving this example along, if you were flying from Adelaide to Sydney versus Adelaide to Melbourne, the difference would be 32°, exactly four times more than the Perth routes. What do we learn from this? The shorter the length of the journey, the bigger the required course correction.

Here are some examples of small and large financial course corrections:

Small	Large
• Acquire new knowledge	• Quit job
• Start tracking spending	• Sell house
• Begin a savings plan	• Sell major possessions
• Have no more debt	• Move overseas or interstate
• Make a debt reduction plan	• Sell your kids (only joking)
• Cash in possessions not used	
• Learn to invest	
• Deploy some investment capital	

The point is this: don't wait until you have to make large or radical changes to achieve financial freedom. The smaller the course correction, and the sooner you make it, the less dramatic it will feel and the easier it will be to implement and stick with. What course corrections do you need to make today?

If you're a little long in the tusk, then imagine if you could go back to your 18- or 19-year-old self and make a series of small but meaningful course corrections to your financial habits that would compound into major financial achievements and benefits today. If only …

Well, that may not be possible, but who do you know in that age group with ears open to listening who could benefit from your wisdom?

Expect in-flight corrections

Back to Apollo 11. Did you know that despite the precise, complex and incredibly detailed pre-flight calculations—which were no doubt checked and checked and checked again before lift-off—the flight crew had to make four minor mid-flight corrections? If they hadn't made them, they would have missed their target entirely.

Expect the same with your financial journey. Situations will crop up that will require a course correction or possibly even plotting a new destination.

Expect situations to crop up that will require a course correction or possibly even plotting a new destination.

The way to eat an elephant is one bite at a time. The way to climb a ladder is one rung at a time. Both illustrations require a solution to a problem that is too big to be accomplished on your own or as circumstances appear at the moment. Don't let that put you off starting. Take that first bite, or take that first step, and then see what happens. Sometimes the going will be easier, sometimes harder. Rest and recover when you need to, but stay engaged and make progress so you don't stall or backslide.

Chapter highlights

- Don't make the mistake of starving what you hope to grow, and feeding what you hope to shrink.
- Based on your financial trajectory, where will you 'land'? Is the destination one you're happy to arrive at?
- Small changes over long periods are a lot more practical and a lot less aggravating than large changes made suddenly.
- It's unlikely that your progress will be even and steady. Experience shows it will be harder at the beginning as you acquire and apply new knowledge, and as you change your behaviour to become more money attractive by trading bad habits for good ones.
- It's unlikely that you'll have all the answers before you launch, or that you won't have to make course corrections along the way, but don't let that stop you from making a start.
- I don't recommend eating elephants. Climbing ladders is much easier.

PART ONE SUMMARY

- The default financial trajectory of your average Aussie is to work for 40 years, pay off the mortgage and retire being supported by family and the federal government via an old-age pension. If that's what you want, then follow the masses.
- If you aspire to a better financial future, one where you are financially independent and self-sufficient, one where you live well above the poverty line and have money to afford the same or a better lifestyle after you've retired than what you enjoyed while you were still working, you need to make and follow a different plan.
- Tomorrow will only be better than today if you plan for it to be so. Things won't look after themselves, because unless you can create a compelling reason to make effort and sacrifice, you'll succumb to instant gratification.
- It's easy to waste what you don't see as valuable. To make your time count, you have to count your time.
- Financial freedom isn't free or easy. But it's not impossible either.
- You've now sketched a blueprint for a better and brighter financial future. How badly do you want to make it a reality? Enough to prioritise long-term gain over short-term pain?

PART TWO
FINANCIAL IQ AND FINANCIAL EQ

The way you think, act and feel financially is no fluke. You've been programmed—probably without even knowing it—and unless you deliberately reprogram, you'll keep thinking and acting the same way. Furthermore, you'll pass that programming on to those who follow you: your kids, grandkids and others you influence.

Are you programmed to be poor? Let the evidence speak for itself. Take a look at your current financial situation and ask yourself, 'Is this a picture of someone who has mastered money?'

If the answer is no, then it's time to book yourself in for a free 'software upgrade' to improve the way you 'run' your finances, while also getting rid of some of the marketing malware that's slipped in without detection and is stealing your dollars without you knowing or realising it.

CHAPTER ELEVEN
FINANCIAL LITERACY

Recruit for attitude and train for skill.

Money is a mystery to many people. It's not because they're dumb, hopeless at maths, unlucky or inherently ill-disciplined. It's because they've never been taught, or shown, how to think and act in a way that will allow them to successfully make, manage and multiply their way to a fortune, or, more simply put, to become and remain a money magnet.

Money is a mystery to many people ... because they've never been taught, or shown, how to become and remain a money magnet.

Young'n

Meet Blair, or, as I affectionately call him, Young'n.

Young'n is an 18-year-old lad who came to do some casual farm work at my property in north-east Victoria where we've planted 300 000 trees to establish a new native forest. While splitting wood one afternoon, Young'n and I started up a conversation.

'Young'n,' I said. 'How are you with money?'

'Not great,' he replied. 'I'm not good at maths, and my family doesn't seem to be very lucky.'

'So, you think you're not smart enough, and not lucky enough, to be wealthy?'

'That's right,' said Young'n.

Then I asked, 'Say I put you behind the wheel of a racing car and told you to drive it as fast as you could around the track. What do you think would happen?'

Not sure of the right answer, and not wanting to give the wrong answer, Young'n looked down at his boots while kicking the dust. After a while he replied, 'Well, I'd probably crash, I guess'.

'That's right!' I replied. 'And why?'

'Because ... I don't know how to drive a race car?'

'Exactly,' I beamed. 'And so it is with money. If you're not taught the basics of how to attract wealth, and how to keep it — how to drive the money car — then you're likely to crash financially. And now to the important point: have you ever been taught, or shown, how to attract and keep money?'

'No,' he said.

'That's a pity. And it wouldn't be because your parents deliberately withheld the information. It's likely they were not taught, or shown, and as we can only teach from what we know and do, they couldn't "know or show" you the right path.'

'If you want to be wealthy, Young'n, first you need a desire to *find out*, and then to *seek out* someone who has the knowledge, and also the experience, to teach you, and show you, what to do. It's that simple.'

How financially literate are you?

How did you learn to read? In my day, before whiteboards and PowerPoint presentations, when blackboards were at the front of every classroom and kids had to bang out the chalk dusters from time to time, we learned by identifying letters with sounds, progressing to combinations of letters, words, sentences, paragraphs and then finally to books of increasing complexity. It took hundreds of hours of learning and practice at school, over many years, supplemented with reading at home.

Now imagine you never went to school. How would you learn to communicate? Most likely you'd cobble together a functional understanding of the spoken word based on the conversations you heard and observed — say on TV, radio, in the home, workplace, social settings and so on — but you wouldn't be able to read or write.

Sasha

A close family friend, Sasha, was born in Germany. When he was one, his family moved to Croatia, the country of his parents' birth. Eight years later, Sasha's family moved back to Germany to pursue work opportunities. Three years later Sasha, his sister and his parents moved again, this time to Australia, with the hope of a better life.

Arriving Down Under, Sasha could speak German and Croatian, but not English.

'Our first thoughts after arriving,' Sasha told me, 'were "What the heck? Where have we come?" We'd left Munich, a world-class city, to arrive in the backblocks of Bacchus Marsh'.

(*continued*)

Sasha (cont'd)

'My first year at school in Australia was in year 7. Because I couldn't speak English, I was put in "Special English" class with two other non-English speaking students. It was a struggle through years 7, 8 and 9, but watching TV and being forced to speak English at school and in social settings gave me the ability to converse with confidence. That said, and even to this day, I feel a bit intimidated when called on to read aloud or express my thoughts without enough time to think them through.'

'Another factor that held me back was the people I associated with at school. The pack I ran with weren't bad people, but they preferred hanging out rather than doing homework.'

The point is this: if you've never been taught, the maximum level of language proficiency you'll accomplish will be limited by the calibre of the people you associate with and the circles you move in.

Now let's apply this discussion to financial literacy. No doubt you can 'converse' financially—that is, use money in day-to-day settings—but how well can you 'read and write' financially: to make plans, track spending, comprehend financial reports, use debt safely, understand what drives returns, evaluate investments and prepare for retirement?

No doubt you can 'converse' financially, but how well can you 'read and write' financially?

Learning financial literacy

While numeracy—the ability to understand, reason with and apply numerical concepts—is taught at kinder and thereafter through primary and secondary school, financial literacy—the ability to make informed judgements and to take effective decisions regarding the use and management of money (ASIC, 2003)—is not.

An ASIC discussion paper titled *Financial Literacy in Schools* (2003) found that financial literacy is not a formal course of study in any Australian state or territory school, nor is there any systematic approach to its teaching. A small amount of content that might be relevant is taught in social science, and a bit in mathematics. Sadly though, it appears that playing the board game 'Monopoly' is likely to deliver more financial skills than what you'll pick up after 14 years of formal schooling.

It appears that playing the board game 'Monopoly' is likely to deliver more financial skills than 14 years of formal schooling.

The Young Achievers (YA) program

When I was in year 11, I participated in a nationwide program called Young Achievers. While advertised as being available in schools, it was not taught in schools. Rather, teams of about 20 kids were formed from multiple schools and mentored in a business setting weekly after school for a couple of hours.

In my case, some managers from Coopers & Lybrand (chartered accountants) would meet with our YA team at their business offices for two hours one night a week for about twelve weeks. The task was to set up a small enterprise, elect directors, create a business idea and produce and sell it. Our team, 'YA Future', created printed shopping lists to 'make shopping easier'. We created a template

(*continued*)

The Young Achievers (YA) program (cont'd)

and had it typeset, then sold the shopping list door to door and at markets. My role was Marketing Manager, and I'm pleased to report that we turned a small profit. Little did I realise how valuable and useful this experience would be. I've used what I learned many times in my adult life.

In the absence of financial schooling, which we now know doesn't exist, how do people acquire their financial thoughts and habits? The only way they can: by watching and listening to conversations over time, and in particular, how their parents and peers use money. This is why, without a course correction arising from the injection of new ideas or information, the highest level of financial literacy you're likely to attain will be an average of that of your parents and friends.

That last paragraph is an important one, and it explains why financial disadvantage can be generational. It's not that parents want their children to be poor; it's just that they don't know, and so can't pass on, the skills needed to better make, manage and multiply money.

The consequences of financial illiteracy

Just as low levels of literacy and numeracy hobble a person's career and social prospects, so too does a lack of financial literacy impact a person's chances of attracting and keeping wealth. For example, the Australian Competition & Consumer Commission (ACCC, 2021) estimates that $328 000 000 was lost to investment scams in 2020. Aside from the risk of being ripped off, other consequences arising from a lack of monetary skill include the use and abuse of debt, lack of retirement planning, inability to properly assess financial risks and opportunities, and lower credit scores leading to higher interest costs.

Another consequence of financial illiteracy is a reliance on receiving advice that the recipient can't independently assess the quality of, and must therefore assume to be true. This can result in a dangerous situation because an inherent risk of any financial recommendation is that it will be biased by the benefit derived by those giving it. The awful stories recounted at The Royal Commission into Misconduct in the Banking, Superannuation and Financial Services Industry bears witness to that and led to the following observation, which should be remembered by anyone receiving financial advice (Hayne, 2019):

> *The interests of client, intermediary and provider of a product or service are not only different, they are opposed.*

That is, you might think that your adviser is primarily working for you, when it is more likely they are primarily working for themselves.

It seems to me that some sort of basic financial schooling will be required to break the cycle of financial illiteracy. Regretfully, the bureaucrats in charge still can't agree on a curriculum, and even if they could, the desire for teaching money skills in schools seems to be a low priority because for something new to be taught, something old must be left out. Seriously though, which is more needed in real life: calculus, or calculating how much you need to retire without relying on a pension?

The desire for teaching money skills in schools seems to be a low priority because for something new to be taught, something old must be left out.

Take the test

How financially literate are you? If you dare to find out, take the following quick, five-question quiz, which was included in the 2016

Household, Income and Labour Dynamics (HILDA) survey in Australia (Melbourne Institute: Applied Economic & Social Research, 2018).

Question 1 Suppose you put $100 into a no-fee savings account with a guaranteed interest rate of 2 per cent per year. You don't make any further payments into this account and you don't withdraw any money. How much would be in the account at the end of the first year, once the interest payment is made?	**$**
Question 2 Imagine now that the interest rate on your savings account was 1 per cent per year and inflation was 2 per cent per year. After one year, would you be able to buy more than today, exactly the same as today or less than today with the money in this account?	**MORE /LESS /SAME**
Question 3 Do you think that the following statement is true or false? 'Buying shares in a single company usually provides a safer return than buying shares in a number of different companies.'	**TRUE /FALSE**
Question 4 Again, please tell me whether you think the following statement is true or false: 'An investment with a high return is likely to be high risk.'	**TRUE /FALSE**
Question 5* Suppose that in four years' time your income has doubled, but the prices of all of the things you buy have also doubled. At that time, will you be able to buy more than today, exactly the same as today or less than today with your income?	**MORE /LESS /SAME**

* A slight modification was made to the wording of this question to remove the original time context, which is now redundant.

Once you've answered all five questions you can check your answers in Appendix 2.

Findings

If you got all the answers correct, then well done because as you'll see in the following table, fewer than half of those who completed the HILDA survey managed to get them all right, with fewer women (35.4%) compared with men (49.9%) scoring 5 out of 5.

Number of correct responses					
	None	1 or 2	3 or 4	All 5	Mean score out of 5
All persons	2.3%	11.1%	44.0%	42.5%	3.9
Males	1.5%	7.1%	41.5%	49.9%	4.1
Females	3.2%	15.0%	46.5%	35.4%	3.7

If you're interested, the table that follows provides a breakdown of how survey respondents performed on each question, with Question 2 (inflation) being the most problematic, and Question 1 (numeracy) being the best answered, just ahead of Question 4 (risk-return).

Proportion answering each question correctly					
	Q1	Q2	Q3	Q4	Q5
All persons	85.5%	69.8%	74.9%	83.5%	77.0%
Males	91.9%	76.6%	77.2%	88.1%	79.2%
Females	79.4%	63.3%	72.7%	79.0%	74.9%

The ultimate consequence of low levels of financial literacy is a dependence on welfare in retirement.

In my mind, the ultimate consequence of low levels of financial literacy is a dependence on welfare in retirement. If we really want that to change, the A-B-Cs of how to make, manage and multiply money need to be taught at school starting from an early age. This won't happen any time soon though because of the difficulty in reaching agreement on making changes to the national curriculum. If you want to improve your financial literacy you'll need to do it off your own back. The same applies to teaching your kids and others you love.

Chapter highlights

- The better your ability to read and write the language of money, the more financially attractive and empowered you'll become.
- If you've never been shown, how are you expected to know?
- The highest level of financial literacy you're likely to obtain is an average of the level of your family's and friends' financial literacy. If you want to aspire to something more than that, then you'll need a course correction: the input and implementation of new ideas and information.
- Low financial literacy will place you at the mercy of the integrity of your financial adviser.
- Financial literacy isn't currently, and probably won't ever be, taught in school. If you want to improve or be able to better instruct others, you'll need to take responsibility for your own up-skilling.

CHAPTER TWELVE

FINANCIAL PEDIGREE

Things are the way they are only until you decide for them to be something else.

Deoxyribonucleic acid.

There's not a whole lot I remember from high school biology, but I've never forgotten what DNA stands for. I can also still recite the first 20 elements of the periodic table—a handy skill at trivia nights.

Genetics

DNA is your genetic code, the building blocks of what makes you, you. You inherit it from your parents, who inherited their DNA from their parents, and so on and so forth back through time. Which of your parents do you physically resemble most? Which do you act like the most?

Environment

After birth, your DNA is affected by your physical environment. For instance, you might be genetically predisposed to being tall, but poor nutrition, injury, disease or hazardous life choices such as smoking, drinking alcohol or taking drugs could stunt your growth.

My mum and aunt were identical twins. And I mean *identical.* They shared the same DNA because after conception the fertilised egg split into two and made an exact genetic copy of itself.

Aside from looking the same, Mum and Aunty were spiritual twins. They even once shared the same dream, on the same night, and when one woke before the other, the other explained how the dream ended. Freaky!

Genetics may explain why Mum and Aunty looked the same at birth, but it doesn't explain why they looked less and less alike as time passed. One got married and had children, the other remained single and had no children. One worked as a teacher. The other as a full-time mum. One developed a brain tumour and had complicated health issues. The other didn't. These variances weren't because of genetics, they were because of differing environments and life experiences.

The point is this: how you look, think and act is determined by a combination of your DNA and the environments you've lived in.

How you look, think and act is determined by a combination of your DNA and the environments you've lived in.

Biology and behaviour

Just like your hair and eye colour are inherited, so too is the way you think and act around money. No, not via the fusion of financial chromosomes, but the combination of biology and behaviour.

Biology

Your genetic code programs how your body functions. That code may make you more susceptible to certain influences and behaviours, such as addiction. An article published by the American Psychological Association (Price, 2008) claimed that genetics accounts for 75 per cent of a person's inclination to begin smoking, 60 per cent of the tendency to become addicted and 54 per cent of their ability to quit. That is, if your parents smoked, you're much more likely to try smoking, and so too are your children.

The brain has the highest proportion of genes expressed in any part of the body (NIH, 2010) and given the brain controls the body, your genes directly affect the way you move, think, feel and behave.

If you're wondering how your DNA affects your financial behaviour, then you'll be interested to learn that a link has been established between genetics and gambling addiction (Mandal, 2010). It's not too much of a stretch to think that your brain chemistry affects the degree to which you are obsessive, impulsive and compulsive, which in turn affects your ability to be persuaded by marketing, make and stick to a plan, control spending, and so on.

It's not too much of a stretch to think that your brain chemistry affects your ability to be persuaded by marketing, and to make and stick to a plan.

ADHD

ADHD is thought to affect over 800 000 Australians, and tens of millions of people around the world. The condition is characterised by difficulty paying attention, being impulsive and hyperactivity. It's no wonder, then, that adults with ADHD may experience difficulty managing their money.

(*continued*)

ADHD (cont'd)

For instance, they may find it difficult to track expenses, pay bills on time and save for the future. They may make purchases impulsively, the consequences of which they may not always fully understand.

This doesn't doom someone with ADHD to financial oblivion. In fact, it makes the need for training, structure, support and accountability even more important.

Behaviour

You'll be familiar with the saying 'monkey see, monkey do'. While I'm sure you're no monkey's uncle or aunt, it's instinctive to model and parrot your parents' behaviour. Have you ever promised yourself that you won't do something your parents did, only to find yourself doing the exact same thing as a parent?

It's been established that genetics influences behaviour, so aside from the DNA you've directly inherited from your parents, you will have been indirectly 'programmed' by their behaviour and the way they talked about and interacted with money.

When I was little, I can't ever remember Mum or Dad putting money in those kiddie rides you see at shopping centres—the big plastic cars or animals that vibrate and make sounds. 'They're a waste of money,' I was told, many times over. So, that became my reference, and to this day I walk past them and think, 'What a waste of money'.

Here's the principle: your experiences while growing up will have influenced your reference point for what constitutes 'normal'. For instance, if your parents or guardians argued, you probably thought it normal that all adults argued. If they played the pokies, you probably thought it was normal for everyone to play the pokies. If you had dinner at 4 pm, you probably thought it was normal to eat at that time. In fact, if you knew someone who didn't do these things, the difference might have struck you as odd or abnormal.

Furthermore, the way you're living now will be defining normal for your children. Unless you tell them otherwise, if you work 16 hours a day, they'll think everyone does. If you have fish and chips on Friday night, they'll think everyone does. If you fight about money, they'll think that talking about money leads to arguments, and therefore it's better not to risk talking about it. Is the role model you're demonstrating the one you want your children to emulate?

Adam

Adam (aka Ads) and I met decades ago when we played junior basketball together.

Growing up, Adam's mum worked three jobs to raise four kids on her own after his dad lost the family home. They moved 11 times in 11 years, causing Ads to change homes and schools over and over again during those notoriously difficult and formative teenage years.

Ads is proof that despite experiencing difficulties, you can hope for improvement. 'It's monumental, Steve. At age 48, I'm only now learning about money. I never knew how strongly my beliefs had been pre-programmed. I was taught that rich people only got that way by being dishonest, money doesn't grow on trees and that "honest money" was hard to come by.'

'To change,' Ads shared with me, 'I had to learn new habits. It was hard. It took time'.

Ads admires and loves his mum for her effort, struggle and sacrifice. He also sees that the understanding and beliefs he inherited needed to change. 'A poverty mindset is a generational curse,' he observed astutely. 'Change begins with awareness and a new mindset.'

I've already shared with you that my dad is known for being frugal, so part of my inherited financial genetic makeup is a dislike of wasting money, and the love of bargains. Mum, on the other hand, is extremely generous, possibly to a fault. I've inherited that too! The combination is an odd mix: the desire to be generous, but only towards people and causes where I can see that the money will be valued and not wasted, and never taken for granted.

Stopping to think about it, which of your financial thoughts and behaviours can you attribute to your parents? Here are some ideas:

- Did your parents buy lotto tickets or scratchies? Do you?
- Did your parents play poker machines? Do you?
- Did your parents pay for things using credit cards? Do you?
- Did your parents budget? Do you?
- Did your parents save? Do you?
- Did your parents invest? Do you?
- Did your parents fight about money? Do you?
- Did your parents link money to faith? Do you?
- Did your parents say disparaging things about wealthy people? Do you?
- Did your parents say you'll never be good enough, successful or rich? Are you?

The clash of what's considered normal can be the cause of friction and fights in marriages. Your expectations and assumptions of what's expected may be very different from your partner's, and if you haven't talked about it beforehand, can lead to a substantial expectation gap. An example of trouble brewing would be one partner who grew up with parents who had little money and saved every cent, while the other partner's parents spent lavishly. The clash in attitudes towards what's the normal way to use money will need to be resolved until the tension eases.

Environment

In addition to what you've inherited from your parents, your monetary attitudes and actions are shaped by your environment outside the home, particularly once you've become an adult and left home. This could be the impact of a spouse or significant other, a mentor, a book or a course that you've studied. What you learn may cause you to question and redefine normal, and sow new seeds, new ideas and new possibilities that expand the boundaries of what you thought was once possible.

Sharon and Oliver

'The concept of financial freedom simply didn't exist in our minds,' said Sharon and Oliver. 'Normal was working until you retired in your mid-sixties.'

Sharon's parents were sheep farmers. Oliver's were public servants.

When I asked them what triggered a change in their thinking, they said reading books.

'Anita Bell's *Your Mortgage and How to Pay It Off in Five Years by Someone Who Did It in Three* challenged our thinking that it took 25 years to pay off your mortgage. Robert Kiyosaki's *Rich Dad Poor Dad* gave us the idea of passive income. Your book, *From 0 to 130 Properties in 3.5 Years* taught us about achieving financial freedom using the power of positive cashflow property.'

Not only did they read, Sharon and Oliver implemented. They applied what they'd read and learned by modifying their behaviour to set a different financial trajectory. One that elevated and

(*continued*)

Sharon and Oliver (cont'd)

expanded their financial horizons over and above what they thought was possible given the financial DNA they had inherited.

It took 18 years, but today their investments allow them to live a wonderful life split between Australia and Europe. Neither needs to work for money ever again. Sharon competes in mature-age professional tennis tournaments. Oliver's contract role recently ended and he is presently enjoying a sabbatical before moving on to whatever comes next: maybe a role in a start-up, or maybe something else.

'Freedom is choices,' they say.

The money mystery

Was money a topic of open conversation in your home growing up? You'd be fortunate if it was, because quite often I'm told that it is either not discussed at all, or worse, a taboo topic that can never be mentioned. A good friend recalled to me how, when he was 10 years old and faced with the task of completing a school assignment, he asked his dad a seemingly innocent question over the dinner table about the family's income and expenses. His dad reached over and hit him so hard with the back of his hand that he was he knocked clear off his chair. His dad said, 'Don't ever speak to me about money again!' He hasn't.

Just as you've inherited financial DNA, so too will you pass it on. The way you talk about and use money is being watched, and your habits will be inherited by your children and others you closely influence. What kind of legacy will that be?

Just as you've inherited financial DNA, so too will you pass it on.

If you want your kids to be ignorant about money, then keep them in the dark. If you want them to be empowered, then make money something that is openly talked about, and include them in conversations at a level appropriate to their age and ability. Here's an example: your kids will observe you using a magic plastic card to buy things. 'How cool,' they must think, 'to have something like that!' No doubt they can hardly wait for the day they'll get their own magic card too. But have you explained how credit works, and shown them (yes, sat them down and actually shown them) how it needs to be repaid?

All too often we give an answer without explaining why.

'Can I have ... ?' says little Johnny.

'No,' says Mum or Dad, for the tenth time that hour.

While answering no is certainly sometimes necessary, would it not be more empowering to redirect the answer to 'Yes, we could buy that, but then we couldn't buy ... '? Or, 'Yes, we could buy that, but remember we're saving for ... '? Or 'Yes, if you want to, you can buy it from your own pocket money and share it with the family'?

Why this approach? Because as an adult you can buy just about anything you want using credit. The decision needs to be reframed away from 'can you or can't you' to 'should you or shouldn't you'. If you can help your kids make good decisions, then that skill will be carried through life.

How much more mature would your money habits be today if your parents had made the time and gone to the effort to include you in their everyday and important financial discussions? Who will educate your kids if you don't or won't?

Breaking the mould

Remember that it's not where you start, but where you finish, that counts most. Things are the way they are only until you decide for them to be something else. If you had the advantage of growing up in a house where your parents talked openly about money and passed on positive habits, then count yourself lucky. If you didn't, then don't let that become baggage you carry around for a lifetime. It's more likely than not that your parents did the best job they knew how to do, which may have been a long way from perfect, but it was a genuine effort. Forgive and move on, accepting the challenge to improve upon their efforts if you're lucky enough to get the chance to be a parent.

Chapter highlights

- The way you think and act around money will have been 'set' based on what you inherited from your parents, both biologically (genetics) and behaviourally (by defining your expectation of normal).
- Those thoughts and actions will be shaped by your environment, particularly your experiences as you grow older and seek insights and influences outside the family unit.
- If you want your kids to be ignorant about money, then keep them in the dark. Don't be surprised, though, if they struggle financially as adults. Don't hide from your mistakes: share them so they're not repeated.
- Having good parents will give you a head start, but any advantage will be more than made up if you commit to learning new money magnet habits that help you to become more financially attractive.
- Just as the way you think and act was inherited from your parents, so too will you pass on behavioural patterns to your children and others you closely influence. What legacy are you leaving?

CHAPTER THIRTEEN

THE FINANCIAL FAMILY TREE

What you plant today you'll harvest tomorrow.

One of the most important matters raised in this book is that without a course correction you're unlikely to exceed the financial pedigree you've inherited from your parents, and your children are unlikely to improve the financial pedigree they've inherited from you. That is, without adding new ideas and information, you don't need to consult the stars or see a fortune teller to predict your family's financial future. Just look at what you have, or your parents had.

The financial family tree

Have you ever attempted to trace your ancestry? If so, then you probably know about 'family trees': diagrams that illustrate family relationships over time. They start with you, and then 'branch out' above as you trace your parents, grandparents, and so on, back through time, until available records and recollections become foggy or forgotten.

Let's attempt something similar: let's trace your *financial* family tree. Not only will we identify your ancestor's name, but also their:

- vocation or occupation — their predominant line of work
- highest level of schooling
- financial pedigree — whether or not they were known to be money attractive or money repellent.

You may be quite surprised by the results. When I've done this exercise at live seminars, participants have demonstrated a range of feelings and emotions, from acceptance and understanding — even forgiveness — to anger, profound sadness and tears.

Gathering information

Expect to do some digging to find information, perhaps by asking relatives or looking through family archives. The more you know, the better you'll be able to understand why you are the way you are.

Format and instructions

Please read all the instructions before starting to fill in the template.

On page 131 you'll see a pre-populated family tree that contains four levels (i.e. generations) of blank boxes like the ones here. Your job is to complete each box using the instructions given.

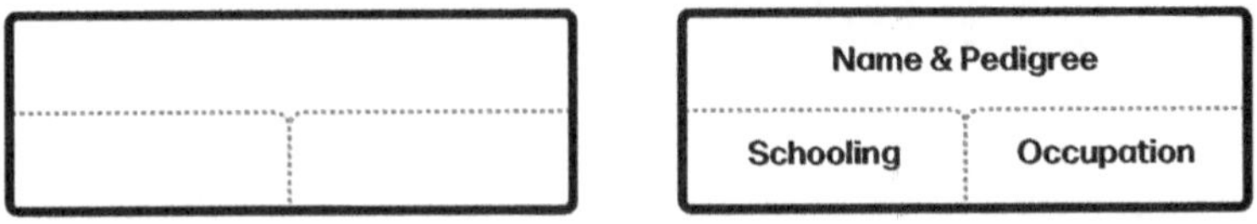

Name and financial pedigree

The first row of the box is reserved for the person's name, and to the right of that, an assessment of their financial pedigree using the scale that follows for how renowned they are (or were) for making, managing and multiplying their money. A clue would be their life after retirement and the extent to which their lifestyle could be maintained (i.e. not downsized) and supported without welfare (i.e. without the aged pension or family support) or greatly eating into capital (i.e. how wealth was preserved and distributed as an inheritance or used to fund a legacy).

Home ownership does not automatically demonstrate financial literacy because a home is a lifestyle asset bought for enjoyment, rather than a financial asset purchased for return. A financially literate person would limit their lifestyle assets to less than one-third of their total wealth.

A financially literate person would limit their lifestyle assets to less than one-third of their total wealth.

?	Not known
+	Financially literate – demonstrated by a good ability to make, manage and multiply their finances
–	Financially illiterate – was reliant on others for financial decisions or had a track record of financial mishaps

You may like to add more pluses or minuses to give a weighting to your assessment of how financially literate (+, ++, +++) or illiterate (–, – –, – – –) a person was.

Schooling

Note the highest level of completed schooling. Use the codes overleaf as a guide.

?	Not known
(N) Nil	No completed schooling
(P) Primary	Primary school
(S) Secondary	High school *Completed Year 12, Intermediate, Leaver's Certificate, 'Matric'*
(T) Trade	Tradesperson *Plumber, electrician, builder*
(C) Certificate	Undergraduate qualification *Certificate, Diploma*
(D) Degree	Bachelor degree *University-issued qualification*
(PG) Post Grad	Postgraduate study *Professional certificate, Masters, Doctorate*

Occupation

What is / was the person's main occupation, field of expertise or vocation? The usual way to describe someone who devoted their working life to keeping the house and raising the children is 'home duties'.

• • •

Right! Grab a pencil and a highlighter and let's make a start. By the way, if you're thinking about skipping the exercise, then I'd say at least attempt it for the sake of your children so you can document and understand the calibre of financial DNA you'll be passing on to them.

My Financial Family Tree

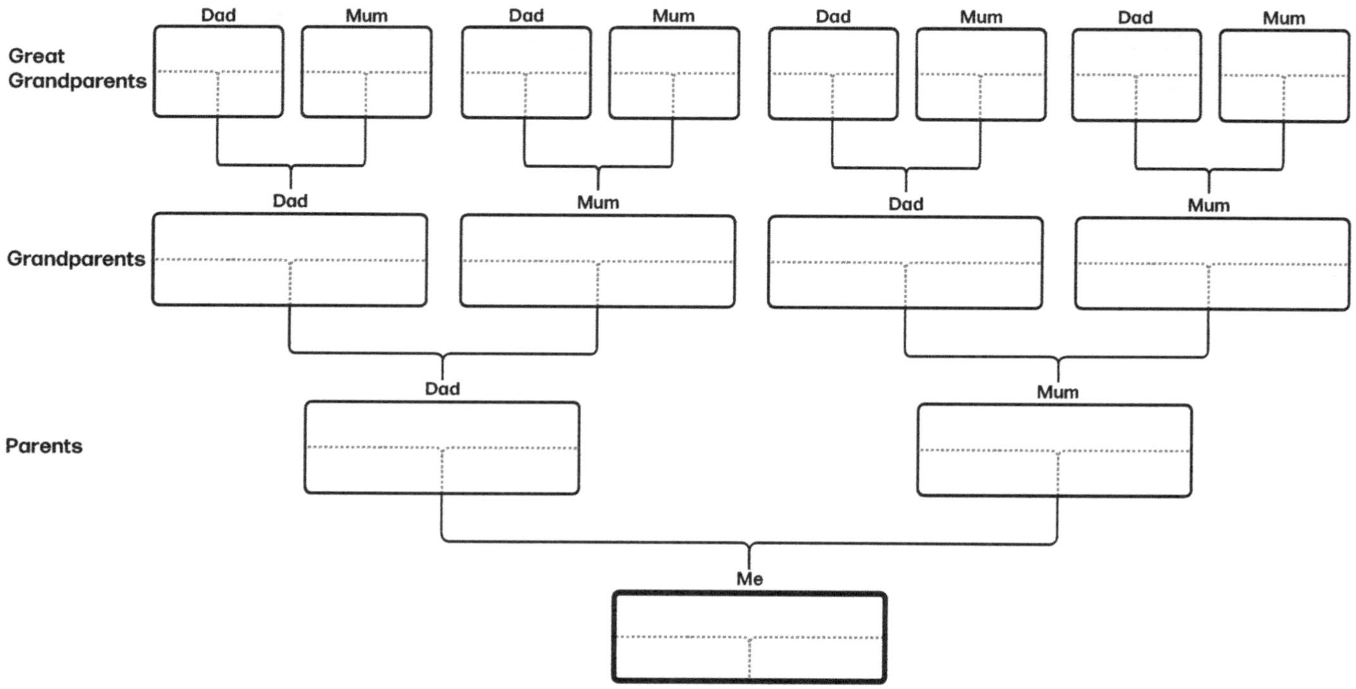

Template download and tutorial

If you'd like more room, then you can download a free A4-sized version from **www.moneymagnet.au**

You're also welcome to do this exercise with me via a video tutorial, which is available at the same website.

Level 1: Me

Refer to the diagram on page 131.

Locate the box at the bottom of your financial family tree titled 'Me', and:

1. Write your name in the top row of the box. To the right of your name give yourself a plus or minus rating to reflect your ability to attract or repel wealth. If you're not sure how to rate yourself, then a simple test is how much more wealth you have today compared to this time last year. You can also ask someone who knows you well and who will provide you with an honest appraisal.
2. Enter your highest level of schooling in the left column of the second row.
3. Write your (current) occupation or vocation in the right column of the second row.

Level 2: Parents

Next, complete the boxes for your parents. If you were raised by guardians, write down the names of two people you felt were major influences in your life, for good or otherwise.

Grab the highlighter and highlight the pathway to the parent you feel you resemble most with respect to your financial DNA.

Level 3: Grandparents

Once you've done this, it's time to move up the family tree and trace another generation: your parents' parents—that is, your grandparents. Depending on how old you are, sourcing this information might be a bit hard and you may need to consult with family members, but it will be worth the effort.

Don't forget that higher education, especially for women, was not the norm in Australia until after the 1960s. It was usual to finish school, move straight into paid employment and start climbing the corporate or career ladder. Women planning on being mums usually worked temporarily before permanently leaving the workforce to start raising their families.

As you did before, try to trace the pathway to each of your parent's parents who you think your parents most resembled with their attitudes to financial matters. If they're still alive it would be a good conversation starter.

Level 4: Great grandparents

Finally, if you can, gather the same information for your great grandparents: your parents' parents' parents. Remember that you can put down a question mark for those fields where information is missing.

If possible, use the highlighter to trace the pathway to which of your great grandparents your grandparents resembled most with their money acumen. If you don't know, then don't highlight anything.

Further thoughts and interpretation

Once you've completed as much as you can, you'll be ready to self-interpret the findings. Here are some suggested topics to work through.

Gaps

What branches are missing in your financial family tree? Sadly, the story of these valuable pieces of your ancestry's jigsaw puzzle—the lives, livelihoods and life wisdom of your ancestors—might be lost forever. A benefit of studying history is the lessons we learn from the mistakes others made. If those mistakes are forgotten, we are consigning ourselves and future generations to repeating them.

Education

The results are in. Higher education leads to higher total incomes, more diverse sources of income and a reduced reliance on the age pension (Australian Government, n.d.).

Boom! Crack! Omph! That's a very powerful trio of money magnetism forces everyone could benefit from. The opposite is also true: leave school early and you're at risk of stunting your full financial potential.

Leave school early and you're at risk of stunting your full financial potential.

A survey conducted for the ANZ Bank (Roy Morgan Research, 2003) identified that those who left school in year 10 or earlier, the unemployed and those in low-skilled employment had the lowest levels of financial literacy.

If financial literacy is not taught in schools, why would it matter when you left school? Perhaps because early school leavers didn't have parents who could teach them—or show them—the habits needed to attract and keep money. More so, in my opinion, it is because leaving school early will deprive that person of the opportunity to improve their reading, writing, numeracy and comprehension skills, meaning it will be harder for them to self-study and self-improve the financial DNA they've inherited. Finally, lower education usually results in lower paid work, making it harder to save, leading to less capital to invest.

Looking over your financial family tree, can you see a connection between the level of schooling accomplished and the wealth accumulated by that family unit? It's unlikely there was a major change in a single generation. Rather, the level of education improved over time, with the financial fortunes trailing behind it.

Being smart is not a sole determinant of being rich.

Note: As you'll see in chapter 14, being smart is not a sole determinant of being rich. Sometimes smart people find it harder to act without the certainty that they'll be right, and the over-abundance of caution results in analysis paralysis.

Lisa

When completing her financial family tree, Lisa observed that she had a superior education to her father, but the same level of employment seniority: a manager. However, her higher education empowered her to reach manager level sooner than her dad, and also gave her the skills to read and understand books and other material to course correct her financial future.

A sudden change for the worse in financial literacy can quickly undo the good work done by earlier generations. A family business left in the hands of someone who doesn't know how to operate it, or a windfall inheritance in the hands of someone who lacks the ability to manage and multiply it, can result in decades of diligence being squandered in quick time. In many ways, the fortunes of a family unit is like a game of snakes (money takers) and ladders (money makers). Which will you be: a ladder up, or a snake down?

Occupation and vocation

Your job describes the way your skills are employed, and your pay reflects how scarce and in demand your abilities are in the workforce. The more skilled you are, and the more in-demand those skills are, the more you'll get paid.

As a rule, higher levels of schooling lead to higher paying jobs because the extra study results in more, and more specialised, skills. If those skills are in demand, then those who have them will be highly compensated for providing them. The lowest level of pay is usually awarded to unskilled labourers who have little to sell other than the strength of their bodies and the time they have available to use it.

For instance, a doctor will get paid more than a checkout operator because the qualifications and skills needed to become and remain a doctor are complex and difficult. Relatively few people have the intellect and inclination to complete that level of study, so those who do are paid more than those who don't.

Looking at your financial family tree, can you identify a pattern of higher education leading to more specialised occupations? Perhaps the progression (or regression) from manual work or lower paying positions (factory workers, farmers, clerks) to more senior or even professional appointments (managers, doctors, lawyers, accountants)?

Looking at your financial family tree, can you identify a pattern of higher education leading to more specialised occupations?

How's your money magnetism?

Some people can sing. Others can juggle. Others still have a natural 'affinity' for financial matters because of the way their brains are wired, which, as we saw in the last chapter, is reflected in their habits and behaviours.

My mum's older sister, Patricia, married Michael, a fisherman and son of Greek immigrant parents. Although Uncle Michael left school early, his tenacity and entrepreneurial flair, matched with my aunt's intelligence, saw them create an enormously successful family empire that spanned marine engineering, fishing and even pearls.

Remember, while a natural affinity is helpful, everything you need to know to make, manage and multiply your money can be learned and mastered if you're willing to put in the hard work.

Everything you need to know to make, manage and multiply your money can be learned and mastered if you're willing to put in the hard work.

Have a go at tracing your money magnetism through your financial family tree to see if you can identify a particular individual who was a major turning point in your family's financial fortunes. What was it that they knew, or did, that made them noteworthy?

Customs and culture

Don't underestimate the impact that customs and culture may play. Someone may have been expected to take on a particular role or responsibility, and if they didn't, shame would be heaped upon them and / or the family name. Wealth may also be disproportionately allocated or distributed according to birth order, rank, title, bloodlines, gender, and so on.

For instance, my grandfather on my mother's side, as the youngest son, was told he would never inherit the family farm. He had to find another occupation and build his own asset base from scratch.

Women and financial disempowerment

Not long ago—and indeed in some countries it's still the case—women were expected to leave school early to learn how to look after the home. They were kept back from the workforce and sheltered from the family's finances.

The consequence of such a well-meaning but dreadfully misguided male ego was a dependency on the man of the house to look after the money. If the man was inept, or pre-deceased his partner, then the whole house could easily be forced into financial disadvantage.

A well-rounded house relies on more than one financial brain.

A well-rounded house relies on more than one financial brain.

Skipping generations

Like biological DNA, it is possible for your financial DNA to have skipped a generation. For example, you may have had an especially close bond with a grandparent whose influence upon you was more profound than your parents'. Alternatively, you may have been grafted onto another family tree: perhaps that of another relative (uncle, aunt) or even a particularly influential friend or mentor.

Timelines

Don't forget that conditions have changed over time: booms and busts, famines, wars and other changed circumstances all affect the level of schooling, types of jobs and family fortunes. For instance, children of the Great Depression tended to be more focused on job security and less risk tolerant because they lived through very difficult times of shortages and high unemployment. That bias would have been passed on to their children, so it will take a few generations for risk appetites to re-emerge.

Graham McKnight

Dad's parents, my grandparents on his side, were both school teachers who were well educated but quite poorly paid given their expertise. There was never much money around when Dad was growing up: bread and dripping was a common meal.

It's become evident that frugal wasn't a choice so much as a necessity, and it was drummed into him from a very young age, and then galvanised as an adult by his lack of consistent pay (he was paid on commission, rather than a steady salary). Dad's attitude can be summarised as 'you live lean, and when you have more, you save it so you can survive when you have less'. Although he has done extremely well for himself, he struggles to enjoy his money. He's hard-wired to never want to need money and not have it, so he always acts like there may not be enough.

Now, turning to my grandparents on Dad's side ... what made them the way they were? Again, they were products of their environment. As children during the Great Depression, they experienced first hand how grim life can be during severe financial hardship. Their frugal habits were a product of their parents, my great grandparents, William – a garden farmer – and Bella – a post mistress, who would have been children during the depression of the 1890s, which was both longer and more severe than the 1930's depression.

Truly, this was a huge revelation for me. For a long time I blamed, even perhaps resented, my dad for not being 'better' – or maybe 'more generous' – with money, and in particular his extremely

(continued)

Graham McKnight (cont'd)

frugal mindset, without ever understanding that it wasn't his choice so much as his pedigree to be so. Only relatively recently have I been able to repent from my adolescent ignorance and come to appreciate, even greatly admire, him for his financial achievements, given the challenges he faced growing up.

Personal attributes

As we saw in chapter 12, a person's characteristics and environment will affect their outcomes. For instance, a younger sibling may have more drive and ambition to prove themselves worthy of their parents' and older sibling's approval. Someone else may have a more determined ingrained work ethic because their parents seemed distant, so in order to make something happen, it was up to the individual.

Negative role models

Just as there are positive role models, there can also be role models you want to steer away from because they've demonstrated behaviours that repel money. You can sometimes learn even more from these people than those who seem to have their financial act together, if their flaws and foibles are more evident. Looking at your financial family tree, can you identify any negative role models, and if so, what was their legacy?

Tree roots

So far, we've been looking up the branches of your family tree. Now let's look down at its roots: the network that's growing out from under you. Grab a pencil and draw your financial family tree's 'root structure', with each line representing one generation under you. For example, if you had two children, and they each had two children, your root structure would look like the diagram overleaf (you're the box with the thick black line at ground level).

Complete the boxes for your descendants, as you did for your ancestors. If their level of money magnetism is not yet known, write in what you hope it will be.

Remember, the starting point for your children and grandchildren is your money magnetism, highest level of education and type of occupation. Are you happy with that, or do you hope for them to aim higher? That is, will you leave your family's financial future to chance and fate, or do you want to cast a deliberate and improved vision, and then resource it as needed to nurture success into fruition?

The starting point for your children and grandchildren is your money magnetism, highest level of education and type of occupation.

What information, skills and habits do you need to acquire and pass on to those who depend on you to help them attract and keep more money? It'll be the best investment you ever make.

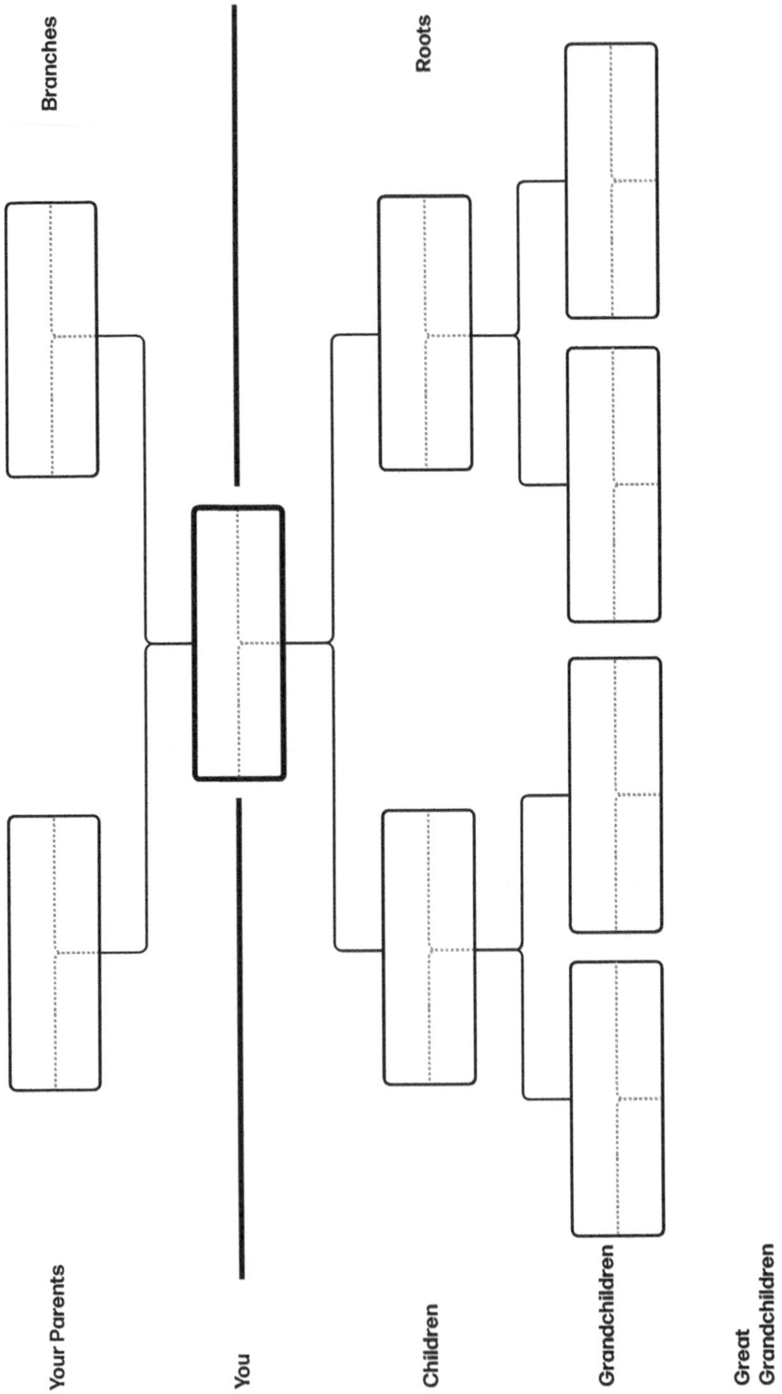
Branches
Roots
Your Parents
You
Children
Grandchildren
Great Grandchildren

Chapter highlights

- You are the way you are because of those who went before you. What mistakes have others made that you can learn from and not repeat?
- If you don't know much of your past you won't know what's shaped your parents' attitudes about money. You might then erroneously think they chose their beliefs and actions, as opposed to them being *shaped* and *influenced* by their environments and experiences. This may cause you to blame them for not being better, when really they did the best job they knew how to do.
- If you want to improve, a course correction is needed. That course correction requires the ability to study, understand and implement new information to form new productive habits and behaviours – and to phase out unproductive ones.
- School is important because it teaches you how to read and think. Without those skills, your financial future – as well as that of those who follow you – may be compromised
- If you want to financially empower your children, don't give them money to buy their favour; encourage and incentivise them to do well at school.
- Change is more likely to be small and incremental than instant and radical. For instance, breaking the cycle of financial disadvantage may take several generations, led by improved schooling as a precursor to higher paid employment opportunities. That said, higher pay without the financial diligence to keep and multiply your money won't result in the accumulation of wealth.

(*continued*)

Chapter highlights (cont'd)

- Are you willing and able to take on the role of patriarch or matriarch for your family and cast a vision for your children, grandchildren and descendants thereafter rather than letting chance and fate alone determine what will happen? Imagine how your life might be different if a parent or grandparent had done that for you?

CHAPTER FOURTEEN

PROGRAMMING YOUR FINANCES

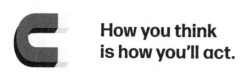

How you think is how you'll act.

Is your financial programming—the way you think, act and feel about money—working for you or against you in your efforts to accumulate wealth? The best way to tell is to work out whether you're an under accumulator, average accumulator or prodigious accumulator of wealth.

Hardware and software

Run with me on this imperfect illustration.

To function, a computer relies on hardware—physical items such as the box and what's inside it, monitor, keyboard; and software—programs that contain 'code' or instructions telling the hardware how to act and behave.

Now, using the computer as a metaphor, you have hardware and software. Your hardware is your physical body: arms, legs, brain, heart and so on. Your software is your habits and beliefs: ideas and thoughts that are the programs or instructions that direct your hardware how to perform.

We actually run many different software programs at the same time, among them health, exercise, parenting, driving and speech. Those programs function according to their programming. If the programming is good, the software will run efficiently and effectively. If the programming is poor, then the outcome from running it will be sub-standard.

How do we become programmed? We've already established that people and events influence our thoughts and behaviours. However, we also learn from trial and error—by giving something a go—and if the outcome is favourable, we 'save' that action so it can be recalled the next time we need it. This example raises the idea of conscious and semi-conscious thoughts. The former is like manual override; the latter are the things we do without thinking much about them: swallowing, blinking, breathing, chewing, scratching, walking and so on.

The way you think and act financially is like a program that runs in the background – in your semi-conscious – most of the time.

The way you think and act financially is like a program that runs in the background—in your semi-conscious—most of the time. Without much effort, you 'operate' your finances according to your programming. Like your choice of paying for petrol after you've filled up the car, or how you pay for a coffee. Occasionally a big decision crops up that requires manual override—perhaps a first-time situation, or solving a complicated variation of a problem you've encountered before. In these cases you rely on your intellect to reach the right conclusion. The question is: *Is the outcome of the financial programs you're running leading to the outcome you want, or do you need some reprogramming?*

Intelligence quotient (IQ)

Have you ever sat an IQ test? They're usually a series of questions that measure your grasp of language, numeracy, spatial matters and logic. For instance, here's a question you might find on an IQ test:

Water is to a pipe as ? is to a wire:

a. cord
b. heat
c. electricity
d. gas.

The answer is provided in the footnote[7].

IQ stands for intelligence quotient. Technically, IQ is a number representing a person's ability to reason, compared with others their age. A score of 100, give or take, represents average intelligence. A score above 130 indicates 'gifted'.

Practically, IQ is more widely used to summarise a person's general level of intelligence. Intelligent people, for instance, are said to have a high IQ, whereas fools are thought to be of low IQ—that is, a classification without a specific number attributed to it.

Having a high IQ doesn't necessarily make you 'real-world' smart. General intelligence is not just what you think (your cognitive ability), but also how you act (your cognitive disposition). It is definitely possible for a person to be a genius and yet be challenged in the company of others. Do you know someone like that: intellectually smart, but socially awkward?

Simple over smart

It's worthwhile quickly differentiating between intelligence and wisdom. The former relates to the ability to know the right answer in theory, the latter to the ability to apply the knowledge astutely. Which would you rather: knowing 80 per cent of a topic but only astutely applying that knowledge 20 per cent of the time; or knowing 20 per cent of a topic, but astutely applying that knowledge 80 per cent of the time? I'd prefer

[7] The answer is (c) electricity. Water flows through a pipe, and electricity flows via a wire.

the latter: to know less but to apply what I did know more successfully. When it comes to being a money magnet it's more important to apply fewer skills well, than more skills poorly.

When it comes to being a money magnet it's more important to apply fewer skills well, than more skills poorly.

People make the mistake of thinking that you have to be smart to be wealthy. I've found the opposite to be true: that a simple-to-understand goal, with simple-to-understand strategies for achieving it, outperforms smart and sophisticated every time. Smart people tend to have a character flaw in that they think they have to be experts at something before they'll give it a try, lest they fail and appear foolish. This leads to analysis paralysis and procrastination. Your goal should be to be smart enough to understand the basics of how something works, wise enough to learn from others' mistakes, and courageous enough to start small and scale as you succeed.

Financial IQ (FQ)

Expanding on the concept of IQ, I use the term 'financial IQ', or 'FQ', to summarise a person's financial intelligence: their ability to reason, think and solve monetary problems and to apply those skills in the real world to attract and retain wealth. That is, a combination of having the intelligence to know and the wisdom to apply.

Some advisers have a high level of technical financial intelligence, meaning they know the relevant theory, but have a low functional capability to apply that theory in their own life. An example that comes to mind is someone who might teach financial planning, or give financial planning advice, but have below-average personal wealth. Such people are happy to tell others what to do, but seem unwilling or unable to act on their own advice.

How financially 'bright' are you? There isn't a test you can take to determine a score for your FQ as such, but a good exercise to complete to gauge your ability is to compare your current net worth with how much net worth you should have for your age and income.

A financial IQ benchmark

A benchmark for net worth was devised by the authors of a book I highly recommend reading and studying, *The Millionaire Next Door* (Stanley & Danko, 2010). Their rule of thumb, which is applicable for those aged 30 to retirement age, is to take your age, multiply it by your total annual income (pre-tax, excluding any inheritance) and then divide it by ten. The resulting number is your target net worth.

However, that's a bit of an eyeful and a brainful, so let's simplify it by taking out the effect of inheritances, and re-express it as outlined in the following diagram.

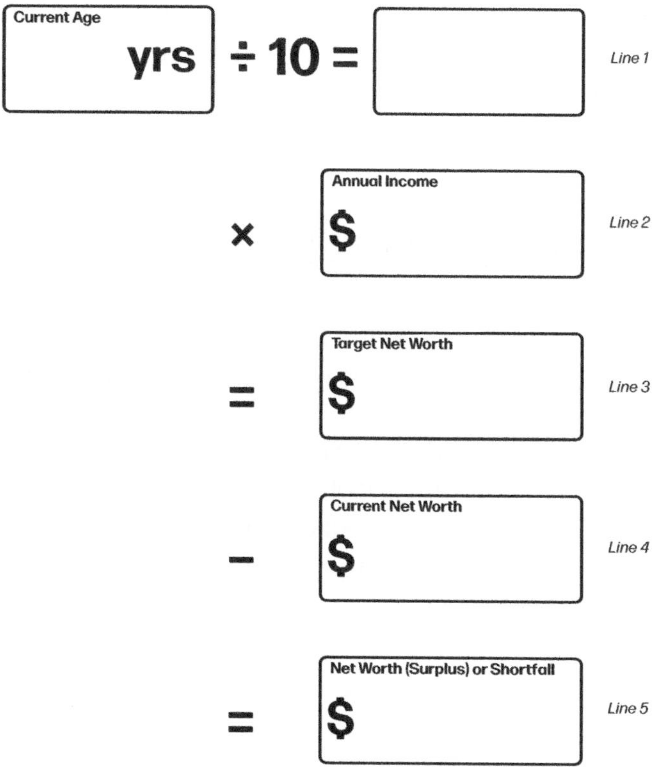

- *Line 1 (Age):* Input your current age, divide it by 10 and write the answer in the blank box on the first line.
- *Line 2 (Annual Income):* Add up your annual income from all sources.
- *Line 3 (Target Net Worth):* Multiply your answer in Line 1 by your Annual Income in Line 2. This is how much net worth (i.e. the value of all your assets less the value of all your debts) you should have managed to accumulate.
- *Line 4 (Current Net Worth):* Enter the total value of all your personal and investment assets (including your home and superannuation), less the total value of all your personal and investment debts. *Note:* You tallied up your assets and debts back in chapter 9.
- *Line 5 (Surplus or Shortfall):* Write in the surplus (if a negative value) or shortfall of your Current Net Worth compared to your Target Net Worth as per Stanley and Danko's rule of thumb.

Sample calculation: Jane

While doing a read through of the draft manuscript for this book with friends, we ran through the real-life situation of one member of the group. Let's call her Jane. Jane agreed to be included in the book to help readers understand her real-life scenario. In her case, she is 40 years old, earns $120 000 per annum and has net assets of $250 000. Here's the calculation for Jane's target net worth according to Stanley and Danko's rule of thumb:

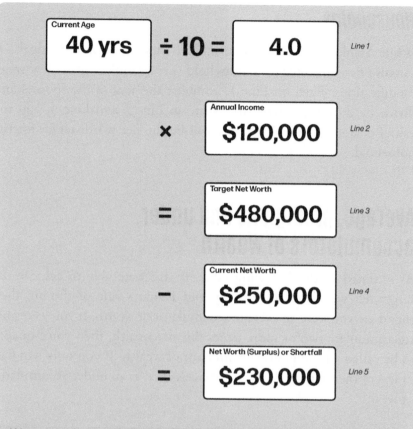

Current Age: 40 yrs	÷ 10 =	4.0	Line 1
	×	Annual Income: $120,000	Line 2
	=	Target Net Worth: $480,000	Line 3
	–	Current Net Worth: $250,000	Line 4
	=	Net Worth (Surplus) or Shortfall: $230,000	Line 5

Worried that my friend might feel deflated by the result, I sought to reassure her that she was in much better financial shape than many poor souls I meet.

'Oh no Steve,' she said. 'This is a great result! Until my husband and I met you a few years ago we had a negative net worth. Our result reflects the progress we've made, and the work we've still got left to complete.'

Households

While Stanley and Danko's formula is designed for individuals, it can also be completed as a household (i.e. a family) with a few small modifications. First, on Line 1, combine the ages of the spouses and divide by 20 (rather than 10). Next, on Line 2 and Line 4, add the values of both adults. The result will be the net worth target for the household.

Average, prodigious and under accumulators of wealth

As outlined in the following table, if you were able to achieve the target net wealth set by Stanley and Danko's rule of thumb, then they'd say you were an average accumulator of wealth. If you were able to accumulate two or more times this net wealth, then you'd qualify to be called a prodigious accumulator of wealth. If you only had half or less of their target, then you'd be classified as an under accumulator of wealth.

Your net wealth compared to Stanley & Danko's target	Accumulator of wealth status
Half or less	Under
At	Average
Double or more	Prodigious

You can use the following diagram to work through the numbers to determine whether you're an under, average or prodigious accumulator of wealth.

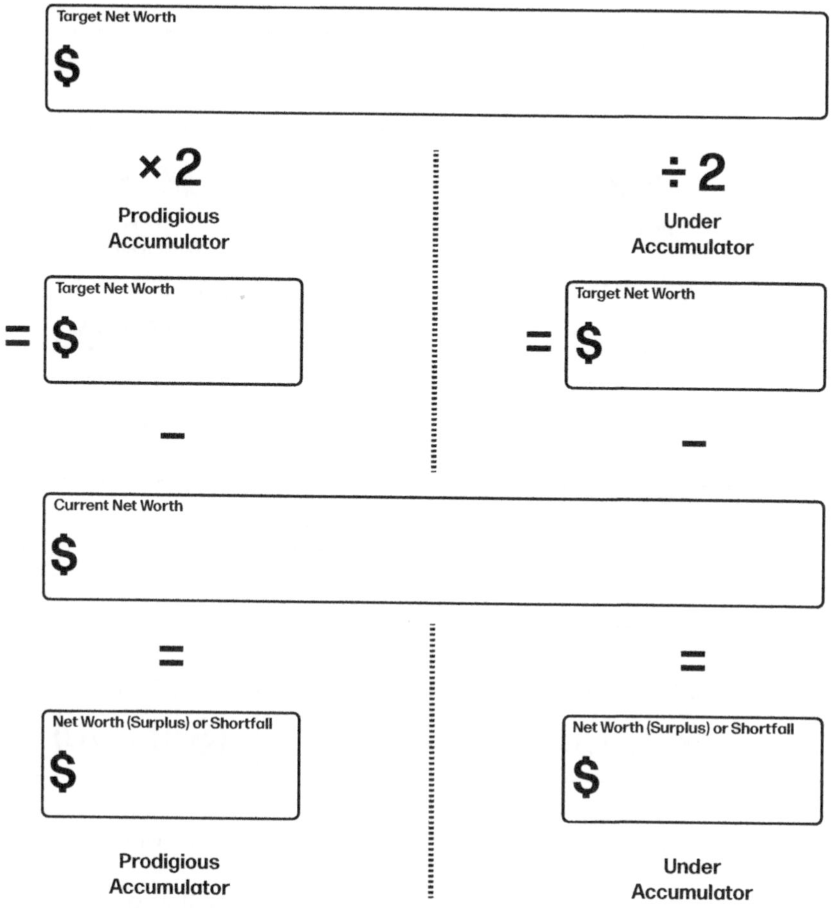

Sample calculation: Part 2

Here's Jane's calculation and classification.

Target Net Worth
$480,000

× 2 Prodigious Accumulator	÷ 2 Under Accumulator
= Target Net Worth **$960,000**	= Target Net Worth **$240,000**
–	–

Current Net Worth
$250,000

=	=
Net Worth (Surplus) or Shortfall **$710,000**	Net Worth (Surplus) or Shortfall **($10,000)**
Prodigious Accumulator	Under Accumulator

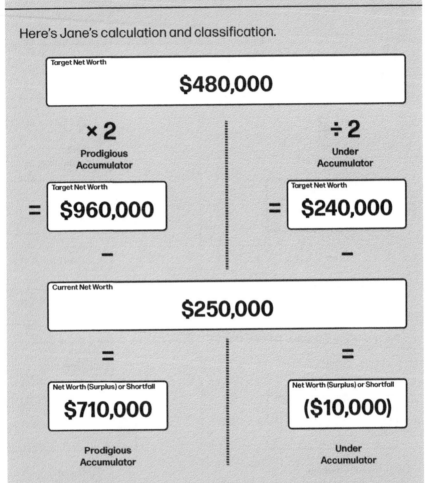

I know it seems counter intuitive, but if your result is a negative amount then that number represents the surplus above the threshold. For instance, Jane is $10,000 above the threshold for 'Under Accumulator', but $710,000 below the threshold for 'Prodigious Accumulator'.

She might have been disappointed with the result, as she is much closer to being an under accumulator than an average accumulator of wealth. However, when you consider her progress in just a few years, she's definitely on the right path.

What's your result? Are you a prodigious, average or under accumulator of wealth? You can link your situation back to your FQ: high (i.e. prodigious), average or low level of financial intelligence. Jane's result indicated that she had a low FQ, which was true a few years back. However, in her case, her progress rather than her score reflects her current FQ.

Oh, and just saying, if you didn't bother crunching the numbers, then you're displaying the behaviour of someone with a low FQ. By your deeds you shall be known!

Emotional quotient (EQ)

Someone with a high level of emotional intelligence (EQ) has a strong ability to perceive, use, understand and manage their feelings and emotions.

Financial EQ

In the context I use it, a person with a high financial EQ has the ability to control and harness their emotional responses to monetary matters, rather than being led and dominated by them.

A person with a high financial EQ has the ability to control and harness their emotional responses to monetary matters.

Whereas someone who has a high FQ would be able to accumulate wealth, in order to also have a high financial EQ, that person would need to demonstrate that they have not become lovers of money. That is, that they maintain control over their financial emotions.

The greed gland

I jokingly say that scientists have made a major discovery about the human body: the existence of a greed gland. Located inside your skull, when it starts secreting greed into your bloodstream, your ability to be reasonable and apply common sense are foregone in favour of believing the unbelievable and expecting the impossible to be possible.

Consider Ebenezer Scrooge, a character from Charles Dickens' *A Christmas Carol*. He's known for being a person of wealth, and therefore would have a high FQ. Yet he is also mean spirited and miserly, demonstrating a low financial EQ—at least until he encounters three spirits who change and brighten his monetary disposition.

The important topic of making your money count—that is, giving it meaning and making it matter—is discussed in more detail in Part 4. For now, I want to point out that the sweet spot of financial enlightenment is where your FQ and financial EQ overlap.

One way to look at the concepts of FQ and financial EQ is using the illustration of a tree. Your FQ determines the tree's size: the more wealth you have, the bigger your tree. Your financial EQ corresponds to how healthy your tree is, and how much life lives in it. How big is your tree? How much life does it support?

The relationship between FQ and financial EQ

Here are four scenarios that explain the relationship between someone's FQ and their financial EQ.

Scenario 1

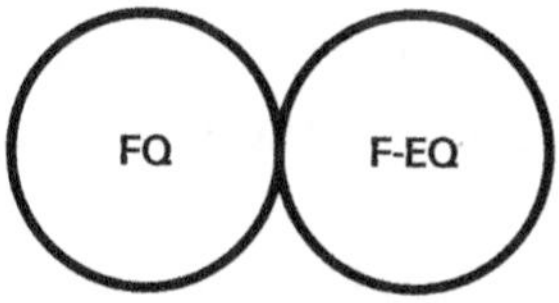

Under scenario 1 the person would have a low FQ and a low financial EQ, indicating an inability to accumulate wealth and a counter-productive emotional attitude. For instance, the person may live paycheque to paycheque and believe that all wealthy people are crooks.

The circles are drawn separately and apart as the connection between thinking / acting and feeling is not known or understood.

Scenario 2

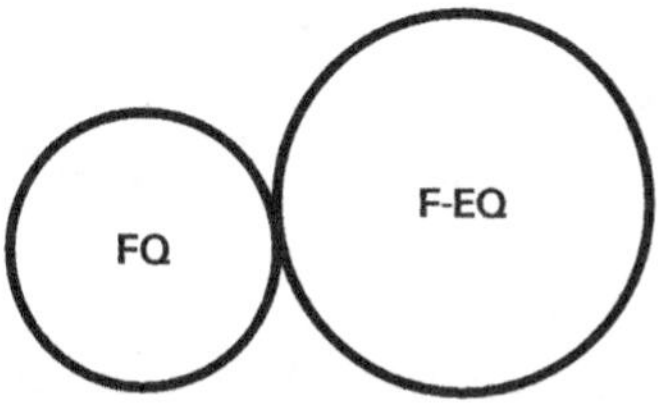

Under scenario 2 the person would have a low FQ but a high financial EQ, indicating an inability to accumulate wealth but a very good grasp on how money could be used to add meaning and purpose to life. Their lack of personal resources limits their financial contribution; however, such people may make careers out of their high financial EQ by working for not-for-profit organisations or outreach programs where they can give or add meaning to other people's money. I call these people the wealthy-poor: rich in spirit, poor in means.

Scenario 3

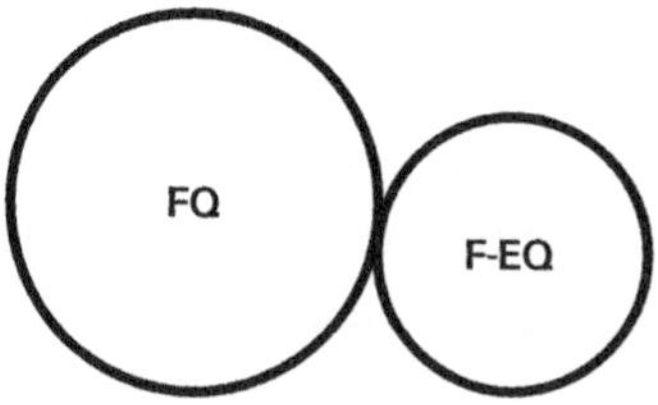

A person in scenario 3 would have the substance of material wealth that they have accumulated over time from their superior financial intelligence, and may also have the appearance of wealth as they use their resourcing to add comfort and status to their life. However, as a result of their low financial emotional intelligence their wealth would be inwards focused rather than being applied to leaving a lasting legacy. Scenario-3 people I've met are focused on increasing the amount of their net wealth as a way of proving their ability, but are unable to give that number a non-financial meaning. I call these people the poor-wealthy: rich in means, poor in spirit.

Scenario 4

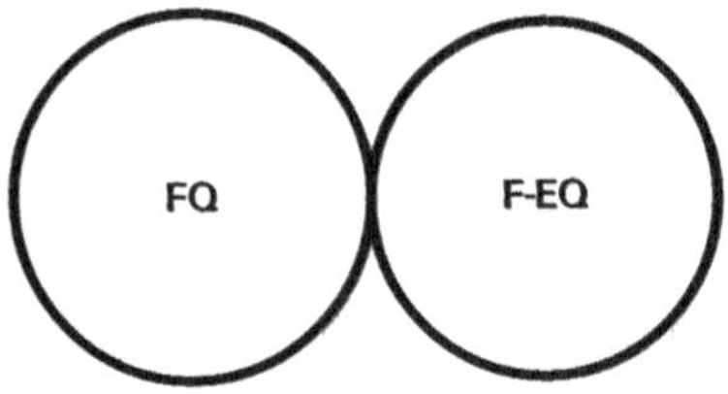

A scenario-4 person has equal measures of high FQ and high financial EQ, but like the earlier scenarios, there is no overlap, indicating such people see the acts of accumulating wealth and giving it purpose as separate rather than complementary. That is, they'll focus on maximising their FQ until they've accomplished their goal, and then shift across to working on their financial EQ and making their money matter. The separate circles become two phases in life: the pursuit of making it, and the pursuit of giving meaning to it.

Scenario combos

It's worth pointing out that partnerships or relationships where the parties have a similar financial EQ and FQ mix will work, up until someone changes. For instance, imagine that two people team up to make money. They are very successful and gradually one person drifts towards being less interested in making more money, and more interested in giving their money meaning. This can cause tension, which if not resolved, can end up fracturing and ending the relationship, potentially in an acrimonious way.

Partnerships or relationships where the parties have a similar financial EQ and FQ mix will work, up until someone changes.

Alternatively, if one person has a dominant FQ, but is lacking financial EQ, and the other has a dominant financial EQ but is lacking FQ (i.e. is the opposite), then neither may feel completely valued or understood — a relationship of convenience rather than understanding. An example is when you're asked to give to a cause that then turns around and shames or degrades those giving or providing the financial resources. Sadly, I have personally experienced this in some of the faith communities I have attended where they ask for a donation or contribution, but also seem to have a culture of shame or guilt about acquiring wealth in the first place. But you can't give from what you don't have.

The ideal situation is for all partners to respect and admire the skills different individuals offer and bring to the table. If both are valued, both are needed.

Overlapping circles

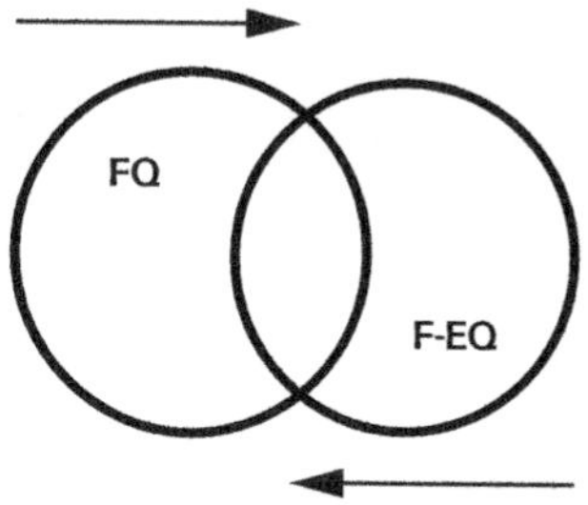

Ideally, instead of being separate, the circles would overlap, indicating that money is being accumulated (financial IQ) and also being used in an emotionally savvy way to add meaning to the person's life (financial EQ), enabling them to give meaning to their money.

As noted back in chapter 3, doing this gives meaning to your money as you accumulate it, and can help you overcome the plateau you'll experience as the compelling reasons that spurred you into action in the beginning start to wane as your situation improves.

The ultimate goal would be to have one single but overlapping circle. I'm yet to meet anyone who can lay claim to that level of money mastery.

Have a go at drawing your financial IQ and financial EQ circles in the box. Use the size of the circles to indicate your level of mastery of both concepts, and draw the extent to which you believe they overlap.

The following diagram may help you appreciate the relationship of the different scenarios. Financial EQ is measured on the vertical axis, and financial IQ on the horizontal axis. Each quadrant is given a number that corresponds to the scenario being described. Place a cross on the diagram where you think you are at the moment, and a cross for where you aspire to be in five years' time.

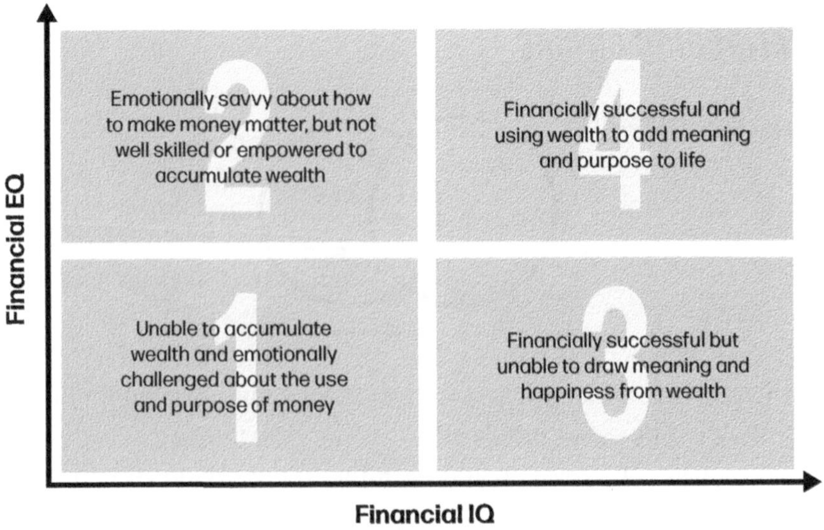

Marketing malware

Malware is software designed to disrupt and destroy, and there are plenty of 'wolf in sheep's clothing' financial programs doing just that to people's financial futures. Some that come to mind are programs (yes, they're actually called 'programs') that make it easier to spend and / or reward and incentivise spending.

Flybuys

Allow me to explain how the trickery works using the real-life example of Flybuys, a rewards program where you generally receive one Flybuys point for every dollar spent.

Here's a question:

How many real dollars would you have to spend to earn 1 000 000 Flybuys points?

(a) $10 000
(b) $100 000
(c) $1 000 000
(d) $10 000 000.

Hint: This is not a trick question. The answer is provided in the footnote[8]. If you got the answer right, then high-five and well done. Let's up the ante.

According to one source (Loo, 2021), the cash value of one Flybuys point is 0.5 cents (i.e. $5 per 1000 Flybuys points). If that's right, how much real buying power does 1 000 000 Flybuys points represent?

(a)	$50
(b)	$500
(c)	$5,000
(d)	$50,000

[8] $1 000 000 = 1 000 000 points, so the answer is (c).

If your brain is starting to short circuit from trying to work out the answer then that's exactly what the head honchos in marketing land want. In what can only be called cunning genius, they've created a system where you think you're being rewarded on a one-for-one basis (i.e. one dollar spent equals one point) when really you're being rewarded at the rate of half of one cent for every dollar spent. So the answer is (c) 1 000 000 Flybuys points requires $1 000 000 worth of spending, but only returns $5000 worth of value.

When it comes time to redeem your points, the products you can 'purchase' are valued at top dollar, rather than at any discounted price you might be able to find if you shopped around. Heads you lose. Tails they win.

Now, let's turn to the real world. Imagine you're at the supermarket and you have a choice of two brands of pure peanut butter. The ingredients and taste are exactly the same; only the packaging and price are different.

Product A is yellow and brown and sells for $5. Product B is blue and white with a cuddly bear on the front label and sells for $5.20. However, Product B is currently being promoted as earning triple Flybuys points.

Your choice is whether or not it's worth spending an extra 20 cents to get triple Flybuys. That is, to spend $0.20 to receive an extra $10.60 worth of Flybuys points. Which brand would you be more likely to buy?

(a)	Product A for $5 with 1 × Flybuys points = 5 Flybuys points
(b)	Product B for $5.20 with 3 × Flybuys points = 15.6 Flybuys points

Surely Product B is the better value, right? Wrong!

The cost to the supermarket is the real-world equivalent of the extra 10.6 Flybuys points (i.e. 15.6 points less 5.0 points). Remembering that one Flybuys point is estimated to have a cash value of 0.5 cents, the supermarket's cost of those extra points is about 5 cents.

However, for that 5-cent cost, they receive an extra 20 cents of income (i.e. $5.20 less $5.00). That may not seem like much in one transaction—a mere 15 cents profit—but it's a 300 per cent markup[9]. This example assumes all the extra revenue and profit is kept by the supermarket, which may not be the case, but it also ignores any money paid by Brand B for gaining access to the promotion.

If you're thinking 'Meh, it's only 20 cents', then you're forgetting about the accumulative effect of rewards spending. This was one small example on one fictitious product. Multiply the extra spending by hundreds or thousands of transactions, across hundreds or thousands of products, across many years and we're talking big bucks!

Is there anything wrong with this? Well, one person's marketing genius is another person's moral dilemma. You can't expect big business to put your financial welfare ahead of their corporate profits. The best you can do is gain the skills and awareness you need to know when you're being played.

You can't expect big business to put your financial welfare ahead of their corporate profits.

Buy Now Pay Later

Another example worth mentioning is Buy Now Pay Later (BNPL) schemes.

Back in the day, most major department stores routinely offered something called lay-by. This was where you could grab a product off the shelf, take it to the store's lay-by counter and enter into an arrangement with them to pay it off over two or three instalments. Once you'd made the final payment, the product was yours to own and take home.

Lay-by was a great option for people who couldn't access, or didn't want to use, credit products such as credit cards. There were usually no

[9] (15 cents divided by 5 cents) × 100

upfront fees associated with lay-by, and there was certainly no interest charged. The only downside was that if you didn't go ahead with your purchase, or didn't pay it off before the agreed deadline, then you may have had to pay a termination fee.

More recently, the concept of lay-by has been reborn and rebadged as BNPL. The same concept of paying by instalments is offered; however, you can take the product with you immediately. A usual feature of BNPL is that you won't pay any fees provided you make the required instalments in full and on time. If you don't, then you'll be slugged with fees such as establishment fees, late fees, account-keeping fees and payment processing fees.

The danger of BNPL is that it can be easier to access than traditional debt options such as credit cards because BNPL is not technically credit since providers don't charge interest. This seems a bit indefensible in my opinion: if it looks like a duck, walks like a duck and quacks like a duck, then it's a duck. BNPL is consumer debt, and that makes it credit in my book.

I doubt you need me to tell you that bypassing the normal checks that a credit provider has to complete is good for business, plus you don't have to enquire about the user's capacity to afford the repayments.

BNPL programs facilitate instant gratification to purchase items that are worth less, or worthless, immediately after acquisition.

So what's the harm? Lots and plenty! BNPL programs facilitate instant gratification to purchase items that are worth less, or worthless, immediately after acquisition. Given that most BNPL programs are based on four instalments, those with low financial literacy and low FQ may have the cash to make the initial downpayment, but are unable to foresee or comprehend the consequences of the future payments.

Afterpay: Buyer Beware

Afterpay advertises on its website that it is a 'free service', provided you pay on time.

And that's the rub of it. Many people don't pay on time. One survey (Shepard & Huang, 2022) of 1500 customers revealed a whopping 42 per cent had incurred a BNPL late payment.

In Afterpay's case, the late fee is $10 per missed payment, plus an additional $7 if the payment is still outstanding after a week. It doesn't sound like a lot, but if you only bought something that cost $20 and forgot to make a $5 instalment, then the $10 fee is 200 per cent of missed payment. Ouch!

Don't forget that the fee is for each missed payment. If there were other purchases made then the fee would compound. For instance, let's imagine Letty uses Afterpay to purchase a $60 shirt on Monday, and a $25 pizza on Tuesday. According to the terms, Letty must pay 25 per cent of each purchase at the checkout, with the balance split over three instalments two weeks apart.

Letty makes her first (of three) instalment payments when due, but due to a glitch with her pay landing in her bank account three days later than expected, she misses her second instalments payments. She is charged a late fee of $10 on the pants (i.e. 66% of her $15 installment due), and another $10 late fee on the pizza (i.e. 160 per cent of the $6.25 instalment due).

The seemingly small late fees can quickly cascade into a significant sum of money, potentially many times more then the instalment due or even the price of the item purchased. There may be other consequences of missed payments—black marks on credit records, difficulties borrowing for other debt such as a home loan, and possibility of additional fees as debts are passed over to debt collectors.

(continued)

Afterpay: Buyer Beware (cont'd)

Afterpay says that it 'hates' charging the late payment fee (Afterpay, 2022). If that was true, they wouldn't charge it. But they do, and once again you need to be aware that your best interests and theirs don't necessarily align. Here's the principle: there's no such thing as a free lunch, even if you pay for it using Afterpay.

BNPL organisations profit from users who fail to meet their repayment obligations, and so part and parcel of running a successful business and growing profits would involve doing well when others do poorly. Once again we're faced with a situation where corporates are incentivised to put their own financial welfare ahead of their clients'. The principle is this: outside of being compelled to do the right thing by law, you can't expect corporates to do the right thing by you if it's the wrong thing by them.

What we have here is the equivalent of a rip at the beach. If you don't know how to spot the danger, you can inadvertently get into trouble in relatively shallow water and quickly find yourself being carried out to sea. It would be a lot safer to swim between the flags.

The consequence of malware is that it corrupts your ability to make good financial decisions.

The consequence of malware is that it corrupts your ability to make good financial decisions.

Ideally, you'd avoid using it at all, but if it's too late for that, then you need to clean up your code as soon as you can.

Program update

No matter your current situation, your financial programming for making, managing and multiplying your money, and your ability to use it in an emotionally intelligent manner, can be improved and updated. Updates are not automatic. You have to seek out the information you desire, incorporate it and then begin to execute the new code by changing your behaviour.

Consider the following equation. If you wanted to make progress, what could you do to improve?

Good Habits		Bad Habits		Progress
50	–	50	=	0

You could look to increase the value of your good habits, while keeping your bad habits constant. Perhaps you could get better at a good habit you're already proficient in, or add new skills. Alternatively, you could hold your good habits constant and reduce the value of your bad habits, perhaps doing them less often or stopping them completely. Finally, you could increase your good habits while decreasing your bad habits and accelerate your progress.

The same approach will work with your financial reprogramming. In most cases, it is unlikely that you'll need to adopt a radical new regime, a complete reboot or a system makeover. Instead, try to make small yet regular improvements because small changes over long time periods will result in profound differences.

Try to make small yet regular improvements because small changes over long time periods will result in profound differences.

What reprogramming or program updates do you need to attract to keep more money and to use it in a way that adds substance and meaning to your life? We'll find out the answer to that question in Part 3.

Chapter highlights

- Your FQ is your monetary thoughts and habits: the way you think and act. Your financial EQ relates to your emotions: the way you feel about money, and your capacity to use it to create and fund a lasting legacy that touches, moves and inspires others.
- You don't need to be smart to be wealthy. A small amount of productive knowledge applied over a long period of time will produce impressive results.
- The best indicator of your FQ is whether you are an under accumulator, average accumulator or prodigious accumulator of wealth. The best indicator of your financial EQ is the extent to which you love your money more than your money loves you.
- Emulate success to become the change you want to be. If you want to act like a person with a high FQ or high financial EQ, imitate how you expect such a person would act.
- Marketing malware disrupts your ability to accumulate wealth by tricking you into believing you are getting a better deal than is the case. Sadly, you can't expect corporates to put your financial wellbeing ahead of their own, especially when their profits rise if you fail to meet your obligations.
- Updates and upgrades to your financial programming aren't automatic. If you want to achieve progress you'll need to seek new information to improve your good habits and / or diminish your bad habits.
- You're undertaking a major financial reprogramming by reading this book, completing the exercises and thinking about how you can implement the ideas contained herein.

PART TWO SUMMARY

- While some people seem to have a natural affinity with money, no-one is born a money magnet. It's something you become if you invest in learning how to make, manage and multiply your money, and apply your knowledge profitably.
- Your level of financial literacy reflects your ability to speak, read and write the language of money. The better you can understand it, the more money you will attract.
- People with poor financial literacy are more likely to become dependent on welfare, have low-paying jobs or be unemployed. If parents want their children to be empowered with money, they must take on the responsibility of being positive role models as the basic skills and knowledge needed to attract and keep money aren't taught in school.
- Financial literacy begins in the home, with children observing and taking on their parents' beliefs and habits. Later, these skills can be improved with self-study, but this requires a level of schooling that supports the acquisition and implementation of critical thinking skills.

- Be the change you want to see. If you're unhappy with the financial DNA you inherited, don't blame your parents. Instead, take ownership and responsibility for improving so you can do something for your children and loved ones that your parents couldn't do for you.
- You're the product of those who came before you and the custodian of skills, knowledge and resources for those who will come after you. Will you allow chance and fate to shape destiny, or will you cast a positive multi-generational vision and do what you can to begin nurturing it to fruition?
- People who apply their high FQ will accumulate wealth. People with a high applied financial EQ will use their wealth in ways that add substance and depth to their existence by improving the lives of others.
- What does your financial programming say about your ability to accumulate wealth? You will continue to get the same results while you keep running the same programs. Updates and upgrades are available, if you have the desire to find and use them.
- Beware marketing malware. It will disrupt and damage your ability to become and remain a money magnet.

PART THREE
MAKING, MANAGING AND MULTIPLYING

Remember Young'n — the son of my friend you read about back in chapter 11? Did you wish you knew someone, or could find someone, with the knowledge and experience to teach you, and show you, how to attract and keep a fortune?

As you'll soon see, you don't need a complicated approach. If anything, the simpler, the better, because the more intellectually and administratively difficult your method, the harder it will be to implement and maintain.

The approach that's worked best for me is a model I call Y–E=S. It explains that savings accumulate when you spend less than you earn. Here's something I've discovered: while you need savings to be wealthy, you won't get wealthy from savings. You must deploy your capital, not store it.

If you're leaking money, then it's sensible to find the leaks and plug them because a dollar saved is worth more than a dollar earned. That said, there's only so much money you'll be able to save by being thrifty, and it's unlikely to be enough to make you rich. As my grandpa Geordie was fond of saying, 'There's no use saving pennies while the pounds are flying out the window.' What he meant was that it's foolish to focus your efforts on trying to save a few extra cents while being blind to the income you could be making if you invested astutely and multiplied your money.

CHAPTER FIFTEEN

Y-E=S

The most important rule of wealth creation is to spend less than you earn and invest the surplus.

To become and remain a money magnet you only need to master two things:

1. spend less than you earn
2. invest the surplus.

The better you become at doing these, the more powerful your money magnetism will be.

No-one learns to swim in the deep end of the pool. It's too risky. You start in the shallows where it's safer and progress from there as your skills improve. So it is with wealth creation: you need to know and master the basics before you attempt the more complicated money-multiplying manoeuvres. Yes, big profits will get your greed gland going, but with high return comes high risk. If you don't have the skill to manage and tame risk, then it's only a matter of time until you get hurt. Trying to make a financial killing carries the constant risk of getting killed.

Trying to make a financial killing carries the constant risk of getting killed.

So, let's start with the basics in the shallow end of the wealth pool. If you already have some money management knowledge, try to forget it, lest you be like the person turning up to their first swimming lesson believing they know how to swim when all they're really doing is thrashing and splashing about.

Oh, it's also worth pointing out that if you feel you already 'know' what I'm sharing, but you're not doing or practising it, then perhaps you don't really know it at all. In fact, in my book you only really know something when you're doing it and teaching others.

Keeping afloat

Keeping afloat financially (i.e. keeping your head above water) requires that you learn and master the most important money skill that exists: to spend less than you earn.

If you can't float, you'll sink.

No matter how much you earn, if you get into the habit of spending all of it then any money you attract won't stick. I know people who earn lots of money—hundreds of thousands of dollars a year—but have nothing of substance to show for it because their consumption is as massive as their incomes. If you can't float, you'll sink.

The way I teach financial floating is via my Y–E=S formula:

Y – **E** = **S**

- **Y** stands for income[10]
- **E** stands for expenses
- **S** stands for savings.

And there you have it: so long as your income is higher than your expenses you'll accumulate savings and remain financially afloat.

Yes, I know, Y–E=S is kindergarten stuff—so why isn't it taught in kindergarten?

In my experience, every financial woe imaginable stems from not understanding, forgetting, or trying to trick or game the formula. Trust me, you won't stay afloat if you do.

Here's some more information on the Y–E=S formula:

- *Y = income:* ideas on how to maximise your income are included in chapter 16
- *E = expenses:* ideas for how to keep more of the money you make by better managing your spending is provided in chapter 17
- *S = savings:* the surplus left from spending less than you earn is accumulated as savings. As explained in chapter 18, savings are better viewed as a store of wealth, rather than a source of wealth. That is, you won't get rich by saving, but you won't get rich without saving.

Rules and re-expression

The Y–E=S formula creates the following fundamental rules of wealth creation:

- S increases when Y > E
- S decreases when E > Y
- When E > Y and S = 0, you must borrow the shortfall.

You can, of course, re-express the Y–E=S equation to solve for Expenses or Income as shown in the following diagram.

[10] Y is actually the symbol that economists use for income, so it ties in nicely.

Y	−	E	=	S
E	+	S	=	Y

Deficit

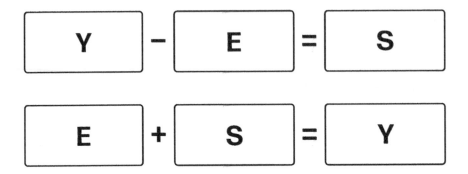

If your expenses are more than your income, you'll need to reach into your savings storehouse and withdraw some of the surplus you've previously accumulated. But what happens if you don't have any savings? You have to go into debt.

What is debt? According to the rules of the formula it can only be Y, E or S. Which is it: borrowing income not yet earned, borrowing expenses not yet spent or borrowing savings not yet saved?

The answer is borrowing income not yet earned.

Appreciating the link between debt and borrowing income not yet earned is a lightbulb moment for many because they think they are borrowing money, when really they are borrowing time. That is, the higher your debt, the more future income not yet earned you're borrowing and the more tomorrows you'll have to work to pay for items you've already consumed. So when you get into debt you're spending tomorrow's pay, today. How many tomorrows do you owe to repay yesterday's spending?

When you get into debt you're spending tomorrow's pay, today.

Grab your highlighter because what's written next is the most important sentence in this entire book: spending income you haven't yet earned is the surest and strongest way to repel wealth.

Using the Y-E=S formula

Given its importance, let's spend a bit more time making sure you absolutely and completely understand how the Y–E=S formula works by filling in the blanks in a couple of easy examples. I'll help by providing two worked examples—then it's over to you.

Note: I'm colour blind and it makes me appreciate that people 'see' different ways. While the numbers used are simple enough, some readers may benefit by viewing the relationship between income, expenses and savings (debt) as pictures that 'balance' rather than sums. I've provided both for you: sums and pictures.

Worked example 1: Juan

Juan earns $20 of income and has $10 of expenses. How much does Juan save?

The following diagram illustrates that Juan's income is balanced, or offset, by expenses and savings. The picture always has to balance.

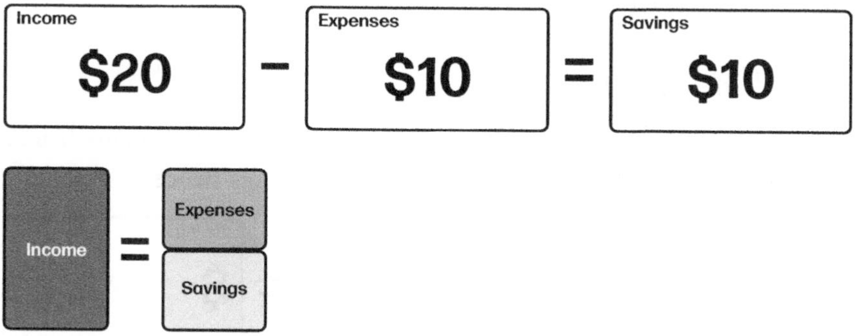

Worked example 2: Bernadette

Bernadette earns $50 of income and has $75 of expenses. She has no savings. What does her Y–E=S situation look like?

Remember that a negative number depletes savings reserves, or else represents debt.

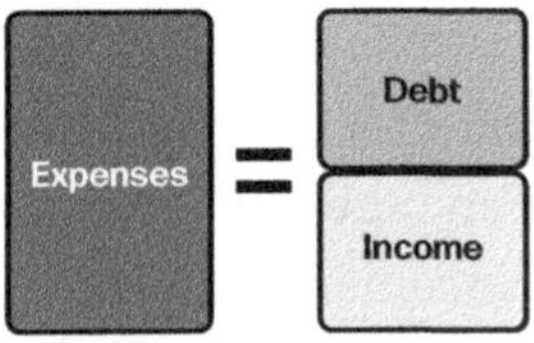

Okay, now it's your turn. See if you can work through these examples.

Example 1: Ana

Ana earns $28 of income and has $23 of expenses. How much does Ana save?

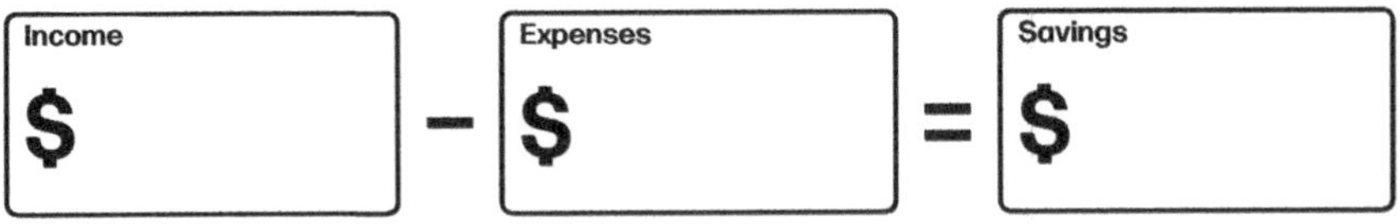

Answer: savings (surplus) of $5.

Example 2: Bruce

Bruce earns $33 and spends $36. He has $10 of savings. Calculate Bruce's Y–E=S situation to determine how much in savings Bruce has left.

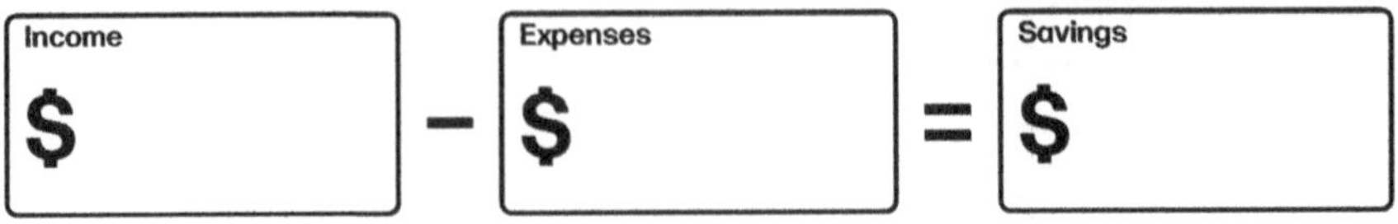

Answer: savings (deficit) of –$3. Bruce has $7 of savings left.

Example 3: Sandra

Each year, Sandra earns $18 and spends $24. She has no savings. What does Sandra's Y–E=S situation look like?

Income		Expenses		Savings
$	–	$	=	$

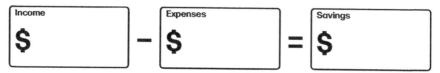

Answer: savings (deficit) of –$6. As Sandra has no savings, she must borrow $6, meaning she is reaching into tomorrow to access $6 of her future income to spend now. That is one-third of her income, which in simple terms equates to four months of work time she owes.

Example 4: Regina

Regina doesn't track her expenses but earns $20 each month and ends up with $2 extra in her savings account. How much does she spend?

Income		Expenses		Savings
$	–	$	=	$

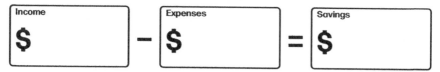

Answer: expenses of $18

Your situation

Now have a go at filling in the boxes for your situation based on your income and expenses over the past month (or any other time period you choose).

Income		Expenses		Savings
$	–	$	=	$

What do the results say about your ability to understand and successfully apply the Y–E=S equation?

Earn more, or spend less?

Right then, can you use your knowledge of Y–E=S to answer this question: 'How can I increase my savings?' It's not rocket science, is it? You can either:

- increase your income
- decrease your spending.

Spoiler alert: how to achieve each of these outcomes is explained in later chapters, but the answer is that you want to increase your income without permanently working harder, and at the same time manage your spending so that you're not haemorrhaging money, and invest rather than consume your extra income.

The Y–E=S formula works in all contexts, irrespective of whether the sums of money are large or small, or the scenario is simple or complex. If someone or something is failing financially, the root cause will always be because their expenses are higher than their income. Failure will always result if the deficit can't be met from savings or debt.

Here's a challenge

If you're up to it, try to explain Y-E=S to a friend or family member to demonstrate your understanding of how it works.

Chapter highlights

- Staying financially afloat is also the cornerstone of all wealth creation. It's something so simple a kid in kindergarten can comprehend it: always spend less than you earn.
- You become more magnetic if you invest your savings, and less magnetic if you spend and consume them.
- Having more income than expenses will result in savings. If you aren't saving, you must be overspending relative to your income.
- Debt is borrowing tomorrow's income and spending it today. The result is you end up owing time and money.
- If you feel like your finances are crazy, complex or out of control, then bring everything back to the simple principle of Y-E=S. You're either earning too little, spending too much or both.
- The wealth-building principle of Y-E=S works all the time and in every context. It's also easily forgotten or dismissed as too simple, resulting in all kinds of financial mismanagement and misfortune.

CHAPTER SIXTEEN
'Y' IS FOR INCOME

Working harder won't usually work.

Swapping your time for money might be unpleasant, but it is a vital component to nearly every wealth-creation plan. The money you earn can be used to purchase investments and to secure access to other people's money so you can take advantage of leverage and purchase investments that you otherwise couldn't afford.

Swapping time for money

The quickest and easiest way to attract money is to get paid for your time. Not only will your wages pay the bills, they'll supply the capital to invest and support your ability to borrow and use (but hopefully not abuse) the power of leverage.

The quickest and easiest way to attract money is to get paid for your time.

Irrespective of whether you get paid by the hour, by the month or by the task, your pay is a function of this formula: Pay = Time × Rate. The formula provides the answer to how to earn more: you can either work harder (i.e. work more hours) or smarter (i.e. earn a higher rate).

Working harder

168. That's how many hours there are in a week. It's an unchangeable, fixed allotment. You can't have more, or less. All you can do is prioritise and allocate the 168 hours allotted to you. Let's do a countdown to calculate how much free time you might have to work some extra hours.

Sleep

How many hours of sleep do you need a night? The doctors at the Mayo Clinic suggest a minimum of seven hours (Olson, 2019), so let's be a bit more generous and allow eight hours. That's 56 hours per week.

Work

Most people work a standard 38-hour week, but let's bump it up by an extra hour a day for travel time. See ya later 43 hours.

Leisure

According to one study (US Bureau of Labor Statistics, 2021) people spend an average of five hours each day pursuing leisure activities: going out, watching TV, surfing the web, reading, exercise, and so on. There goes another 35 hours.

Cleaning, care and grooming

That same study reported that people spend a little less than three hours a day doing housework, caring for others and engaging in personal grooming. Rounded up, we can cross off another 21 hours a week.

Eating

And finally, we've all got to eat. Three meals a day, 20 minutes a meal... let's agree on one hour a day, or seven hours a week.

• • •

As shown in the following table, you have six hours left over—that's less than one hour of free time each day. Not much, eh? No wonder there never seems to be enough time in the day to get new things done.

Activity	Hours allocated	Hours left
	Opening balance	168
Sleep	56	112
Working	43	69
Leisure	35	34
Cleaning, care & grooming	21	13
Eating	7	6

Conclusion: Monetising your free time won't make you rich.

Reorganising your time

What about re-jigging your 168 hours and doing less of something else to free up time for something new? That's easier said than done.

The cup riddle

Imagine you fill an empty cup to the brim. How do you get the cup to hold more water without it overflowing and spilling the contents? Get a bigger cup? Yes, but what if the size of your cup is fixed, like the hours you have available in a week? The answer is to pour some old water out, so you can pour some new water in.

Let's apply the answer to the cup riddle to your available time. If you're planning to work more, what will you stop, in order to start?

- *Less time eating?* Perhaps you could save a few minutes a day, but that's not going to add up to much.

- *Less time cleaning, caring and grooming?* Halving your time cleaning will leave you with a half-clean house. It's unlikely you can care less without it affecting your relationships, and compromising your grooming might impact your self-esteem.

Overall, there might be a little time you can claw back, but nothing substantial.

- *Less leisure time?* This is definitely possible, but everyone needs down time to rest and recuperate. If you don't do this, you risk burning out, leading to exhaustion and job dissatisfaction. Thirty-five hours a week sounds like a lot of time, but it's not really considering the time needed to unwind after a long day at work and to rest over the weekend.
- *Less sleep?* I don't know about you, but less sleep brings out grumpy Steve, plus it makes me more foggy headed and more prone to getting migraines. Again, you might be able to pinch a few hours here and there, but probably not enough to make a material change in your available work hours.

Efficiency gains

You might invest in acquiring some 'do more in less time' skills that offer efficiency gains, but from my experience time hacks tend to be temporary rather than permanent and result in small changes rather than radical results.

• • •

Heck. That was a long-winded explanation to arrive at a disappointing conclusion: working harder won't usually work.

Working smarter

How about working smarter and getting paid more per hour?

Quick fix

The easiest way to do this is to get a pay increase. Don't wait for your boss to make the first move—they'll be more preoccupied with running their business than fussing over your pay. Take the initiative and hit your boss up for a pay increase. It might be a bit nerve-racking, but make a time to sit down and, once all the niceties have been exchanged, say, 'Boss, what can I do to get paid more?' Be sure to come prepared to argue your case by being able to list the things you do that add value and might not have been noticed or understood. If you don't get any joy, you can always look for a higher paying job elsewhere for the same hours worked.

Solving problems

Asking for a pay increase, or switching jobs, is getting paid more for the skills you have. You can also increase your pay rate by gaining new skills.

Everyone gets paid to solve problems. The following equation reveals the relationship between the four ways to increase your pay by increasing your skills:

1. Solve more problems
2. Solve bigger problems
3. Solve more complex problems
4. Be one of only a few people who can solve a problem.

$$\left(\frac{\text{Number of Problems} \times \text{Size of Problem} \times \text{Complexity of Problem}}{\text{Number of People who can Solve the Problem}}\right) = \text{Pay}$$

The difficulty with skilling up, or re-skilling, is that it requires time to obtain new skills and experience, and that makes it a long-game. Still, if you have time up your sleeve or the kids need some career counselling, it's a useful discussion, so let's have it.

Income accelerators

If working a lot harder isn't a long-term answer, and working smarter is a long-game, what can you do to earn some extra income? The answer is to implement an 'income accelerator'.

An income accelerator is best described as a side-hustle you do in your spare time to earn some extra money. By definition, it is not your day job, but watch out because your side-hustle might take off and even replace your salary, if all goes well.

An income accelerator is best described as a side-hustle you do in your spare time to earn some extra money.

Monetising ideas

Towards the end of a seminar I attended in May 1999, Robert Kiyosaki dropped an off-the-cuff comment that anyone interested in building a serious amount of wealth in a short period of time ought to attend an upcoming seminar in Vancouver, Canada that Robert was going to participate in as a student. 'If it's good enough for Kiyosaki,' I thought, 'It's good enough for me!'

So it was that I convinced Julie, my newly married wife, to deplete our savings and go on a honeymoon to Vancouver, Canada. She was all for that, but less so the proviso that we had to sit in a direct marketing seminar for a few days at the start. How romantic! Two important events occurred at that seminar: meeting a fellow participant, Chuck, who shared with me his strategy for buying positive cashflow properties for low money down (and sometimes even no money down), and learning from Corey Rudl and his business partner Derek Gehl.

Corey and Derek—a couple of young Canadians—were selling a course about how to make money on an emerging technology that was steadily gaining traction: something called the internet. During their presentation they earnestly outlined their belief that selling information online was a trend that was only going to grow and grow. 'If you know how to solve a problem,' they said 'you can bet your bottom dollar there's someone on the internet that would be willing to pay you for the solution.' I must be a sucker for buying stuff because I ran to the back of the room, jostling people out of the way, to buy one of their courses.

With the honeymoon over, and the marriage still intact, I returned to Australia to begin building two businesses with Dave. We agreed that he'd keep selling his time doing accounting, while I worked on buying positive cashflow property using the approach Chuck had shown me, and selling information over the internet.

Fast forward a few years and I can faithfully report that both worked marvellously well. Dave and I used Chuck's model to buy a heap of houses for low money down and generated tens of thousands of dollars of recurrent investment income, and my knowledge of real estate became the source of information we sold at our internet site—www.propertyinvesting.com—which over the past two decades has sold millions of dollars' worth of real estate education and training. Not bad for a side-hustle.

Derek and Corey: Epilogue

Sadly, Corey Rudl died in a car accident in 2005. A brilliant life that came to an end far too soon.

Over the years Derek and I stayed in touch, gradually building a great and enduring family friendship. We've stayed at each other's houses, and watched each other's kids grow up and each other's businesses flourish.

When it comes to making money on the internet, there is no-one in the world I endorse more highly, nor trust more implicitly, than Derek.

An entertaining video that Derek and I recorded about how to make money on the internet in the modern era is available at **www.moneymagnet.au**

In my opinion, the lowest cost and quickest way to earn extra income is to monetise your knowledge over the internet. As Corey and Derek predicted more than two decades ago, the World Wide Web has made it easier than ever to find, attract and monetise an audience. If you have information of interest, there's money on the internet waiting for you to mine it.

The lowest cost and quickest way to earn extra income is to monetise your knowledge over the internet.

That said, you might prefer to go the more traditional route, such as cashing in on a hobby, delivering flyers or maybe even finding a network marketing idea that works for you. If you like property investing, you may be able to become a bird-dog and get paid for finding deals for other investors (be sure to do it legally!). Other folks may give day-trading shares a go, or maybe even attempt something in the cryptocosm. Neither are in my sphere of expertise.

Time Multiple of Money (TMM)

Your TMM is the number of times you get paid per hour you work.

It is possible to have a TMM of zero (e.g. unpaid work), or infinity (e.g. payment without having to work), but most folks earn money at a TMM of one: one hour of work in exchange for one payment. If they want another payment, they need to work another hour.

TMM > 1

To have a TMM greater than one you need to be paid more than once per hour worked.

Here are some examples:

- *Mortgage brokers*, who write and place loans, receive two streams of income: an upfront commission when the loan is written, and also a smaller commission, called a 'trail', that is paid monthly or quarterly as long as the loan isn't repaid. As the time taken to source the loan, write it up and get it approved will result in more than one payment, the TMM is greater than one.

- *Financial planners*, who receive recurrent commission (also called a trail) for their recommendations (paid by the entity providing the investment), rather than an upfront fee for the advice (paid by the client). As long as their client's money remains invested, the financial planner will receive a trail, so their TMM for the time taken to meet with the client, research and provide a financial plan is recouped over multiple payments, making it greater than one.
- *Affiliate and networking marketing programs*, where a client (i.e. affiliate) makes a purchase and a portion of it is paid to the person who introduced them. Each time the affiliate makes a subsequent purchase, the person who introduced them receives an agreed affiliate commission.
- *Music artists and authors*, who spend hours writing and recording for no money, but thereafter receive a small payment when their material is purchased or played in public.

Can you see how in these examples you have to accept getting paid less upfront (TMM < 1) in order to create a product or service that will pay you on a TMM >1?

In order to earn more, you might have to first earn less.

Different approaches

Income accelerators where you swap ideas for income over the internet are the perfect way to access a TMM of more than one, while also allowing you to take advantage of temporarily working harder, and monetising your ability to work smarter. Here's an example of how it might work.

Ronnie's side-hustle

Let's flesh this concept out using the idea of selling information over the internet as a side-hustle. Ronnie loves shopping and has an eye for finding bargains. Ronnie decides to use the 'intellectual property' they know from years of smart shopping to create an online program that explains the 'three easy steps for buying brand-name clothes at discounts of up to 75 per cent'.

It takes Ronnie 50 hours to write the course, which, at their day-job rate of $30 an hour, gives an opportunity cost of $1500 for creating the course, plus a further $2000 to set up a website: total $3500. Ronnie's only ongoing cost is the $100 a week spent on social media advertising and two hours of time to answer emails and do other general admin.

Ronnie sells the course for $25 a unit. Sales currently average 10 courses per week.

After six months, a summary of Ronnie's position is:

Sales [260 units]	$6,500	(26 weeks × $25 × 10)
– Set-up costs	$3,500	($1,500 + $2,000)
– Advertising	$2,600	(26 weeks × $100)
= Profit	$400	

Start-up hours	50	
+ Admin	52	(26 weeks × 2 hours)
= Total	102	
Pay per hour	$3.92	

That looks like a pretty ordinary result, but let's look at the next six months, keeping in mind that Ronnie's set-up costs and time have been recouped in the first six months:

Sales [260 units]	$6,500	(26 weeks × $25 × 10)
– Advertising	$2,600	(26 weeks × $100)
= Profit	$3,900	
÷ Admin hours	52	
Pay per hour	$75	

Do you see how the initial 50 hours Ronnie's spent writing the course for no upfront pay is now providing an impressive ongoing payment every time a sale is made: less money upfront but more money overall?

Ronnie's example illustrates that working to unlock a time multiple of more than one might look a bit disappointing at the start, but once the time and costs associated with setting up are recouped the results can look very impressive indeed! It also reinforces that selling information, which has a very high profit margin because of its low cost, is an excellent income accelerator. If Ronnie was smart, after setting up and establishing their first online side-hustle with a TMM > 1, they would set up another, and another ...

But here's the catch: it's likely you'll have to go backwards (i.e. TMM from one to zero) in order to move forwards (i.e. get a TMM of greater than one).

Here's the catch: it's likely you'll have to go backwards ... in order to move forwards.

If you're thinking, 'This all sounds great, but I'm too busy at work, and too tired after work, to get cracking at dreaming up ways to increase my TMM', then obviously your cup is full. Rather than overfilling it and ending up with a mess, stop doing something else before starting something new. It doesn't have to be a permanent change: you might be able to free up enough temporary time, like deciding to take some paid or unpaid leave from work.

Joint ventures

You can still build wealth without a job, but your inability to borrow will make the going much harder. Unless you have access to large sums of money and don't need to borrow, you will have to combine your time with someone else's capital. Being a time-partner in a joint venture sounds like a job to me, just with a different name.

Being a time-partner in a joint venture sounds like a job to me, just with a different name.

And finally, investing

So far we've concentrated on the income you can earn from swapping your time and ideas for money. You can also earn income from investing, which is the return you earn from letting someone else borrow or use your money or assets. It's a big topic, so let's save that discussion for chapter 22.

Chapter highlights

- Swapping your time for money is a proven way to earn income, and your output adds value to the community. There's nothing wrong or demeaning about having a job, but bear in mind that needing your job more than your job needs you is a very risky proposition.
- If you don't have a job, then you'll struggle to borrow money and won't be able to take advantage of the wealth-building power of leverage.
- If you want to get paid more for your time, focus on working smarter by gaining new skills that solve bigger problems, rather than working harder by putting in more hours – especially if that comes at the cost of your health and wellbeing.
- Having money chase you by pursuing a career you're interested in will result in a better outcome than chasing money by selecting a job purely based on how much it pays.
- You have a finite amount of time available each week: 168 hours. It's financially astute to maximise your return for the hours you work.
- The number of times you are paid for an hour of your time is your Time Multiple of Money (TMM). The higher your TMM, the stronger your money magnetism and the faster you'll build wealth.
- Employees swap their time for money. Entrepreneurs swap their ideas for income. Unlike time, which is finite, ideas are infinite. Monetising ideas and intellectual property leads to TMMs of greater than one.
- Before doing more, do less. Otherwise the contents of your cup might overflow and end up as a mess on the floor.

CHAPTER SEVENTEEN
‘E’ IS FOR EXPENSES

If your spending isn’t *under control*, then it’s *out of control*.

You can only live three ways:

1. Below your means (expenses < income)
2. At your means (expenses = income)
3. Above your means (expenses > income).

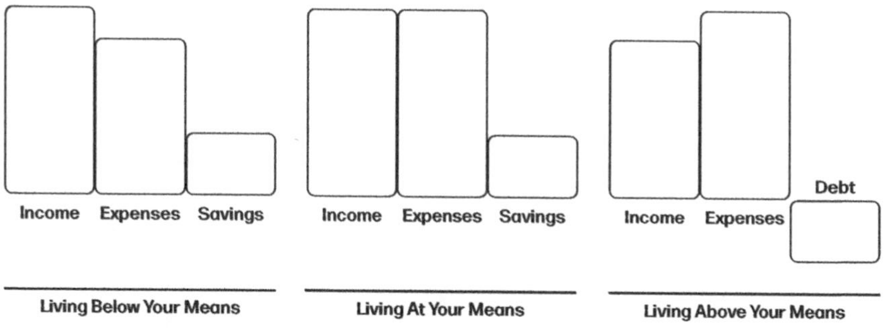

The difference between your income and your lifestyle spending quantifies how much under or over your expenses are relative to your means. Those who spend more than they earn will struggle to attract wealth that sticks..

Those who spend more than they earn will struggle to attract wealth that sticks.

Living above your income can only be sustained if the gap between your consumption and income can be filled by depleting your savings or getting into debt. Given you have a finite amount of savings and borrowing ability, the following must be true: no matter how much you earn—lots or little—if you can't persistently and consistently live within your means, then the money you attract won't 'stick' and can't accumulate. Furthermore, the less money you have accumulated, the riskier and more precarious your financial position.

Spend less, or earn more?

Dave, my co-adventurer in purchasing 130 properties in 3.5 years, had a good way of distinguishing those who could attract wealth from those who couldn't: the number of holes in their money bucket. 'Wealthy people,' Dave would say, 'have only one hole at the top where money pours in. Their bucket fills up and they live on what spills over. A poor person has one hole at the top, and many holes at the bottom where their money leaks out. Their bucket is always nearly empty'. The lesson here is 'before trying to earn more, try leaking less'.

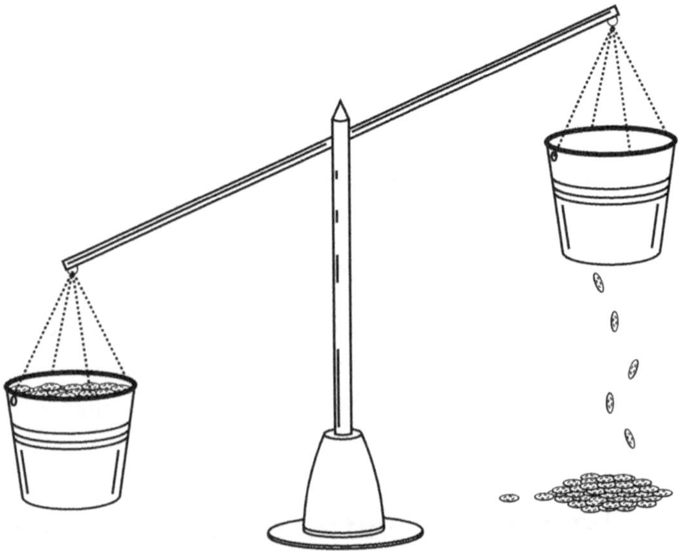

Before trying to earn more, try leaking less.

If you're struggling to accumulate wealth, then before trying to find new and better ways to funnel more money in, first identify and plug the leaks at the bottom of your money bucket.

High-impact, low-motivation

Trying to convince someone to become a smarter spender is like trying to convince a smoker to give up their cigarettes. It sounds good in theory, but it will be difficult to change behaviour because addictions are habitual, not intellectual.

Saving to spend is like dieting to binge eat. As I explained back in chapter 3, unless you have compelling reasons that provide sufficient momentum to push through the pain barrier of change, you're only likely to make yo-yo, rather than permanent, progress. By that I mean you will improve until the pain is no longer compelling, then plateau as you slip back into old habits, and then start regressing until you're back at the point where you're motivated to rein in your spending, resulting in progress, resulting in plateauing ... and so it goes.

Saving to spend is like dieting to binge eat.

Everyone has something different that will trigger their motivation to change. Finding your trigger, and keeping the motivation switch 'on' even when you feel like it would be okay to turn it 'off', is necessary if you want to transition from okay to good, and from good to great.

My desire for time freedom (i.e. a carrot) and dislike of working in accounting (i.e. a stick) were sufficient motivating factors to compel me to change. I couldn't do it alone though. I also had to convince my wife, Julie, to live frugally for a number of years while we accumulated and then deployed our savings to purchase investments. Julie and I struck a deal that we'd live off her salary until we had children, and thereafter she'd never have to work again if she didn't want to because the income from our investments would replace the salary she earned from her job.

This sounded good as a plan and a policy, but it was much harder to live in practice. At the time, all our friends were buying homes while we rented a subsistence-style unit on a busy road with paper-thin glass windows that did nothing to stop the sound of trucks roaring past at night. I didn't know it at the time, but the irritation of the trucks interrupting my sleep ensured my flames of motivation didn't flicker or fail.

Remember there is nothing free about financial freedom.

The biggest challenge to your success is likely to be finding the motivation to undertake and keep making sacrifices that will result in the *reality* of having less pleasure now, for the *promise* of more pleasure tomorrow. Remember, there is nothing free about financial freedom. It comes at the cost of sacrifice and delayed gratification. Is that a price you're willing and able to pay?

The power of saving

The pithy proverb 'a dollar saved is a dollar made' makes good sense, but the 'nuck, nuck, nuck' accountant in me can't help correcting it because in actual fact a dollar saved is better than a dollar made. How so? Because you have to pay income tax on the money you earn, whereas there is no income tax on the savings you make by reducing or eliminating your personal spending.

Bob's options for saving

Bob wants to save $100. His options are to earn more, or spend less.

If Bob decided to try for extra income, and assuming he paid income tax at an average rate of 30 per cent, he would need to earn $143 to end up with $100 after tax[11]. Alternatively, he could cut back on his personal spending by $100. Since reducing personal spending has no income tax effect, every dollar Bob doesn't spend translates to a dollar saved.

Spending ≠ earnings

A big money mistake I see people making time and time again is spending their gross pay, rather than their net pay. That is, spending based on what they earn in their head, rather than what they receive in their hand.

A big money mistake I see people making time and time again is spending their gross pay, rather than their net pay

Gross pay

Let's say you spy a job with a salary package of $100 000 per annum. The $100 000 is your gross pay and it's natural to think, 'I get paid $100 000, so I have $100 000 to spend'. This is not the case though because the salary you receive 'in the hand' (i.e. your net pay) is after payroll adjustments have been deducted.

[11] $100 ÷ (1 – tax rate) = $143 (rounded)

Net pay

The biggest payroll deductions are income tax instalments and superannuation. Your employer must set these aside and remit them to the ATO. You may also have other money compulsorily deducted (e.g. child support), or voluntarily deducted (e.g. additional superannuation, car lease or loan repayments).

A problem will arise if you don't pay much attention to your payslip, or your bank statement, and instead maintain a loose ledger of your earning and spending in your head. The result can be spending according to your gross salary, but earning according to your net salary. Do you recall what happens when expenses are higher than income (E > Y)? You must raid your savings storehouse, and if there isn't enough in reserve, you'll find yourself reaching into tomorrow and borrow income not yet earned.

Increasing your money magnetism and improving your financial IQ means finding out or calculating your net pay, and then ensuring you spend less than you receive.

Caitlyn's spending scenario

Caitlyn is on a salary of $84 000 per annum, or $7000 a month (i.e. $84k ÷ 12 months). When thinking about buying something, Caitlyn compares the cost of the item against her monthly gross pay of $7000.

Caitlyn has $1625 deducted for income tax, $735 for superannuation and an extra $650 (by choice) for her car loan repayment, leaving only $3990.

When all is said and done, 43 per cent of Caitlyn's earnings is deducted by her employer, and only 57 per cent hits her bank account. If she spends according to her gross pay, rather than her net pay, Caitlyn will be living well beyond her means and getting deeper and deeper into debt.

Spending hacks

I'm not your go-to guy when it comes to small-scale spending hacks. In my mind, trying to save 50 cents here and there isn't worth the time or effort it takes, and it also shifts your focus from abundance to scarcity. As I mentioned earlier, to requote my grandpa Geordie, 'Stop trying to save pence while pounds are flying out the window'.

Stop trying to save pence while pounds are flying out the window.

Channelling the wisdom of my late grandfather, I think you would be much better off if you concentrated on saving dollars off your larger spends, rather than cents off your smaller ones. Also, be reasonable. I don't think sacrificing to the point of regressing to one-ply toilet paper makes any sense. That is, you don't want to cut back on everything because it will become unmotivating and difficult trying to stick to the financial equivalent of a diet of lettuce leaves.

That said, here are a few suggestions for saving on some big-ticket spends. The tips are all based on avoiding paying a 'lazy tax', which is money you voluntarily pay when you forget to negotiate a better deal.

Home loan

Engage the services of a mortgage broker to see if they can find a lower interest rate loan. If they can, ask your current lender to match it, and if they won't, move your business.

Even if you only negotiate a small discount, on a big loan, over a long time, the savings will be significant.

Energy providers

Make it a rule to price shop your power at least once a year. Power providers are always dangling incentives and lower prices to get new sign-ups, and then hope you prefer the convenience of sticking with them rather than shopping round.

Insurance

As for energy providers, price shop your home and car insurance annually to see if you can get a better deal. Before changing, ask your current provider to price match, and if they can't or won't, then move.

Phone and internet

The rule is to pay for what you use, not what you don't. Paying for data and speeds that you rarely use but want 'just in case' is flushing cash down the 'toilie'. If you require more data or more speed for a special occasion, you can usually buy the extra needed by the block.

TV subscriptions

Keep one paid TV subscription at a time, for two months at a time. Binge watch the shows you like, then cancel and move on to the next TV subscription. You'll get through six providers in 12 months, watch all the good shows, but only effectively pay for one membership.

Vices

Finally, name and number your vices and make the call on whether the cost is worth the benefit. It might not be an all-or-nothing decision, but rather a less-is-more mindset. Here's a few on the vice list to consider with the average weekly spend in after-tax dollars next to it (Wallis, 2021), which I have recalculated back to before-tax dollars, assuming a tax rate of 30 per cent.

	After-tax		Before-tax
Spending category	Weekly	Annual	Annual
Recreation and culture	$208	$10,816	$15,452
Hotels, cafes and restaurants	$120	$6,240	$8,915
Alcoholic beverages	$46	$2,392	$3,418
Cigarettes and tobacco	$36	$1,872	$2,675

For instance, if your marginal tax rate is 30 per cent, then $10 816 in after-tax dollars requires $15 452 in pre-tax dollars.

Allowance

If your spending isn't *under control*, then it's *out of control*, and that's a problem because runaway spending repels money. To fix the problem, you need to learn and implement spending control.

The most common spending control mechanism is a budget. While there's no doubt they work, I'm not much of a fan of them because people struggle to stick to them. The more cumbersome a budget is, the more administratively difficult it is to implement, and the harder it will be to stick to. Budgets are the financial equivalent of a diet, and who wants to be on a diet for the rest of their life?

The more cumbersome a budget is, the harder it will be to stick to.

While it arrives at more or less the same outcome, an *allowance* is a friendlier form of spending control because anything and everything is allowed, up to a point. When you hit that point, you can't spend any more.

A simple allowance is the 80:20 rule, where you're allowed to spend 80 per cent, so long as you save 20 per cent. For instance, if your net pay is $5000 a month, $1000 of it is immediately siphoned off to savings, and the balance, $4000, can be spent on anything you like, until it runs out and the cupboard is bare.

The approach I recommend is a bit more advanced, but still only requires a fairly basic level of financial intelligence to understand. I call it my GDR (i.e. Giving–Deductions–Remainder) 70–20–10 program, and it's illustrated in the following diagram.

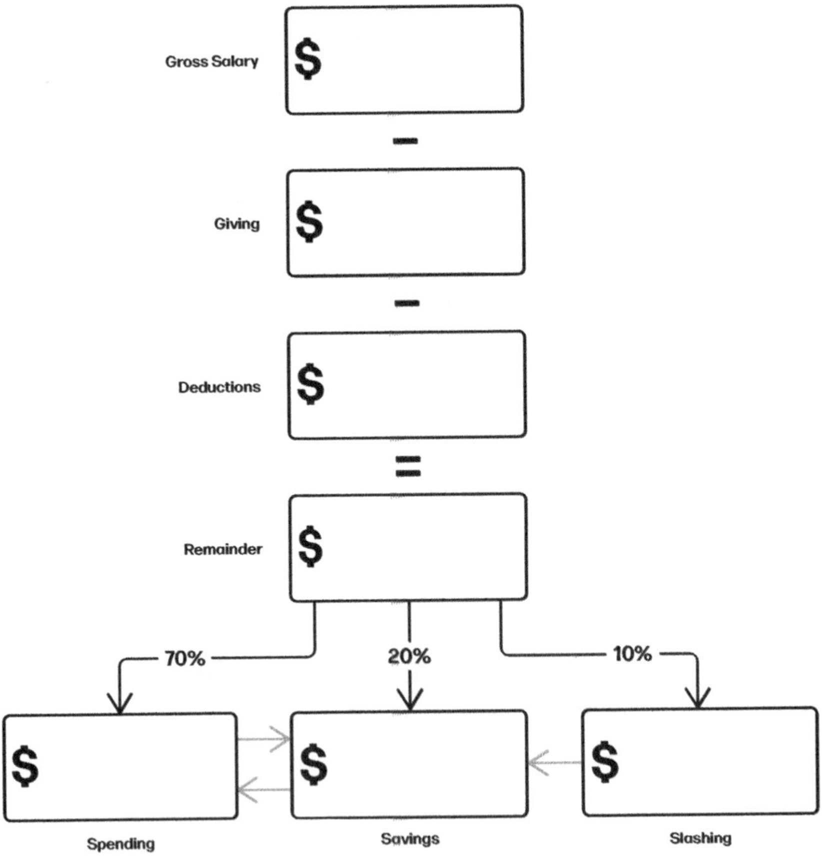

Gross salary

To complete the boxes in the diagram, you begin with your gross salary, which you'll recall is the amount you're paid before any payroll deductions.

Giving

Off the top, in pre-tax dollars, set aside an amount you can cheerfully give to causes that add significance to your life. The principle is to give generously from the first fruits of your earnings, for as you sow, so shall you reap. I don't recommend a set percentage or amount; instead, give as led by your heart, but never to the point that you have to borrow, for you can't give from what you don't have.

Some readers are going to say or think, 'Meh, giving means less for me'. If that's the case, remember that stingy is as stingy does, and that it's unreasonable to expect that you'll achieve abundance with an attitude of scarcity.

It's unreasonable to expect that you'll achieve abundance with an attitude of scarcity.

Deductions

These are your compulsory payroll deductions for income tax, superannuation, and so on.

Remainder

This is the balance of your gross pay after subtracting giving and compulsory payroll deductions, which is then split as follows:

- 70 per cent to spending
- 20 per cent to savings
- 10 per cent to slashing (debt).

Spending

You can spend the 70 per cent of your remainder pool as you see fit. If you don't spend all your allowance, then a good idea is to transfer the balance at the end of the period across to your savings account (as shown by the grey arrow from Spending to Saving).

Saving

Divert 20 per cent of your remainder pool to savings, some of which you'll keep in reserve (to be used to pay for any unexpected expenses, as shown by the grey arrow from Saving to Spending), and some of which you'll use to purchase investments.

Slashing

This is an extra sum that you're going to 'sacrifice' to accelerate the pace at which you pay down your debt. Once you're debt free, this portion is reallocated over to savings (as demonstrated by the grey arrow from Slashing to Saving).

Accounts

Under my GDR 70–20–10 approach you only need two bank accounts: a transaction account for your spending with a debit card linked to it, and a savings account.

Caitlyn's GDR 70-20-10

Back to Caitlyn. The following diagram shows what Caitlyn's GDR 70-20-10 program would look like if she chose to give $500 per month.

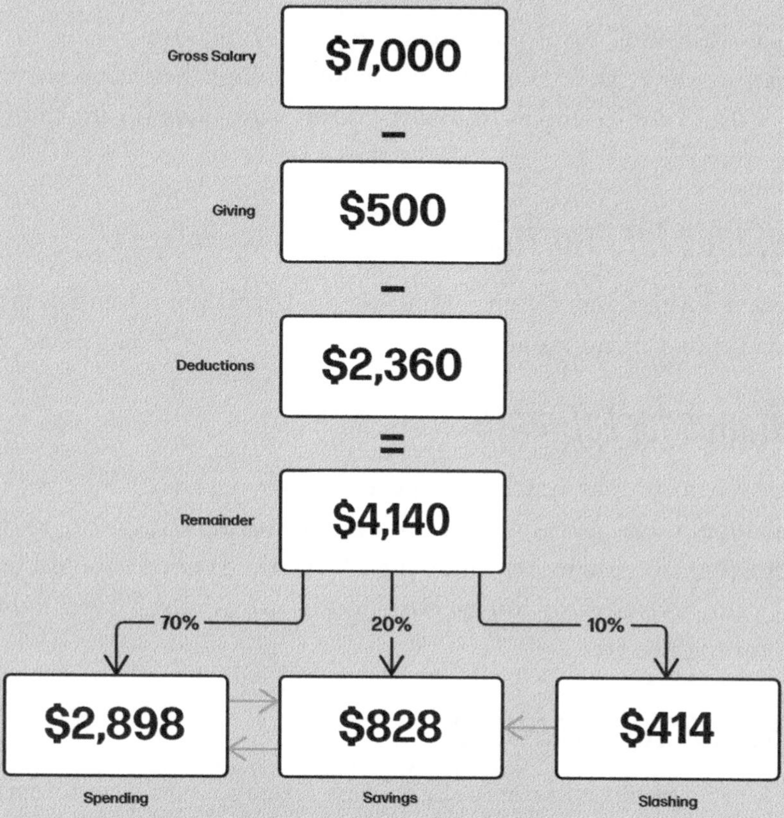

She earns $7000 a month, from which she gives $500. Compulsory payroll deductions of $2360 are subtracted, leaving a remainder of $4140, which is split 70 per cent to spending ($2898), 20 per cent to saving ($828) and the balance of 10 per cent ($414) to slashing her debt.

Note that her $625 car payment is a voluntary deduction, so it would need to be paid out of her spending allowance.

S.P.E.N.D.

How do you control the money that flows through to your spending allowance? Here's a little acronym that might help: S.P.E.N.D.

S stands for Separate

Make a list of all the things you spend money on, group them under broad headings and then separate those headings between essentials (needs) and non-essentials (wants or discretionary spending for comfort and convenience).

P stands for Prioritise

Next, prioritise and number your essentials and non-essentials from most (1) to least important.

E stands for Estimate

Next, estimate how much you spend in each category. Don't get too anal about it, and err on the side of over-estimating rather than under-estimating. You might be wondering, 'What time period should I use?' Use your pay period: if you get paid weekly, use weekly; for fortnightly, use fortnightly, etc.

N stands for Negotiate

Now the fun bit... like a coach or team manager you have to decide what expenses make it 'in', and which ones get 'cut' or 'cut back'. Remember, your salary cap should be how much net pay you receive, not gross pay earned.

Remember, your salary cap should be how much net pay you receive, not gross pay earned.

D stands for Dissect

The final step is to dissect the essential and non-essential expenses to try to find ways to save the dollars without getting caught up chasing the cents. Remember that if you don't spend all your allowance, then the balance carries forward to the next period.

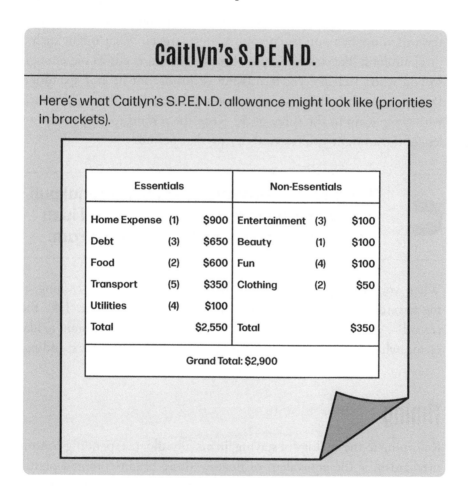

Caitlyn's S.P.E.N.D.

Here's what Caitlyn's S.P.E.N.D. allowance might look like (priorities in brackets).

Essentials			Non-Essentials		
Home Expense	(1)	$900	Entertainment	(3)	$100
Debt	(3)	$650	Beauty	(1)	$100
Food	(2)	$600	Fun	(4)	$100
Transport	(5)	$350	Clothing	(2)	$50
Utilities	(4)	$100			
Total		$2,550	Total		$350
Grand Total: $2,900					

Rewards

Feeling the pain of delayed gratification, when you could be having fun spending and being rewarded for it, is another reason why budgets fail.

Our brain chemistry wires us to seek rewards, so linking spending to some sort of no- or low-cost loyalty program is a marketing department's answer to prayer. The dopamine response of being rewarded provides a pleasurable 'fix', which, in some cases, can result in an addiction to retail therapy.

The way to overcome the gravitational pull of being rewarded when you spend is to create your own even better program that generously rewards you when you reach your savings targets. What might such a program look like? It's up to you, but the reward needs to big enough so you won't feel like you're missing or losing out by not spending. Perhaps something like, when my savings reach *$x*, I'll reward myself with *thing y*, up to the value of *$z*. Keep the reward to 10 per cent or less of the amount you've saved during that period.

The way to overcome the gravitational pull of being rewarded when you spend is to create your own even better program.

When you reach your target, you may feel anxious about cashing in the reward, lest it ruin your momentum. Forget about that. Take the reward—you've earned it! Better still, you'll be training your brain to like saving, which is a great defence against unplanned discretionary spending.

Timing

Returning to the analogy of staying financially afloat, a spending control mechanism is the equivalent of floaties: those bright-coloured plastic rings you pop on the arms of kids who can't swim so they don't drown.

You only need to control your spending while your spending is out of control.

Some people appreciate the structural support that financial floaties (i.e. budgets or allowances) provide and are happy to use them all the time. No shame in that, but it's not necessary. You only need to control your spending while your spending is out of control. Once you have learned how to keep yourself afloat with the floaties on, try taking them off and seeing if you have mastered the habit of controlling your spending intuitively, in which case you can ditch the floaties forever. You'll also be ready to progress to learning a few semi-advanced 'investing strokes' in order to put your savings to work.

Tracking

Finally, there's no way of escaping this: until you're in control of your spending you must track *all* your expenses. This is the accountability piece that is so often missing, but here's the rub: if you're not accountable, then you're unaccountable, and that's when things can and do go wrong because unaccountable people convince themselves that a little purchase here and there doesn't matter, and it absolutely does!

What about earning more?

It's very difficult to earn your way out of a spending problem. If you're living beyond your means, it will usually be easier to reduce your spending, up until the point where there are no more cuts that can be reasonably made. Thereafter, concentrate on earning more income.

It's very difficult to earn your way out of a spending problem.

Some try to invest out of a crisis. This is possible, but factors that will count against you include:

- higher profits leading to greater consumption, leading to higher permanent living costs
- your excess spending will make it difficult to borrow money, so your capacity to invest will be diminished
- your desperation to make money will act as a wealth repellent.

Trying to invest out of a spending deficit is like building a second storey on cracked foundations. Without sure footings, the whole structure can collapse at any time. I can't think of a single person who became and remained wealthy without living within their means. Who knows, maybe you'll prove me wrong, but is it worth the risk?

If you think that controlling your spending doesn't matter, then go back and re-read the first few paragraphs of this chapter. Your money bucket will never fill or overflow while the holes at the bottom leak out all the money you've poured in the top.

Chapter highlights

- If you want to increase your savings, it will be easier to spend less rather than earn more.
- Spending income not yet earned is a strong indicator of low financial IQ.
- Most people have a spending problem, not an earning problem.
- You earn in gross dollars, but receive net dollars.
- If you're not in control of your spending, your spending is out of control.
- Budgets are the equivalent of financial diets. They work in the short term, but are hard to stick to because they feel restrictive rather than liberating. You may get better results with an allowance and accountability approach.
- Don't worry about saving pence while the pounds are flying out the window.
- Before investing, lay a firm financial foundation where your income exceeds your expenditure, otherwise your desperation to build wealth puts the whole structure at risk of crashing down.

CHAPTER EIGHTEEN

'S' IS FOR SAVINGS

Savings are a good store of wealth, but a poor source of wealth.

Here are five scenarios with a question and answer each that you can use to explain earning, spending, saving and borrowing to young children. Grab a young'n and see if they can get all the answers right.

1. **Frankie and Freddie each bake one pie per day.**

   Question: How many pies does Frankie bake each day?

   Answer: One pie. (It's always good to start with an easy question!)

2. **On Monday, Frankie bakes one pie and eats half of it. She stores the remainder in the fridge for later.**

   Question: How much pie has Frankie saved?

   Answer: Half a pie.

3. **On Tuesday, Frankie bakes another pie and eats all of it. She's still hungry so she eats Monday's left-over pie.**

   Question: How much saved pie does Frankie have left?

   Answer: None. She ate the half she set aside the day before.

4. **On Wednesday, Frankie bakes another pie. She eats all of it but is still hungry. She goes to Freddie, borrows one of his pies, and eats it.**

   Question: How many days of baking does Frankie owe in order to pay Freddie back?

   Answer: Frankie owes one pie, which equals one day's baking.

5. **On Thursday, Frankie bakes her pie and gives it to Freddie to repay what she owes.**

   Question: What will Frankie eat?

   Answer: Nothing. She has to go hungry because she 'consumed' Thursday's baking on Wednesday.

If your child can accurately answer these questions, then they've demonstrated they understand the basics of earning (i.e. baking), spending (i.e. consuming), saving, borrowing including the concept of turning debt into time, and repaying debt, which results in going hungry because you have to repay yesterday's consumption.

Back in the adult world we tend to complicate our finances unnecessarily, when mastering money is really as easy as pie. In the example, baking pies relates to how much money you earn, with the more you earn, the bigger the pie. Eating the pies is your monetary consumption. Saving is your surplus of earning over consumption, and borrowing is the excess of consumption over earning when there are no savings to draw upon.

Store, not source

Here's another sentence to highlight: *Savings are better viewed as a* ***store*** *of wealth rather than a* ***source*** *of wealth* because:

1. savings earn no capital appreciation; and

2. the interest return on savings is extremely low (and possibly even negative) after adjusting for income tax and inflation.

Store of wealth

As a store of wealth, your savings represents reserves you can call upon when the need arises, as well as purchasing power and borrowing ability[12].

Mark, a friend who works in the socially disadvantaged sector, once said to me that in his experience the difference between rich and poor is the amount of 'margin' someone has.

The difference between rich and poor is the amount of 'margin' someone has.

'How do you mean?' I asked.

'Most poor people don't have any margin to fall back on, so when something unexpected happens, like a big energy bill or if someone gets sick, they have no margin of error and so they are in an instant crisis. A rich person though, can ride the bumps by drawing on their savings to bail them out and keep going.'

Grab a calculator and let's figure out how much wealth you have in reserve based on work days saved and months of spending up your sleeve.

Work days saved

Savings		Current Annual Income		Work Days Saved
$	÷	$	× 260 =	$

Dividing your savings by your current annual income and multiplying the result by 260 (i.e. number of working days in a year) will tell you how many work days you have 'saved up'. For example, if Sarah had

[12] Savings can be used as a deposit, and the bigger the deposit, the smaller the size of the potential loan.

$10 000 saved up, and she earned $75 000 per annum, she would have the equivalent of 34 work days in reserve. That is, if something happened to Sarah she could absorb up to 34 days of missed income before she would have used up all her margin.

Spending reserves

Savings		Current Annual Expenses		Months of Reserves
$	÷	$	× 12 =	$

You can also calculate the number of months of living costs you have saved up by dividing your savings by your current annual expenses and multiplying the result by 12 (i.e. 12 months). In Sarah's case, if her annual living costs are $70 000, then she would have 1.7 months of living expenses 'in the bank'.

If you're wondering how much you should aim to hold as savings reserves, according to one article (Parker, 2021), a cash stash of six months' living expenses is prudent.

If you want to know how well you stack up on your ability to save each month, then compare yourself against the results of Canstar's Consumer Pulse Report (2021):

Percentage of monthly after-tax income saved	
None	25%
Up to 10%	26%
Up to 20%	16%
Up to 30%	8%
Up to 40%	4%
Up to 50%	3%
Up to 60%	1%
More than 60%	2%
Unsure	15%

Another measure you can use to track your ability to save is to compare your achievements against something called the Household Saving Ratio, a statistic reported by the Australian Bureau of Statistics that measures the portion of a household's total net disposable income not consumed by them in that period.

The following graph indicates that most households save between 5 and 10 per cent of their monthly disposable income, increasing to 10 to 20 per cent in uncertain times (see the spike corresponding with the start of the COVID-19 pandemic).

Household saving ratio, seasonally adjusted

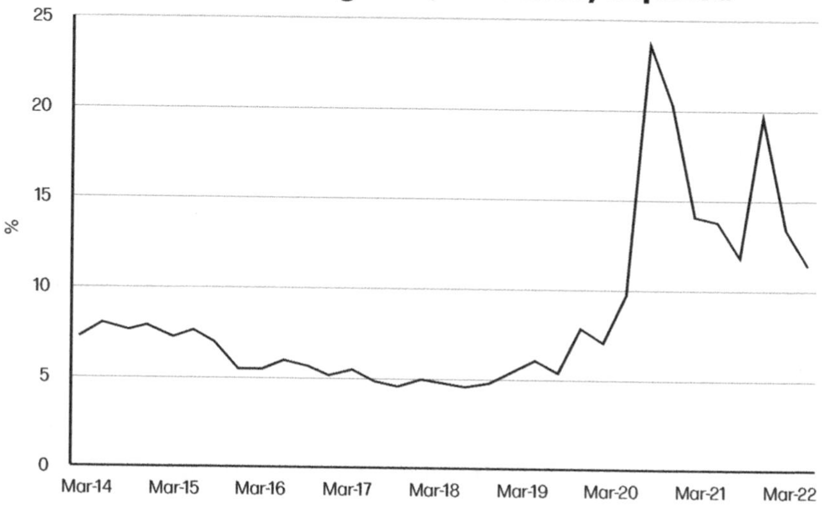

Source: Australian Bureau of Statistics, Australian National Accounts: National Income, Expenditure and Product March 2022

A double-whammy appears to be emerging though, as at the time of writing, the economy is contracting while prices are rising rapidly. Those higher prices will eat into your ability to save, so you may find you have diminishing reserves at a time when it would be more prudent to increase what's in your storehouse for any possible financial famine to come.

Source of wealth

In order for something to be a source of wealth, your money must earn an income and / or capital growth return. Yes, savings can earn an interest return, but after adjusting for income tax and inflation, the return is negligible or even negative.

In order for something to be a source of wealth, your money must earn an income and / or capital growth return.

Inflation

Inflation is a word economists use to describe rising prices (i.e. prices are inflating, resulting in inflation). Inflation reflects higher prices, and therefore lower purchasing power of your savings. A good way to look at inflation is to think of it as salt. A little is good and brings out flavour, too much and the whole dish is ruined.

Inflation reflects higher prices, and therefore lower purchasing power of your savings.

Hot chips (French fries) are not only yummy, they're the perfect inflation illustration. 'Back in my day' when I was a young'n, minimum chips at the local fish and chip shop cost … wait for it … 20 cents (and for good measure, potato cakes, aka potato scallops in some states, were 5 cents each, or five for 20 cents). I've just popped down to my local fish and chips store for, er, research purposes, and can faithfully advise that minimum chips is now $3.50 or 1650 per cent more. That's inflation!

Rising prices are the arch-enemy of savings: the equivalent of a mouse plague raiding your storehouse, stealing and spoiling the value of your precious reserves. Imagine you have $10 000 of savings. You earn 1 per cent interest per annum, but annual inflation is 5 per cent. The following table reveals what your wealth situation looks like, assuming an average income tax of 30 per cent.

Savings buying power at start of year		$10,000
+ Interest @ 1%	$100	
– Income tax	($30)	$70
– Inflation @ 5%		($500)
= Savings buying power at end of year		$9,570

Looking at your bank statement, you have $10 070 at the end of the year, but because prices have inflated, it will only buy $9570 worth of goods, and so your purchasing power or 'value' of your savings has actually gone down.

Comparative asset buying power

The comparative buying power of your savings is relative to other asset classes.

Let's explain the concept with an example:

- Chris is considering investing $10 000 of his savings to purchase XYZ Ltd shares.
- On Monday, XYZ Ltd's shares open at $1.25. Chris is distracted at work and is too busy to buy any shares.
- On Tuesday, news hits the market that XYZ Ltd might be a takeover target and its share price jumps up to $1.30 a share. Chris is upset that he didn't buy yesterday and curses his bad luck.

- On Wednesday, the price of XYZ Ltd shares falls sharply to $1.20 when the news of the takeover proves to be false. Chris is thinking about jumping in, but is now worried about the long-term future of the company.

The following table shows how many XYZ Ltd shares Chris' savings of $10 000 could have bought each day.

	Monday	Tuesday	Wednesday
XYZ Ltd share price	$1.25	$1.30	$1.20
Number of shares	8,000	7,692	8,333

Do you see how Chris' savings remain constant at $10 000, but the buying power of those savings decreases as XYZ's share price increases, and increases as XYZ's share price decreases?

The following table reveals the way the comparative value of savings changes relative to the movement of other asset prices.

When	Then
Asset prices ↑	Savings value ↓
Asset prices ↓	Savings value ↑

The table demonstrates that:

- when non-cash asset values rise, the purchasing power of your savings falls
- when non-cash asset values fall, the purchasing power of your savings rises.

This principle is important because it demonstrates that if you don't deploy your savings and asset prices increase, your savings effectively become 'worth less'. For instance, on Monday, Chris' $10 000 of savings could buy 8000 XYZ Ltd shares. However, on Tuesday the same amount of savings could only buy 7692 XYZ Ltd shares. Did you see how Chris' savings are (comparative to XYZ Ltd shares) worth less on Tuesday than Monday?

If you don't deploy your savings and asset prices increase, your savings effectively become 'worth less'.

The opposite is also true. Not deploying your savings will be to your advantage while asset prices are falling. This is illustrated in the example by Chris' savings buying 333 more shares on Wednesday than they did on Monday.

What do we learn from this? Be careful about how much cash you keep in reserve. You might feel safer with a big bank balance, but the comparative buying power of that cash could be slipping away.

Real estate

The loss in comparative value of savings as asset prices increase could also have been illustrated using a strongly appreciating real estate market. In such times, house prices rise faster than people's ability to save, so their savings buy less house, or price them out of areas they could once afford.

Lazy money

A certain level of savings, adjusted as needed to the prevailing conditions, is sensible. However, from a wealth maximisation and efficiency point of view, there is a point where you can have too much of your seed in your storehouse, and not enough sowed in the pasture, especially in times of high inflation. Grab that highlighter again because here's another important Steveism: *savings are an asset, but they are not an investment.* In order to be productive, your wealth needs to be deployed rather than waiting to be put to work.

Savings are an asset, but they are not an investment.

You can use the following diagram to help you calculate how much of your savings are in the barn, and how much have been planted in the field.

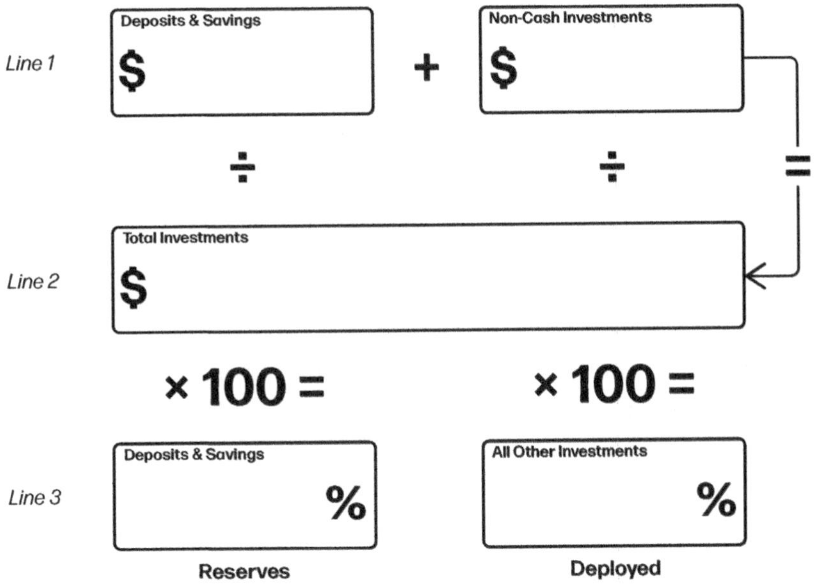

Line 1 requires that you add up and input all the money you have in your deposit and savings accounts (plus cash, if applicable). You also need to add up the current market value of all your non-cash financial investments. Include superannuation if you have retired; otherwise only include the voluntary or non-compulsory superannuation contributions you've made.

Line 2 is the value of your total investments, and is the sum of the two items in line 1.

Line 3 calculates your percentage of capital in reserves (i.e. deposits and savings ÷ total investments), and your percentage of capital deployed (i.e. non-cash investments ÷ total investments).

Maximising your money magnetism requires that you don't under-utilise your savings by overfilling your storehouse, where there are no returns, at the expense of deploying your savings to purchase investments that deliver capital gains and income returns. The message here is: Stores of wealth have low or no money magnetism. Sources of wealth have medium to high money magnetism.

Robyn's capital deployed situation

Robyn is 38 years old and has $5000 in savings and $25 000 in a share portfolio. She also has $45 000 in compulsory superannuation.

Robyn's superannuation is excluded as she does not have access to it.

The following diagram illustrates what her capital deployed situation looks like, with 17 per cent stored in reserve, and 83 per cent deployed.

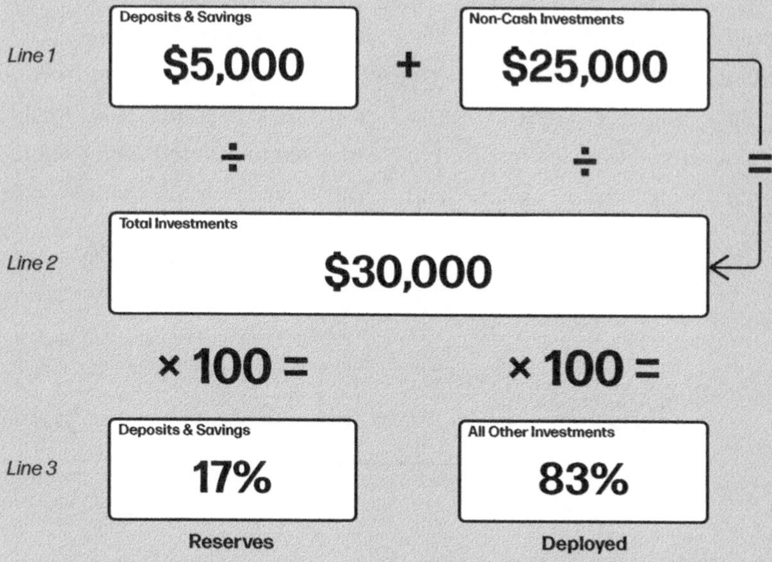

Stores of wealth have low or no money magnetism. Sources of wealth have medium to high money magnetism.

Asset allocation

Asset allocation is the term given to the way you split your wealth into different asset classes with varying risk profiles. An established wealth-planning principle is that as your age increases, your exposure to risk should decrease. Why? Because your ability to recover from losses is reduced given your shortened work life, as is your timeframe to allow financial markets to recover lost value.

An established wealth-planning principle is that as your age increases, your exposure to risk should decrease.

A rule of thumb used in some asset allocation circles (Kurt, 2022), and as illustrated by the following diagram, is to deduct your age from 100 and that's the percentage of your total portfolio you should hold in at-risk assets, with the balance in safe-harbour investments that are backed by high credit ratings and are known for low volatility in all market cycles.

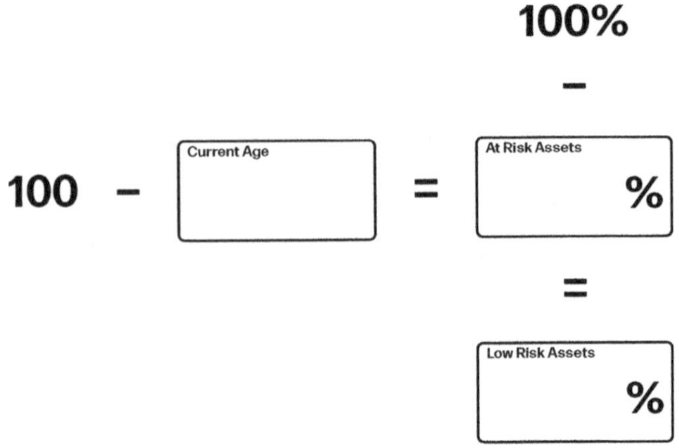

For instance, consider three people: Ben aged 25, Brinda aged 50 and Bobby aged 75. Applying the rule of thumb mentioned before, their general asset allocation guidelines would be:

Asset allocation	Ben (25)	Brinda (50)	Bobby (75)
At risk	100 - 25 = 75%	100 - 50 = 50%	100 - 75 = 25%
Safe harbour	100 - 75 = 25%	100 - 50 = 50%	100 - 25 = 75%

How much of your total capital is deployed in the field versus bunked up in the barracks? There is no perfect right answer. The situation simply needs to reflect your risk appetite and expectations of economic conditions to come. Be aware though, that holding too much in reserve will act as a brake on the speed at which you accumulate wealth because, as mentioned earlier, savings normally earn low-to-no after-inflation interest returns.

If you need specific advice on what asset allocations are appropriate for your age, circumstances and the current economic climate, make an appointment to see an experienced financial planner.

Chapter highlights

- Savings accumulate when your income exceeds your expenses.
- You can increase your savings by earning more and / or spending less.
- The after-tax and inflation return on interest on savings is usually low, or even negative. This makes savings a good store of wealth, but a poor source of wealth.
- Wealthy people have savings, but savings alone rarely makes people wealthy.
- Inflation happens when prices increase. Some inflation is good as it indicates the economy is growing.
- If the interest rate on your savings is lower than the rate of inflation, then the buying power of your savings will be decreasing.
- Keeping some savings in reserve is sensible, but holding back too much will act as a drag on your ability to multiply your money, and weaken your money magnetism.
- Not keeping enough in reserve is risky. My experience is that cash is abundant when you don't need it, and scarce when you do.

CHAPTER NINETEEN
THE DANGERS OF DEBT

Debt is always dangerous and never good.

When your expenses are higher than your income, and you don't have savings to draw down, you'll have to use debt to fill the gap. This is illustrated in the following diagram, where the shortfall of income to expenses is topped up by debt.

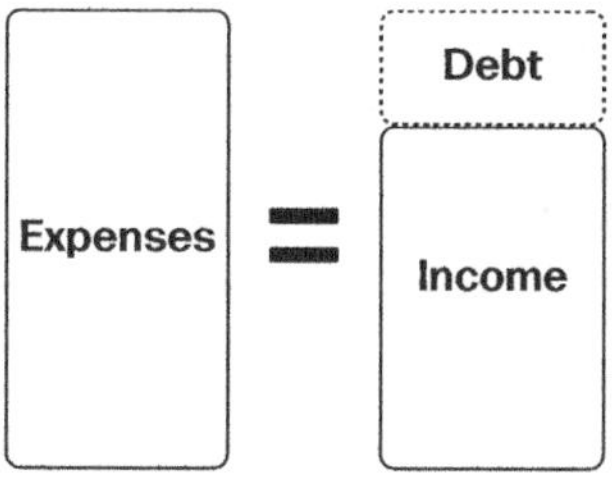

Some say there are two types of debt: good debt and bad debt, but I firmly disagree. Debt is never good. It is always dangerous and should only be used in well-controlled and astutely managed circumstances.

What is debt?

It's easy to think that debt is simply the amount of money you've borrowed and have to repay. There's a bit more to it than that though, and those with a high level of financial literacy are aware of something called the 'debt-time connection': that you borrow dollars and owe time.

You borrow dollars and owe time.

The following diagram shows that getting into debt means borrowing money. You swap time for pay, which is used to repay the money you borrowed. In summary, Debt = Time.

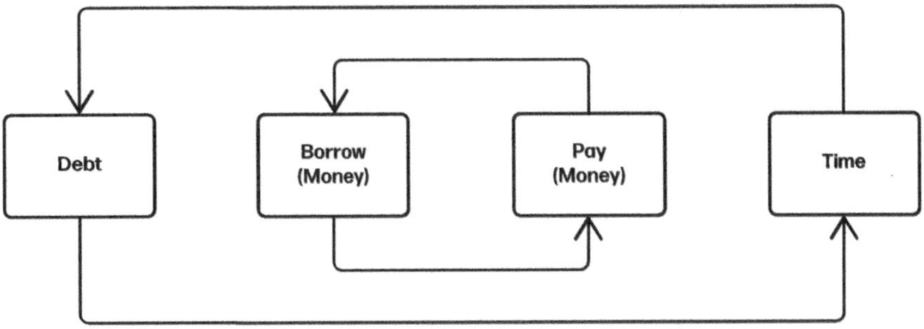

Here's an example: Ebony wants to go on a holiday and borrows $3000. She plans to repay the loan when she gets back to work, deducting money from the monthly salary she earns as a sales rep. At first glance you'd correctly say that Ebony is borrowing $3000 of someone else's money. But if you look *through* the lender to the source of how Ebony will repay her debt, you'll see she is really getting an advance of her future pay. The result is that Ebony borrows money, but owes time. Keeping the maths simple, if Ebony is paid $30 per hour in net pay, then her $3000 debt equates to 100 hours of work time owed.

Here's a true story that demonstrates that you borrow your future pay.

Ralph: Borrowing future pay

Many years ago, my older but less-good-looking brother (grin), Ralph, went into a bank to apply for a new credit card. He'd just returned from a few years of working overseas where he'd managed to save an impressive amount of money. The credit card was for convenience rather than necessity, and the limit he requested was a tiny fraction compared to his savings.

'I see here on your application form,' the teller said, 'that you don't have any income'.

'That's right,' my brother cheerfully replied. 'I'm enjoying a short break after returning from working overseas and I'll be applying for a new job soon.'

Looking at Ralph like he was crazy, the teller said in a scorned tone, 'You realise you have to repay the money, right? How are you going to do that if you don't have any income?'

'From my giant savings account, which is also with your bank,' Ralph replied.

'Oh no,' said the teller. 'We can only lend you money if you have income available to repay it.'

Borrowing is akin to reaching into tomorrow, grabbing hold of money you haven't yet earned and spending it now. Be aware though … your pay can only be spent once. As demonstrated in Frankie's example (see pages 217–218), the consequence of borrowing to live above your means today, is an obligation to have to work tomorrow for income you've already spent and can't spend again. Here's the principle: the more money you owe, the more time you owe.

Borrowing is akin to reaching into tomorrow, grabbing hold of money you haven't yet earned and spending it now.

How many tomorrows do you have to work to repay money you've already consumed? As illustrated in the following diagram, the formula to calculate the number of work hours you owe is to divide your non-investment debt by your hourly net pay. Divide that result by (assuming you work an 8-hour day), and you'll also be able to calculate how many work days you owe.

Non-Investment Debt		Hourly Net Pay		Hours Owed		Days Owed
$	÷	$	=	hrs	÷ 8 =	days

Have a go at calculating how many work hours, work days and even work years Sonja owes.

How much time does Sonja owe?

Sonja's payslip reveals she receives $42.23 per hour in net pay. She has $3000 in credit card debt, owes $12 000 on her car loan, and has $1250 of buy-now-pay-later debt and a home loan with $350 000 outstanding. Sonja works a standard 8-hour day. How many work hours and work days does Sonja owe? Assuming there are 260 work days in a year, how many years of future pay has Sonja already consumed? Have a go at calculating the answers by filling in the boxes below.

Non-Investment Debt		Hourly Net Pay		Hours Owed		Days Owed
$	÷	$	=	hrs	÷ 8 =	days

÷ 260 =

Years Owed
days

Note: Round up the hours and days to the nearest whole unit.

You can check your answer in Appendix 3.

After you've calculated Sonja's situation, go back and fill in the boxes in the earlier diagram to calculate the number of work hours and work days you owe, assuming you had to repay your non-investment (i.e. consumer-related) debt solely from your employment income. What does the answer reveal about the way you've been using, and possibly abusing, debt?

Good debt and bad debt

'There are two types of debt,' the smartly dressed seminar presenter explains.

'Good debt, or money borrowed to buy things that put money in your pocket. And bad debt: money you borrow to buy everything else.'

The audience nods enthusiastically, indicating their agreement, and now believe that getting into debt can be 'good' in some circumstances.

As I've said, I don't agree that debt can ever be good. To demonstrate, try to answer this question: Is it bad to repay good debt?

The answer must be 'yes, it is bad', because good debt is good, which means it shouldn't ever be repaid because to do so would result in a less-good outcome, which must be bad. Capiche?

Look, let's cut through the confusion: debt can never be good in the sense that superheroes are good. Have you ever seen Debt Man or Debt Woman come to the rescue of anyone? No. How about debt causing the demise of someone? Absolutely! Lots of people have been stabbed in the back by debt. Wouldn't it be more accurate to say that debt can pretend to be good, but is actually evil at its core? Yes, and therein lies the truth.

Let's cut through the confusion: debt can never be good in the sense that superheroes are good.

Bad debt and worse debt

Make no mistake: all debt is bad; some is badder than bad—in other words, worse. I teach that there are indeed two kinds of debt, but they are bad debt and worse debt.

Bad debt is something you get into temporarily, and aim to get out of as soon as possible. I call it 'bad' because the consequences of mismanaging it are, well, bad. You could face financial hardship, maybe even financial ruin.

Worse debt is money borrowed to buy stuff that's worth less, or worthless, immediately after buying it. Steer clear of that stink bug, lest your finances start emitting a most unpleasant odour!

Make no mistake: all debt is bad; some is badder than bad – in other words, worse.

Helpful and harmful debt

In some circumstances a villain with an evil nature can still be helpful—even useful—but only so long as your motive aligns with theirs. While it does, you can be frenemies. When it doesn't, you know what to expect: debt is going to drop you like a hot potato and do what's in its interests without regard to yours. I'm only happy to be friends with bad debt if it's temporary and on my terms.

Does that mean you should avoid debt completely? Yes, if it's worse debt, but I'm happy to make friends with bad debt provided all the following conditions are met and maintained:

- Its use provides a return greater than its cost.
- The relationship is temporary for only so long as it suits me.

- Before getting into debt, I have a realistic plan for getting out of debt.
- I repay the debt before I pay myself.

I'm only happy to be friends with bad debt if it's temporary and on my terms.

Getting into debt to purchase positive cashflow investments is an example of 'bad debt' that I'm willing to be mates with. Let's say you find an asset offering a return of 6 per cent per annum. Everything else being okay, so long as you can borrow at an interest rate of less than 6 per cent per annum, then your loan repayments will be covered from the asset's income[13].

'Ah,' you say. 'But what happens if interest rates go up, or your tenant leaves, or your expenses increase and your return no longer services the debt?' That's when your helpful mate becomes your harmful mate, and you'll have to call on the strategies you've put in place to prevent yourself from getting hurt.

Using debt to pay for assets and expenses

Here's a good rule to live by: never get into debt before making a plan for getting out of debt. That is, have a plan for how you'll make your interest and principal[14] loan repayments (also called 'servicing' your debt).

[13] Well, at least the interest will be. The principal loan repayment will still need to be met too.
[14] 'Principal' means the sum borrowed.

Never get into debt if you don't have a plan for getting out of debt.

Servicing debt is an important conversation because a surprising number of people get into trouble with an assumption that is often flawed, and occasionally even financially fatal. I had better let you know about it, but 'heads up': this next bit might be a heavy slog. Hang in there because your financial literacy and financial IQ will be much improved at the end.

Assets

An asset is something that has a future value, perhaps because it can generate income, or be sold, even if its sale price is less than what you paid for it (because the cash you receive has a value).

Assets can either be lifestyle or financial in nature. *Lifestyle* assets are purchased for pleasure or enjoyment. *Financial* assets are purchased for profit or return.

Sometimes the line between a lifestyle and a financial asset can be a bit blurry. Confusing lifestyle and investment assets leads to a muddled mindset. Take a holiday home, for instance. Would you classify it as a lifestyle or an investment asset? If it was bought for enjoyment, then it would be a lifestyle asset, but what about the income that could be earned from renting it out, or the prospect of its value increasing over time? Doesn't that make it a financial asset?

Confusing lifestyle and investment assets leads to a muddled mindset.

Making the distinction between lifestyle and investment assets is important because the strategy and mindset associated with their purchase is very different. Think about the mindset when purchasing a holiday home. If you were trying to maximise your money, then how well the property meets your family's needs (e.g. the suitability of the location and style of the house) is simply not relevant. All you should care about is making the most money, in the quickest time, for the least risk and the lowest aggravation.

An indication of low financial IQ is purchasing lifestyle assets for financial reasons. Here's a simple rule to remember: a financial asset will *never* be used for lifestyle purposes.

A financial benefit from a lifestyle asset doesn't make it a financial asset. It makes it a 'compromised' lifestyle asset, and as you know, when you compromise you make sacrifices rather than getting exactly what you want.

An indication of low financial IQ is purchasing lifestyle assets for financial reasons.

Using debt to buy assets

Debt used to purchase assets can be serviced three ways:

- *Option 1:* from the asset's current realised income
- *Option 2:* from the asset's future realised income
- *Option 3:* from other sources.

Option 1: Repaying debt using an asset's current realised income

Self-liquidating debt is the safest unsafe debt there is.

Realised and unrealised income

If you're unfamiliar with the terms, realised income is real in the sense that it can be measured by a flow of cash, whereas unrealised income is unreal and exists only on paper.

Take an investment property, for example. The rental income is realised as it is a physical transfer of money and can be seen and measured by movements in bank accounts. Capital appreciation – the opinion of how much the property's value has increased – is an unrealised profit; it only exists in theory or 'on paper' until the property is sold, when it becomes a realised profit and converted into cash.

To be self-liquidating, the debt must be used to purchase assets that generate enough realised income to cover the loan's interest and principal repayments.

Referring to the following diagrams, the diagram on the left illustrates an asset that can pay its own way. Say you borrowed to buy an investment property that generated rent (Realised Income) higher than its operating and interest expenses[15] (Realised Expenses). The surplus is sufficient to pay the principal loan repayments[16].

[15] The grey arrow from Debt to Realised Expenses represents the interest.
[16] Shown as a dotted line as principal loan repayments are not an expense, but a capital repayment.

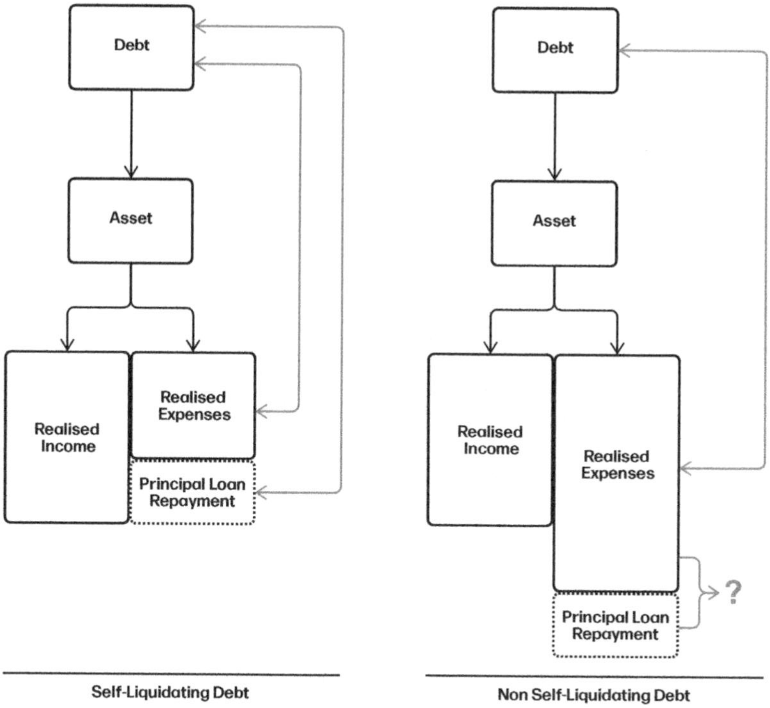

The diagram on the right, on the other hand, shows a property that has insufficient income to cover its realised expenses, including interest, and so the resultant loss and principal loan repayment must be funded from other means.

Option 2: Repaying debt from an asset's future realised income

The following diagram shows the loan's interest and principal repayment being met from the property's realised net income (i.e. Realised Income less Realised Expenses). Often though, a property's realised net income is not sufficient to meet its realised expenses and loan service costs (i.e. this would be a negative cashflow property). Why might an investor still want to buy it?

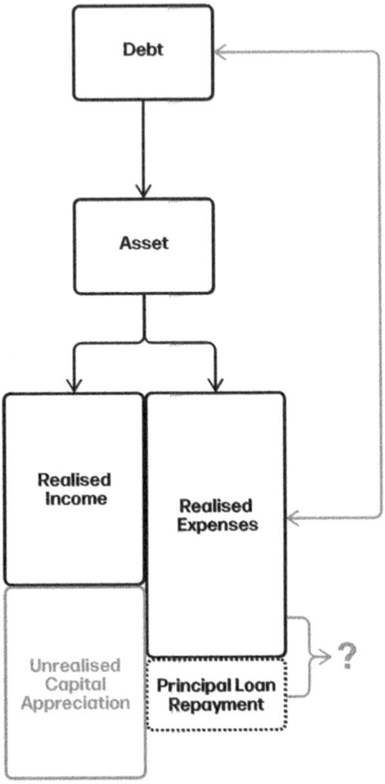

Repaying from Future Income

Because they're willing to speculate that the property's future capital appreciation will be greater than its current realised net income (see the shaded box). This is the premise of negative gearing: an extremely popular way of property investing that I'm particularly wary of. Any investment where you make a certain loss today for the hope of an uncertain profit tomorrow is high risk.

Any investment where you make a certain loss today for the hope of an uncertain profit tomorrow is high risk.

To be successful, the property's eventual realised capital appreciation must exceed the property's cumulative net realised loss. In the meantime, the cash shortfall of the excess realised net expenses and principal loan repayments must be met from other sources.

If you think 'tomorrow's uncertain gain will be higher than today's certain loss' sounds risky, then you'd be right. Such a deal results in a certain realised loss for an uncertain unrealised profit and makes you more reliant on your other sources of income. If that's employment income, then this strategy will cause you to need your job more and more, which is the antithesis of financial freedom (i.e. to need your job less and less). But people do it, in droves, usually because they want to use the loss (i.e. from expenses > income) to reduce their income tax.

Some particularly aggressive (er, foolhardy?) investors take this idea to an even more precarious level by borrowing their unrealised capital appreciation to purchase more non-self-liquidating assets. This double-down-debt strategy is only effective as long as property prices keep rising and the investor can tap other sources to plug their annual cash shortfall. If either or both don't eventuate, and the investor is forced to sell assets in a down market, then the result may be financially catastrophic.

Option 3: Other sources

Finally, the money needed to make debt repayments can be found from sources other than the asset purchased. For instance, employment income, other positive cashflow assets or, most dangerously of all, other debt. There's a word for those who use debt to repay debt … insolvent.

There's a word for those who use debt to repay debt … insolvent.

Expenses

Anything purchased that has no future value, or is quickly consumed, is an expense and not an asset. For example, buying toner or ink for your printer.

Money borrowed to pay expenses must always be funded from other sources.

Death adder debt

For the unfamiliar, a death adder is an Australian snake you definitely don't want to accidentally step on while you're out hiking. It may not be the most toxic snake in the world, but its venom can kill you in less than six hours of being bitten. Not good. Old mate death adder is no sluggard. It has a very fast strike, possibly the fastest of any Aussie snake, I'm told.

Fast, and deadly, the death adder is what's called an ambush predator. It will just about completely conceal itself in the ground cover, leaving only the tip of its tail exposed. Looking like a tasty grub, it will twitch the end of its tail to lure its dinner, and when it comes within striking distance, it's game over.

'Death adder debt' mimics the behaviour of the snake that it's named after. Its danger is largely hidden, and it lures its prey by some seemingly attractive feature. Before you know it—crunch! You've been bitten.

Borrowing to buy assets that depreciate (i.e. fall in value) and don't produce income is an example of death adder debt. Here's how it works.

Let's imagine there's a fictitious car called a 'Nassin Fortuna': a snazzy four-door sedan with all the latest mod-cons.

Helen's death adder debt trap

Helen's car is on its last legs. She was going to spend her savings on buying a second-hand car, but she saw a snazzy new Nassin Fortuna advertised on her social media feed, with the added bonus of low-deposit, no-hassle, no-interest finance. 'I've never owned a new car before, but I work hard and deserve it,' Helen thought. 'This seems interesting ... low deposit and 0 per cent interest. Perhaps now I could afford one after all?' she wonders.

Helen pops into her local Nassin car dealership and is pleased to discover there is currently a run-out sale to clear the dealer's remaining stock ahead of a new model being released soon. 'The car is essentially the same,' the dealer says. 'Just some new trim and an upgraded entertainment system.'

Helen asks about the low-deposit, 0 per cent interest loan terms, and is told that all she has to do is make the easy interest-free monthly repayments over three years, with a 50 per cent balloon payment due at the end of the loan[17].

'Don't worry about the balloon payment,' the dealer says. 'We guarantee to buy back your car for the amount you owe, provided you drive it less than 15 000 kilometres each year and agree to have it serviced at our dealership according to the car's service schedule.'

With no interest to pay, surely this is a great deal. How could Helen go wrong? Twitch, twitch goes the snake's tail.

The dealer checks and confirms Helen's preferred colour is in stock and the car can be ready next week rather than Helen having to wait the usual three to six months. As an added bonus for

(*continued*)

[17] In other words, Helen has to repay 50% of the loan over 36 monthly payments, with the other 50% due at the end of three years.

Helen's death adder debt trap (cont'd)

buying today, the dealer agrees to throw in custom car mats and a free loan car when Helen's vehicle is in for its service. 'It's a done deal!' Helen announces. Here's a summary of what the purchase transaction looks like:

Purchase price	$41,000
Deposit	-$1,000
Finance	= $40,000

Now let's delve a little deeper into the transaction to calculate the car's depreciation: its loss in value from its use and obsolescence (i.e. no longer the latest model, nor having the latest technology). Instead of calling it depreciation, let's call it quasi-interest: the interest you're paying when you're not paying interest.

Purchase price	$41,000
Value of car, year 3	-$20,000
Depreciation	= $21,000
Loan term (years)	÷ 3
Depreciation per annum	= $7,000
Finance	÷ $40,000
Quasi-interest per annum	= 17.50%

Helen thinks she's getting a 'can't-lose' deal with '0 per cent' interest, when in actual fact her cost is '17.50 per cent' per annum. She has been enticed to spend more than she otherwise would and lured into a debt trap. Let's hope it was only a dry bite with no venom, otherwise she's in real trouble.

Other than car loans, can you think of any forms of credit that might be 'death adder debt'? Yep, credit cards, personal loans, buy-now-pay-later loans, store credit and the big one … a home loan. 'A home loan?' you cry. 'Surely not!'

I'm afraid so. Explaining how and why is so important that it warrants its own dedicated chapter, which is coming up next.

Chapter highlights

- Debt is money you borrow and have to repay. It is always dangerous and never good.
- Borrowing money to pay for living expenses is reliable evidence that you're living beyond your means and progressing towards financial hardship.
- The debt-time connection explains that more debt = more time owed.
- Accessing debt and spending money you haven't yet earned is the antithesis of financial freedom since it makes you more reliant on your job.
- Beware speculating and borrowing to buy assets that can't pay their own way.
- Bad debt can still be helpful in limited and carefully controlled circumstances.
- The hidden costs and fees associated with low- or no-interest debt can result in a very nasty bite.
- Death adder debt demagnetises your money magnetism.
- While you may choose to borrow in certain circumstances from time to time, debt-free should be your ultimate goal because as wise Grandpa Geordie said, 'You'll never go broke if you don't owe money'.

CHAPTER TWENTY
THE GREAT AUSTRALIAN NIGHTMARE

Success comes from doing things differently.

Home ownership is portrayed as a great utopian outcome, like all your problems will somehow magically disappear once you're on the property ladder. That's just not true, especially if you need a giant home loan to pay for your purchase. We're told that it is the Great Australian Dream to own a home, but is it actually a nightmare?

The great Aussie property pyramid scheme

Home affordability keeps getting worse and worse because property prices keep going higher and higher. The fix to this problem is for house prices to come down—a lot. Naturally, this will create a different kind of pain as those who own houses will see their wealth diminish, possibly to the point of having negative equity—where the property's value is lower than the debt owing against it. Those who have the majority of their wealth tied up in their home will watch in horror as their nest eggs crack and crumble.

What does a government do when it is politically unacceptable to dash the great Aussie dream or crash home values? It keeps everyone happy, of course, by preserving rules that prop up house prices while also creating schemes that leverage buyers (who otherwise couldn't afford a home) into the property market.

It all sounds like a government sanctioned pyramid scheme to me, where those 'in' the market are propped up by those 'entering' below them. The scheme can continue as long as the existing property pyramidians trade up and not out, and new property pyramidians can be convinced to buy in.

I'm quite impressed with how successive governments have found innovative ways to keep real estate prices inflated while simultaneously encouraging new buyers to enter the property pyramid by co-sponsoring their purchase. In the past few years we've had the government guaranteeing debt so new buyers could borrow 95 per cent of the purchase price without having to pay the usual lender's mortgage insurance, and the latest showstopper is the government co-owning your home via a shared-equity scheme; all you need is a 2 per cent deposit.

Oh golly. My head hurts just thinking about how this could all end in tears. Since when has it ever been a good idea for someone to borrow 98 per cent of a property's purchase price? Now add rapidly rising interest rates into the mix. If (when?) it all turns to custard I think the government will have to nationalise the debt under a program they'll probably call 'Home Saver'. It won't save the nest eggs of asset-rich, income-poor retirees though.

I'd also like to point out the obscure obvious. Giving handouts and handups to home buyers really only transfers wealth to home sellers. For instance, if the government gives a first homebuyer a $10 000 grant to buy a home, who is the ultimate recipient? It passes from the government, through the buyer, into the seller's pocket. Aha! If the penny has dropped that homebuyer incentives are really homeseller incentives, then you've also understood how government intervention props up buyers who overpaid yesterday by getting new purchasers to overpay today, who in turn will be protected by new entrants who overpay tomorrow[18]. The scheme will work, until it doesn't, and when that happens, watch out.

Giving handouts and handups to home buyers really only transfers wealth to home sellers.

All right, McKnight, what's the better option? I'm not sure you can stop the property pyramid scheme now without it toppling over because the Aussie real estate market has become too big to fail. The best I can offer is this common-sense observation: wouldn't it be smarter to educate people to become better makers, managers and multipliers of money, rather than bigger borrowers? Probably, but that will cost votes, so it's unlikely to happen.

Wouldn't it be smarter to educate people to become better makers, managers and multipliers of money, rather than bigger borrowers?

Dreams turning to nightmares

The dream of home ownership will turn into a nightmare when the financial pressure of owning becomes intolerable. That can happen if:

- property prices fall to where the homeowner owes more than their house is worth (i.e. negative equity)
- interest rates rise and home loan repayments become unaffordable

[18] If you've also realised the government's shared equity scheme creates another incentive for them to keep propping up the property market, then that's an astute observation.

- rising living expenses make it harder and harder to make ends meet
- the source(s) of income used to pay the home loan is compromised. For example, loss of employment, falling wages, sickness, relationship breakdown.

While it's unlikely that all these events will occur, it's equally unlikely that none of them will eventuate.

You probably don't need me to point out that the more you borrow, the less margin (see page 219) you have and the greater your exposure to these financial shocks. How will those who have borrowed 98 per cent of their purchase price fare?

The worst possible scenario will arise if borrowers find themselves in a situation where they can't afford to keep their homes because they can't afford the loan repayments, nor can they afford to sell because they're in a negative equity situation and don't have the money to pay out the loan.

Does buying a home make sense?

With the additional FQ you gained from reading the previous chapter, can you answer this question correctly: Is a home an asset or a liability?

The answer, without any doubt whatsoever, is that a home is an asset. But what kind of asset: lifestyle (bought for enjoyment) or financial (bought for return)? Remember, an asset cannot be both; it has to be one or the other. What say you?

A home is a lifestyle asset bought for enjoyment. If buying it happens to result in some ancillary financial perks, then that's a bonus—an encore to the main show, never the main show in its own right.

Now, let's see how well you understood the dangers of debt. What is the outcome when you borrow to purchase lifestyle (i.e. non-self-liquidating) assets? That's right, you reach into tomorrow, grab hold of pay you haven't yet earned and consume it today, resulting in the obligation to have to keep working for decades. Does borrowing to buy a home sound like a step in the right direction, or the wrong direction, if you want a financially empowered future that is less reliant on employment income? The wrong direction for sure.

'But hang on a minute,' you may say, 'isn't buying a home the biggest investment I'll ever make?' It might be, but that doesn't mean it will be the best investment you ever make, and if it is, I dare say you need to up your FQ or else you're on track for a financial future that is asset rich and income poor.

Buying lifestyle assets

The two must-ask questions to work through before buying a lifestyle asset are:

1. Can you afford it? If you can't pay cash for it, you can't afford it. If you can't afford it, don't buy it.
2. Can you rent or borrow it? It's almost always better financially to rent (i.e. borrow) a lifestyle asset than it is to own it because you won't have to purchase it, maintain it or suffer the loss in value as it depreciates. You get to use it when you want, and when you're done, you hand it back.

If you can afford it, don't need to borrow and you can't or don't want to rent it, then go ahead and buy the lifestyle asset and enjoy it. If you can't buy it without using debt and you go ahead anyway, then it may sound harsh, but you're deliberately sabotaging your financial future.

Financial sabotage

Homes make particularly poor financial assets for many reasons, including:

- The money you pay as a home deposit leaves less money to invest.
- As you only have a finite borrowing capacity in your own name, borrowing to buy a home will reduce your ability to borrow for investing purposes, leaving you with less money to invest.
- Having to pay the home loan is going to tie you to your job, which will result in a more risk-averse investing appetite and may cause you to forego opportunities to invest.
- Home loan repayments must be made in after-tax dollars, meaning you have to earn more dollar for dollar than the home loan repayments. For example, if you borrow $500 000 and pay an average 30 per cent income tax, then you have to earn $714 286 (more actually, when you add on compulsory superannuation). In other words, what you have to earn is considerably more than what you have to repay, leaving you with less money to invest.
- The stamp duty paid when buying a house is thousands, if not tens of thousands, of dollars, which is effectively immediately flushed for absolutely no benefit. That could easily equal several years of rent. It leaves you with less money to invest.
- Homes have considerable ownership costs, which again must be paid for in after-tax dollars. Council rates, building insurance, body corporate fees, repairs and maintenance, and so on, can easily add up to several thousand dollars each year, which leaves you with less money to invest.
- Time is the most powerful component for maximising the incredible benefit of compounding returns. Delaying your investing for the sake of buying a home means you will have less

time to benefit from compounding, and in the end, less money from your investments.

- Working 38+ hours a week to earn money to pay the home loan will leave you with less time and energy to invest.
- Homes are emotive purchases and people tend to fill them with goods they feel they deserve, which in the very least will result in less money to invest. If you borrow to buy those goods, then your debt burden will also reduce the money you have available to invest.
- The consequence of buying a home and spending decades paying it off at the expense of purchasing other investments, is that you can end up asset-rich and income poor. That is, having a home but little money to pay for its upkeep or put food on the table.

But Steve . . .

Righteo, let me guess your rebuttals.

1. But I'll *never* own a home!

   I'm not suggesting that you never buy a home. I'm advocating a pathway where you maximise your financial future first, and buy a home using your investing profits second. Doesn't that sound like a better plan than running head-first down a track where you get into debt up to your eyeballs and then spend the next three decades scrambling to keep yourself financially afloat?

2. Rent money is dead money.

   Bollocks. The benefits you get from renting instead of owning are the flexibility to move without transaction costs and the extra money you have available to invest because you haven't paid a house deposit and your rent is lower than your home loan repayments. If you want to talk about dead money, look at how much interest versus capital you have repaid over the first five years of your home loan. Assuming you borrowed $500 000 and have a 30-year P&I loan at 5 per cent per annum interest with monthly repayments, after five years you will have paid $161 046 in loan repayments, of which $120 190, or 75 per cent, was interest. You will only have repaid $40 856 or a little over 8 per cent of the loan's principal. Hmmmm... all that interest sounds more like dead money to me.

3. Capital gains on homes are tax free.

   Yes, it's true that the capital gains made on your principal place of residence (PPR) are exempt from capital gains tax (CGT). But then again, home loan repayments, ownership costs, and so on, are not tax deductible and have to be paid with after-tax dollars. Also, let's see how long homes are completely CGT exempt. I wouldn't be surprised if a future cash-strapped government added a threshold—say $500 000—after which capital gains made on the sale of homes are taxed. You heard it here first! Never let the tax tail wag the wealth creation dog.

Never let the tax tail wag the wealth creation dog.

---

4. Property prices only ever go up.

   Bollocks. While state and federal government policy in Australia facilitates a giant real estate pyramid scheme, where those at the top cash in to the detriment of those at the bottom, everyone knows that pyramid schemes eventually topple over. When that happens, those who couldn't get out get crushed.

   I've lived through several real estate downturns, and I can faithfully advise that property prices do fall. Furthermore, I've been on the ground to witness the misery from a bona fide property crash (USA, 2009–2012) and the misfortune I saw was truly horrible.

You never want to be a seller in a down market, and you won't be if you don't owe money.

5. My kids will never own a home.

   I'm not sure what you mean. Are you saying you want to cheer your kids on to getting into hundreds of thousands of dollars of debt and binding themselves to having to work for three or more decades, to end up asset rich and income poor? Wouldn't it be better to teach them how to become money magnets so they can own a home without debt and have a brighter financial future?

6. Homes provide security.

   Oh really? How secure is your home if you lose your job or interest rates rise and you can't afford your home loan repayments? Or if house prices drop and your lender claims a 'material adverse event' and requires you to make a large lump sum payment to bring your debt back in line with your agreed loan-to-valuation ratio? The best you can say is that your home is as secure as your ability to make your home loan repayments.

7. I'm going to flip my way to financial freedom.

   The plan here is to cash in on rising property values, buying with a large interest-only loan to minimise the amount of the home loan repayments. As property values increase, the property is sold and the tax-free capital gain reinvested into the next property, and the next property, and so on, until there is enough equity to buy a house debt-free.

   Like any strategy, this approach is only as good as the assumptions that underpin it. If house prices fall or interest rates rise, then look out! This approach falls into the high-debt, high-risk category, so buyer beware!

8. I plan to downsize and eat my home equity.

   What about getting the enjoyment from living in a home, gaining the benefit of capital appreciation, and then later on downsizing, selling and cashing in the equity to live off? This is the exact plan of the masses, and as you've seen the vast majority of them end up relying on the age pension to survive. The goal should not be to eat your golden goose equity once, but rather to preserve it and live off the eggs it lays (i.e. recurrent income from your investments). A better question to ask and answer is: how can I live in my house without having to downsize, and without having to rely on any government welfare?

9. Renting sucks.

   Okay, you've got me on this one. Renting is a less heart-warming and less socially satisfying experience than owning a home. But is the personal enjoyment of owning a home worth the financial disempowerment that stems from the debt burden really worth it? Also, the aggravation of renting will make it hard for you to get comfortable and will act as a motivator to keep pushing you forward and prevent you from backsliding.

But I already own a home . . .

To the reader who already owns a home and is wondering whether or not to sell it to maximise their financial future, I can only refer you back to the discussion about lifestyle and financial assets.

You own a home because you can afford it, and because of the enjoyment it brings. If you can't afford it, or it doesn't bring enjoyment, why continue owning it? What about keeping it, refinancing the equity and using that money to invest? You could, but you'll end up with a compromised lifestyle asset. Furthermore, those with a high financial IQ keep their lifestyle and investment assets separate and certainly don't take risks with their homes.

'But Steve,' you may say, 'keeping our home compromises our ability to make, manage and multiply our wealth'. That's probably true, but that's the price you'll pay for buying lifestyle assets before financial assets. The cost of selling your home is the enjoyment you'll forego. Is that worth the benefit of the investing opportunities that selling will unlock? That's your call.

The monkey trap

Perhaps knowing about the monkey trap might help. The story goes that villagers catch small monkeys by setting a simple but effective trap. They put food, such as rice or peanuts, in a container that has a hole big enough for the monkey's open hand to reach in, but too small for a clenched fist to be pulled out. The container is fixed to an immovable object, like a rock or a tree. A monkey comes along, reaches in for the food, and gets stuck. The trap is sprung. It could escape if only it would let go of the food, but it wants the food and won't let go. Instead it jumps up and down screeching. The villagers return with a hessian sack and capture the monkey.

Do you kind of feel like the monkey—wanting to be financially free but trapped by the expense and burden of your ham-fisted determination to own a home, or other mindset traps and lifestyle choices you're not willing to forego?

The best help I can offer is to work through this logic process:

1. Where am I now?
2. Where do I want to get to?
3. How do I get there in the quickest time, with the least risk and lowest aggravation?
4. Am I willing to pay the cost and sacrifice price? If not, what won't I sacrifice or delay, and therefore what's the impact?

Forced savings

Despite everything I've said, there is one group of people who would be better off buying a home sooner rather than later—those who would otherwise spend (rather than invest) their money on lifestyle expenses and accumulate little, if any, assets in retirement. This form of forced saving is a slow and steady grind, and you'll need to work until your mid-to-late sixties—and you'll likely be reliant on the age pension in retirement—but at least you'll own the roof over your head.

I'm guessing that's not you though, because if it were, you probably wouldn't be reading this book.

Chapter highlights

- A home is a lifestyle asset purchased for enjoyment, not an investment asset purchased for return.
- Getting into debt to buy a home is a long-term commitment that binds you to a job and reduces the money you have available to invest. Less money invested now results in less money accumulated later.
- If your biggest financial investment is a lifestyle asset, then your financial future is precariously placed. It's likely you'll end up asset rich but income poor, resulting in having a roof over your head, but needing support to put food on the table.
- Government policy inflates house prices, which makes homes less affordable and transfers wealth from buyers to sellers.
- Rapidly rising interest rates are beyond the government's control and will put downwards pressure on home prices, resulting in improved affordability for buyers, but horrible financial consequences for those whose wealth is tied up in their homes.

- Rent money is not dead money. It provides flexibility and choices and preserves capital and borrowing power that can be used to invest.
- The longer you leave it to start investing, the less time you have to take advantage of the money-multiplying effect of compounding, and the less wealth you'll accumulate. Stop procrastinating … there's not a moment to lose.
- If you think you'll spend rather than invest your savings, then getting on the property ladder sooner rather than later is a worthwhile consideration, notwithstanding the financial servitude getting into debt will bring. Paying off your home loan will be a form of forced savings, and although it will likely result in an asset-rich income-poor outcome, that's better than having no assets and no income.
- You most definitely can have your cake and eat it. If you invest astutely from the get-go, you'll be able to use your profits to buy a home, plus have enough investment capital left over to fully fund your financial freedom. I can say that with confidence because that's what I did.

CHAPTER TWENTY-ONE
THE PATHWAY TO POVERTY

The road to financial ruin is paved with good intentions and well-meaning but ignorant advice.

When I started my accounting career I only knew one pathway to wealth: climbing the corporate ladder and progressing from graduate, to senior, to manager and ultimately reaching the pinnacle of the accounting profession — becoming a partner. Partners seemed to have a great life: large incomes, beautiful homes, impressive cars, status and respect.

The corporate ladder

The problem with the plan was the climb up the corporate ladder required long days (a typical working day was 10 hours) and long years (it usually takes about 15 years to reach partner level). That's a lot of six-minute interval timesheets! Even after becoming a partner, life wasn't expected to be all beer and skittles. There was another 25 or so long years exchanging time for fees to fund that large partner salary and profit share. Any way I looked at it, I couldn't overcome the fundamental weakness in the swapping-time-for-money model: if you stopped working, you stopped getting paid.

It was 1999: the year Lou Bega's 'Mambo No. 5' raced up the music charts. I was 26 and a half years old and after six years of climbing the corporate ladder I decided a life of journals and timesheets, er, accounting, wasn't for me. I started reading widely to see if I could find a magic income pudding that never ran out and didn't require me to work until my mid-60s to make it.

I started attending seminars: a fair number of them were fronts for shonky, get-rich-easy schemes targeting attendees whose greed glands had short-circuited their sensibilities. A friend had recommended that I read a book, *Rich Dad Poor Dad*, by US author Robert Kiyosaki, which I dutifully did. Robert happened to be touring Australia a few months later and I booked to attend his two-hour introductory evening session, and was thereafter upsold into his two-day weekend seminar for a few thousand dollars. It was money I didn't really have and couldn't really afford, but then again, I was becoming more and more desperate to do something other than accounting.

The life-changing moment

There's not much I remember about Robert's two-day seminar, except the bit where he yelled at me (a story for another day) and when my life changed forever.

One of the guest speakers was a real estate agent, and during his presentation he said, 'I don't know why people bother with negative gearing, when you can positively gear and make money'. He then proceeded to show a variety of property deals in the Sydney metro area that delivered positive cashflow outcomes: where the cash received from rent was higher than the cash paid in finance and ownership costs, resulting in a cash surplus.

At that moment the clouds parted and the fog lifted—there may even have been gentle harp music playing and a choir singing faintly in the background—as I caught a glimpse of the positive cashflow pathway to financial freedom. If I could buy enough properties that generated enough positive cashflow, then I'd be able to stop working as an accountant without suffering a drop in income. Bring out the pudding!

Over the next few years, Dave, my business partner (yes, from Ecogen boardroom fame) and I embarked on a *Bill & Ted's* (well, Steve &

Dave's) *Excellent Adventure*–type escapade of buying 130 properties in 3.5 years to achieve our goal passive income of $250 000 each per annum. Exactly how we did it, including some of the bizarre people we met and situations we found ourselves in, is outlined in my #1 bestseller *From 0 to 130 Properties in 3.5 Years.*

In all the books I've read, and seminars I've attended, I was never given the big-picture model. It was only after climbing to the top of the proverbial money mountain that I was able to 'see' the entire journey I'd travelled. Here's what I saw (pause for dramatic music) …

Beware the easy path

The first path I saw seemed the more appealing. It was well worn and mostly downhill, making it easy to walk. You won't need sturdy shoes, indicating the road may be followed without much forethought, training and preparation. Sadly, it resulted in a mediocre wealth outcome at best, and financial ruin at worst. Allow me to explain it step by step.

Step 1: Income and superannuation

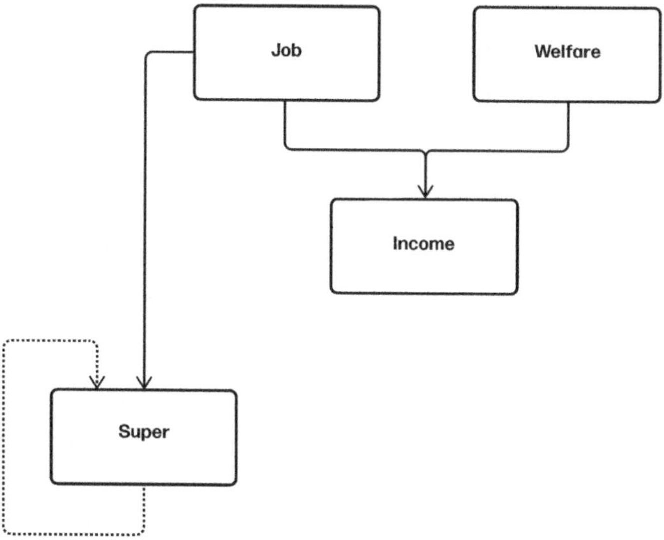

The pathway to poverty begins with incoming money (i.e. in-come = income) in the form of compensation received from monetising your time and knowledge, supplemented with welfare support. Some seminars I attended derided those with jobs, saying that J.O.B. stood for Just Over Broke. I can't see anything wrong with working and contributing your skills to solving problems, can you? It adds more value to the economy and community than playing a round of golf, or sipping chardonnay at the beach house.

Compulsory superannuation (arrow to the left and down) will be deducted from your employment income. The income earned in superannuation must be reinvested until you reach retirement age, which is illustrated by the dashed line stemming from, and feeding back into, Super.

Step 2: Spending

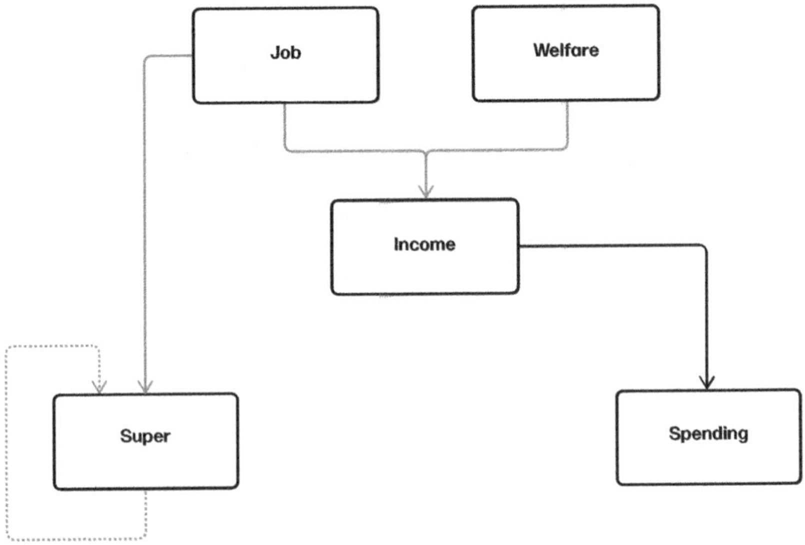

Along the pathway to poverty are many vendors with trinkets and so-called treasures to sell. Those with average-to-low financial literacy and FQ can easily get caught up in the hubbub and swap all their money for comfort and convenience. This is represented in the diagram by the arrow from Income to Spending.

As time goes on and pay increases, so too does the cost of living expenses as bigger and more luxurious purchases are made. Beware the golden handcuffs: a situation where you become bound to your job's income, and are unable to unchain yourself without suffering a fall in living standards.

Step 3: Debt

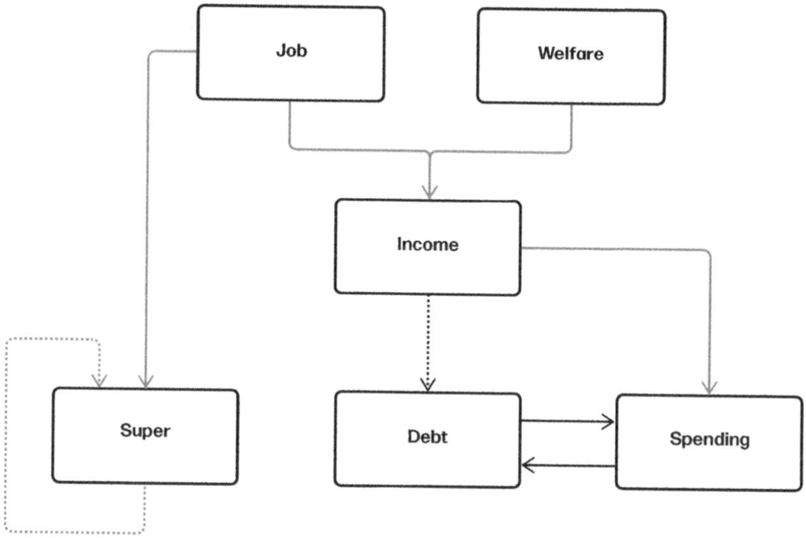

An even worse situation can occur when you live beyond your means and borrow to pay for life and lifestyle expenses (line from Debt to Spending). When you borrow, you're reaching into the future, grabbing tomorrow's not-yet-earned income and consuming it today. Debt demagnetises your money magnet. The more tomorrows you've borrowed, the more days you'll have to work to service and repay what you owe (line from Spending to Debt). Another complication is that you'll be working tomorrow to pay for yesterday's expenditure, which can result in you feeling like you're working for little reward given the gloss of what you bought yesterday will likely have worn off.

Debt demagnetises your money magnet.

Neither consumption nor borrowing seems too dangerous while you're young and have decades of work days up your sleeve. This youthful optimism is financial foolishness in disguise. The flexible dynamic you think exists when you're young—that you'll stay in the job only for as long as it suits you—slowly changes as you age and life becomes more expensive.

Once you move out of home, decide to buy a house and / or have children, your cost of living expenses will increase and won't begin falling until you're in your 50s. As your responsibilities increase, particularly mortgage and mouths to feed, you will become more and more dependent on your job if you don't have other income to call upon. The dynamic you have with your job gradually changes as you need it more and more, with that dependence resulting in you enjoying your job less and less. The struggle at home to pay the bills and raise the kids, combined with the battle to put on a happy face at work when you're feeling frustrated and trapped, while watching the so-called best years of life slip through your fingers, can set you up for a dreaded mid-life crisis.

Around the time you start to feel old because your work colleagues look young, your flexibility and portability to switch jobs and careers becomes more rigid. You're less motivated to lose the respect, status and goodwill you've built up and start again from scratch somewhere else. Furthermore, your seniority makes it difficult to easily switch jobs as there are fewer higher paying opportunities the further up the career ladder you progress.

Retrenchment becomes a real risk. Your seniority and superior pay make you an expensive labour resource, and if your employer needs to find cost savings, they may let you go in favour of younger and cheaper labour.

This situation sounds bleak, and it is. If you can't find another position for the same or better pay, you'll have to reconsider your financial options, and a fall in living standards is inevitable. Cuts to everyday lifestyle expenses will be needed, but bigger changes may be afoot, such as having to sell the family home as you can no longer afford the mortgage payments, or re-schooling the kids to save fees.

Step 4: Retirement

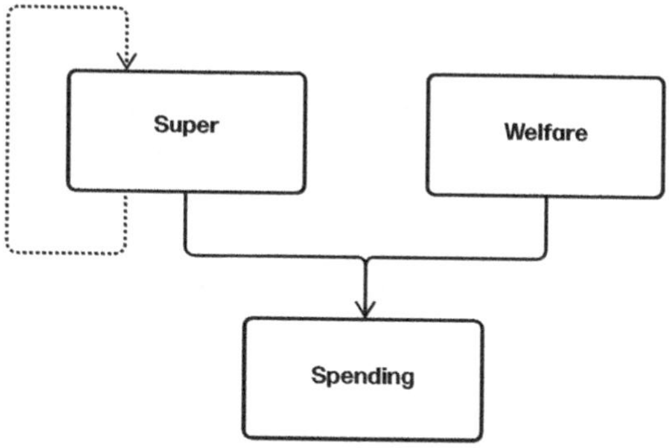

Without other income to rely upon, when you stop receiving employment income your spending will reduce to what you can afford based on your ability to access welfare (see chapter 4) and the income and capital from your superannuation (see chapter 5).

When reflecting on how someone can work for decades and not have more to show for it, it wasn't the last step that led to misfortune but rather the first step and the choice to earn then burn the employment income, rather than save and invest it.

What I've described above is the road most travelled when it comes to managing money. Let's pause for a moment to catch our breath and then resume with an outline of the less travelled, more difficult, but ultimately more prosperous and profitable route.

Chapter highlights

- If you're on the career ladder, pause for a moment and look up. How far do you have left to climb? Will the effort be worth the view?
- The Bible (Proverbs 27:17 NIV) says 'As iron sharpens iron, so one person sharpens another'. It's smart to find people who are where you want to be, and to engage with them so you can sharpen up your knowledge and skills. Who are you sharpening and who is sharpening you?
- The road to financial ruin appears easier at its origin, but arriving at its destination can be financially disastrous.
- Borrowing is accessing tomorrow's pay and spending it now. The more debt you have, the more tomorrows you owe.
- Spending all your income indicates low FQ. Borrowing to spend more than what you earn is financial foolishness.
- Needing your job more than your job needs you is one of the riskiest situations to ever find yourself in.
- Failing to plan means living for now and letting tomorrow look after itself. This is fine, until you stop working and have to live on whatever you can scrounge together. The better approach is to cast a vision for what you want your financial future to look like, and then start resourcing it now so that achieving your goal is a matter of choice, not a matter of chance. As the proverb says, don't wait until you are thirsty before you dig your well.

CHAPTER TWENTY-TWO

THE PATHWAY TO PROSPERITY

You'll never be wealthy if you can't save, but you'll never become wealthy by saving alone.

The path to prosperity begins at the same starting point as the pathway to poverty, but rather than being a pleasant and easy track, the going is mountainous, uphill and tough. Sturdy shoes are needed, as are training and conditioning before beginning, and support along the way. Those that persevere and make it to the top, once there, will enjoy a well-earned rest and an incredible view.

The eight steps to financial freedom

Chapter 5 included four options for funding your retirement: welfare, compulsory super, voluntary super and super sufficient. It's now time to expand upon the last option by outlining the eight steps to achieving financial freedom. The milestones build upon each other; for example, step 2 is 'higher and further along' than step 1, and so forth.

Step 1: Employment income and superannuation

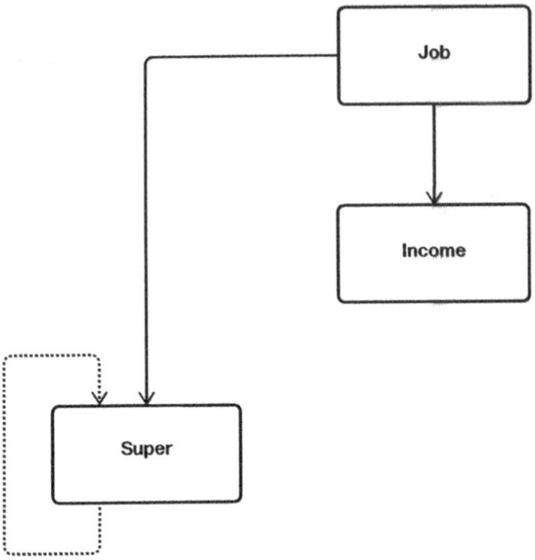

Step 1 is the same as the previous model. Although not shown on the diagram, if you receive welfare support or have other non-investment and non-employment income (e.g. inheritance, scholarship), then that would also flow through to your Income box.

Step 2: Income accelerator

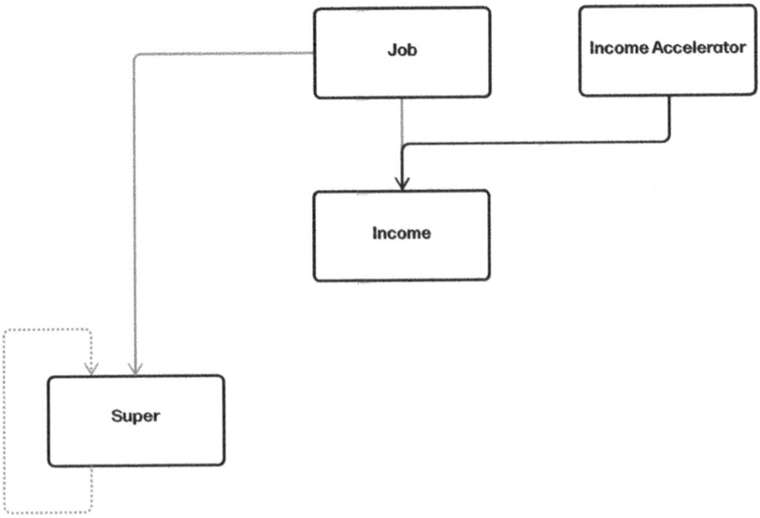

Supplement your income by adding an income accelerator side-hustle as outlined in chapter 16.

Step 3: Spending

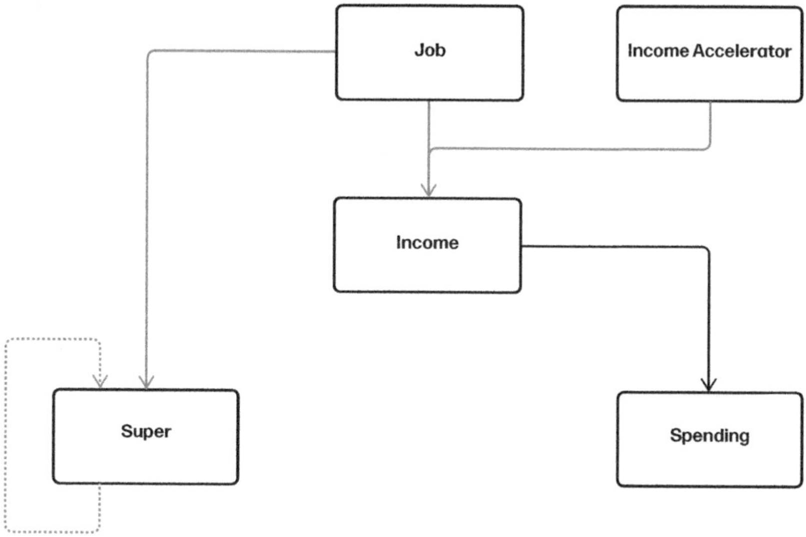

What's left of your employment income after superannuation (and taxes), together with the money earned from your income accelerator side-hustle, is available to pay for your living and lifestyle costs (arrow to the right and down to Spending).

Step 4: Savings

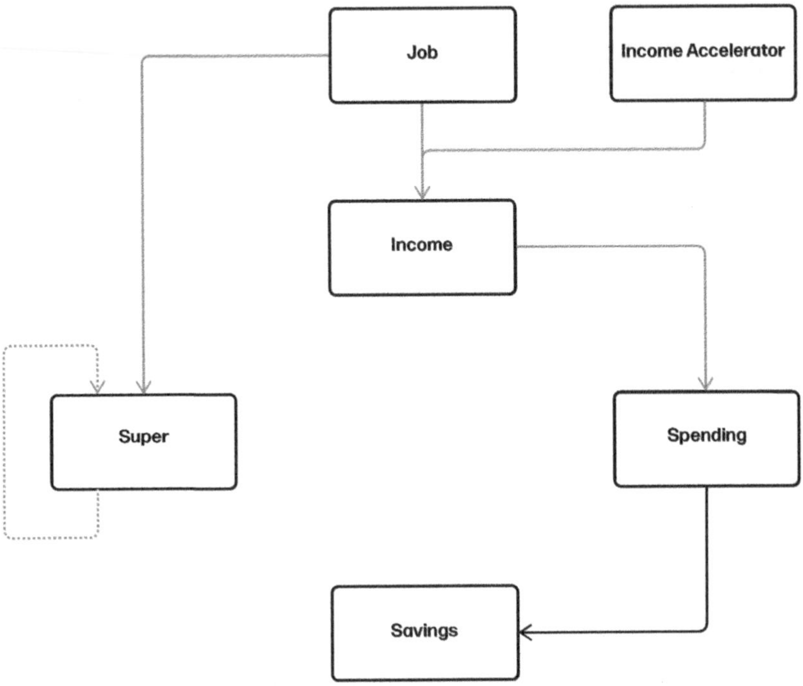

Step 4 is where the two financial paths diverge in a yellow wood.

Unlike the pathway to poverty described in the previous chapter, where all income earned is spent, following the pathway to prosperity requires that you live within your means and spend less than you earn, with the surplus of income over expenses accumulating as savings (line from Spending to Savings).

The pathway to prosperity requires that you live within your means and spend less than you earn.

Now grab a highlighter and get ready to use it, because this next sentence is one of the most important money magnet principles in this whole book: You'll never be wealthy if you can't save, but you'll never become wealthy by saving alone.

Step 5: Deploying savings

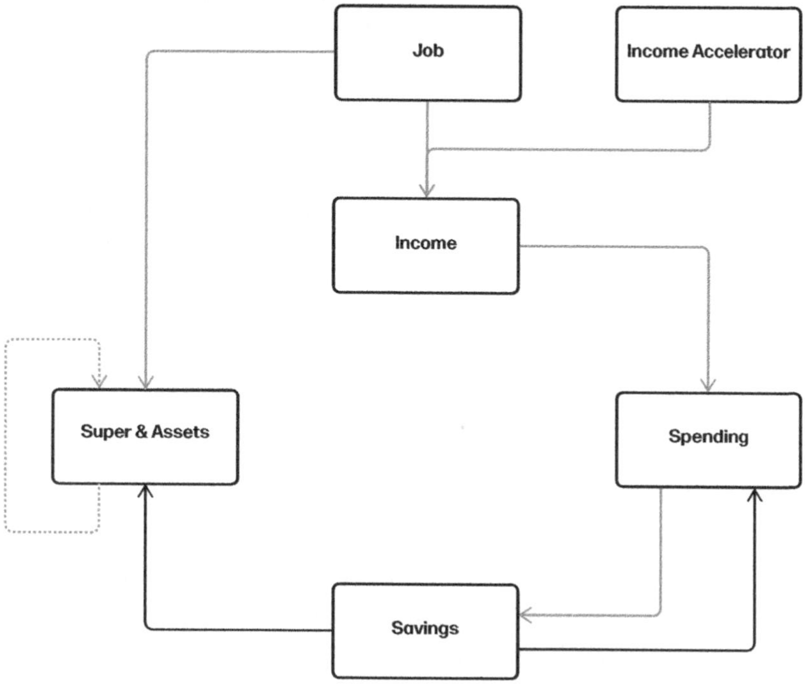

When it comes time to use your savings, you have three options, two of which are discussed here and the third, debt reduction, a little later on.

Consumption

You can consume your savings by spending them on life and lifestyle expenses that you can't fund from your income (line from Savings to Spending). Once spent, those savings are gone forever leading to a flow of wealth away from you, and a loss of magnetic power.

Green army soldiers

At a seminar a few years back I showed the picture of a plastic green army solider and said, 'I want you to imagine every dollar you've saved is one of these soldiers. You're their commander, and it is your job to keep them alive and to use them to conquer new wealth territory. Every time you spend unwisely or on a whim you're sacrificing your soldiers for no gain and depleting your wealth creation army. What kind of general does that?'

Investment

Instead of storing your savings seed in the barn, you can plant some of it in the field by purchasing investments (line from Savings to Super & Assets). We're going to talk about investing in a lot more detail in the chapters ahead. For now, be aware that just as there is no one perfect crop to plant in every field, there is no such thing as a perfect investment for every investor. The right investment for you is the one that makes the most money, in the quickest time, for the least risk and lowest aggravation.

The right investment for you is the one that makes the most money, in the quickest time, for the least risk and lowest aggravation.

Step 6: Debt

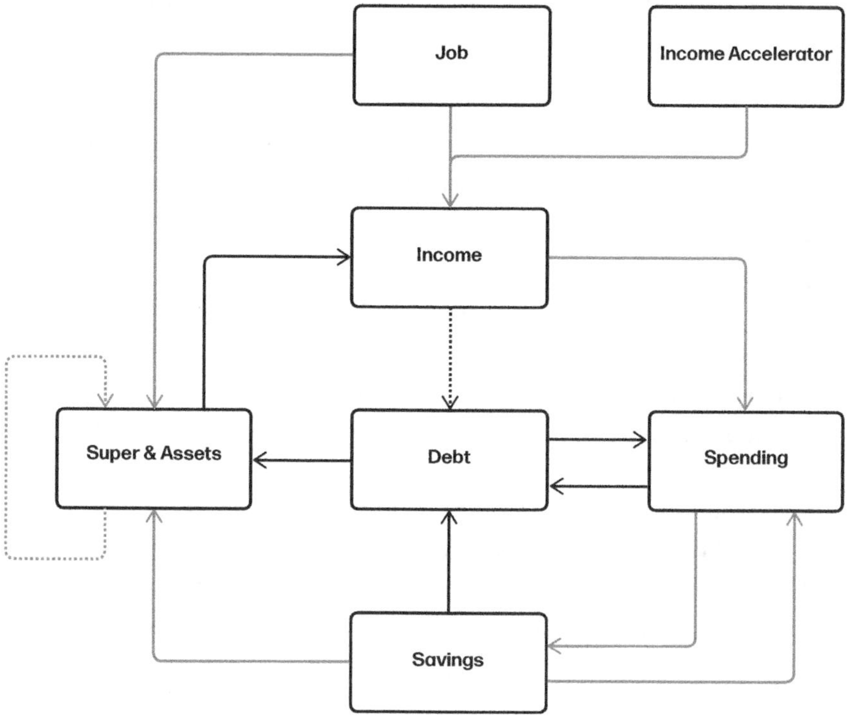

Whereas debt was used to pay for spending in excess of income in the pathway to poverty, in this model accessing other people's money is used as a way of leveraging and accelerating the accumulation of wealth. Naturally, there are risks, and these are explained in chapter 23.

Did you also notice the arrow from Savings to Debt? That indicates the third use of your savings: repaying debt. Oh, and in case you've forgotten, the dashed line from Income to Debt illustrates the twofold truth that your ability to access debt depends on your current income, and that by getting into debt you are borrowing from your future income.

More savings or less debt?

Imagine that Shaun has $5000 in savings and $3000 in debt. What should he do: hang onto his savings or wipe off his debt?

From a pure 'bang for buck' perspective, as shown in the following table, so long as the interest Shaun pays on his debt is higher than the interest he receives on his savings, he will be 20 times better off repaying it (i.e. $300 ÷ $15).

	Left in savings	Repaying debt
Amount	$3,000	$3,000
× Annual interest rate	0.5%	10%
= Annual interest	$15	$300

The decision may not be that simple though. For instance, since Shaun has maxed out his credit he won't be able to borrow more money. That might be a protection mechanism against him spending more until his finances improve. Another consideration is that although Shaun's net saving situation is $2000 (i.e. $5000 less $3000), he may feel more secure knowing he has access to the full $5000 should an unexpected need arise, in which case the $25 a month he pays in interest is worth the convenience of being able to call on the money.

As you can see, there's a right answer in theory, but another answer in real life that depends on the person and their circumstances.

All that said, my personal preference is to avoid carrying consumer debt and paying interest—something that I regard as a 'lazy tax' by not being a better money manager.

Step 7: Investment returns

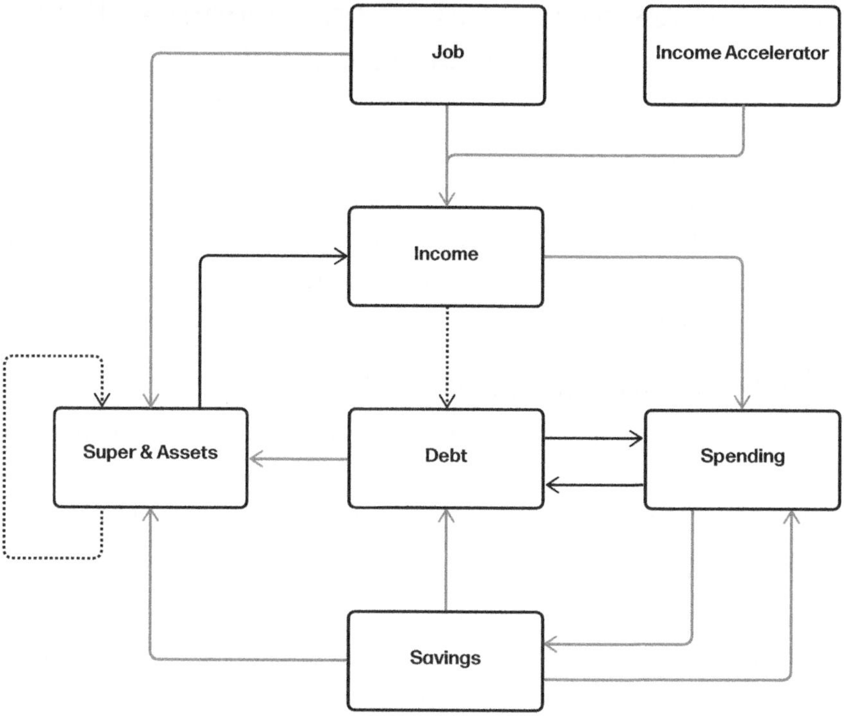

Time for a dad joke. What do you call a boomerang that doesn't come back? A stick! Ha ha.

This joke reminds me that some investments are boomerangs and provide good returns, and others are poor investments and are only useful as sticks thrown for dogs. I have more to say about investing in chapter 23. For now though, I just want to point out the solid line from Super & Assets to Income, which represents the after-tax cash profit from your non-superannuation investments, and the dotted line, which represents the capital gains arising from your non-superannuation assets increasing in value.

Some investments are boomerangs and provide good returns, and others are poor investments and are only useful as sticks thrown for dogs.

You'll also notice new arrows have appeared between Debt and Spending, indicating borrowing for life and lifestyle expenses and the repayment thereof. I've done this to illustrate an advanced way of using money and debt that some people advocate, but I don't. Given that forewarned is forearmed, let's talk about it.

Using investment returns to leverage lifestyle

A school of thought taught at some seminars is to use your employment income to purchase investments, and then leverage or borrow against the after-tax investment returns to upsize your lifestyle. Let's review how it works using an example.

Dimitri and Thea have a property investment portfolio that is generating $25 000 per annum of after-tax net rental income. That's not enough for them to achieve financial freedom, but they recently attended a seminar where the presenter told them that $25 000 could service a principal and interest loan of nearly $500 000[19]. 'Imagine how much bling you could buy with that?' he said.

But wait, there's more. The presenter showed them how the $500 000 could be used as a 20 per cent deposit to buy a $2 500 000 home (i.e. their principal place of residence where they'll live), with Dimitri and Thea's employment income supporting the interest-only repayments on the $2 000 000 loan.

But wait, there's even more. 'The icing on the cake', the presenter said, 'was that you don't have to bother repaying the home loan. It will be

[19] Annual rental income of $25 000 ÷ 12 months = $2083 per month. A $500 000 loan at 5% per annum interest over 25 years would have repayments of $2093 per month.

repaid when you sell the home, at which time the capital appreciation that's been accruing as the home's value increases can be cashed in tax free'[20].

Wow, eh? See how $25 000 can be turned into $2 500 000 of debt? If you think that sounds a bit scary, then you'd be right. Any investment is only as good as the assumptions that underpin it. Provided everything goes to plan, the strategy will work. However, if any of the following happen, its viability is compromised:

- vacancy in the rental property
- reduced rent or increased rental property expenses
- increase in interest rates
- fall in property values
- loss of job or incapacity to work
- reduction in employment income.

It's doubtful that *all* of these contingencies will occur, and it's equally doubtful that none of them will occur. The only question is whether the ones that do will be the financial equivalent of a hiccup or a heart attack.

It's doubtful that *all* of these contingencies will occur, and it's equally doubtful that none of them will occur.

The approach outlined above is high risk, and that makes me nervous to say the least. I prefer that investment income be reinvested (dotted arrow), with the profits compounding back into the asset providing the return, or else being used to purchase more assets.

[20] Gains made on the sale of principal places of residence are exempt from capital gains tax, and so are not subject to income tax.

Of course, until you reach financial freedom, you can 'eat' or consume a portion of the investment income by using it to purchase occasional life and lifestyle expenses. After you've become financially free, all your living and lifestyle costs will be met from your after-tax investment income.

Step 8: Financial freedom / retirement

Speaking of which... here's what retirement looks like under the path to prosperity.

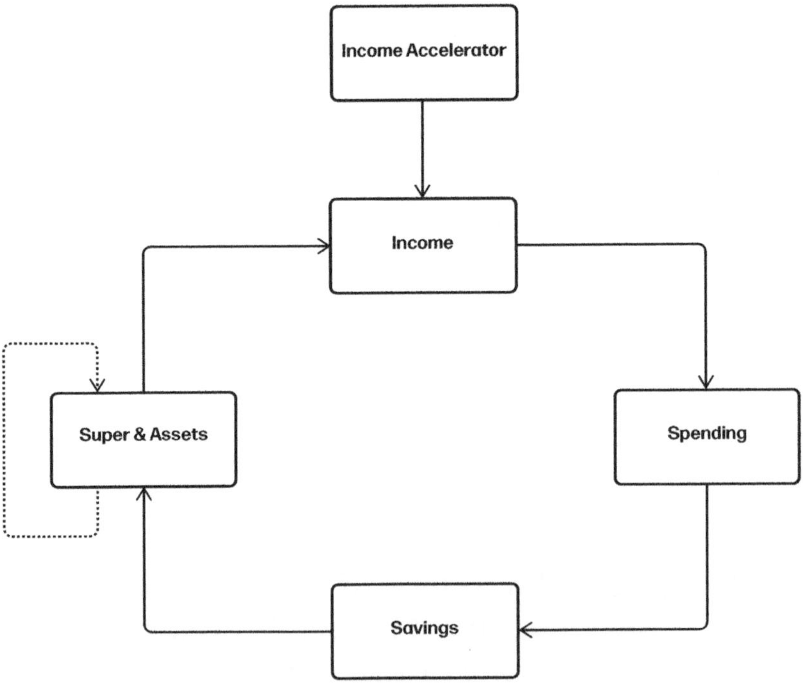

You can keep your income accelerator if it suits, but the goal is for your after-tax investment income to meet all your living and lifestyle spending needs. If there is a surplus left over, that will flow to savings, where it can be accumulated for reserves or deployed to buy more assets. The assets you own ought to appreciate in value, as represented by the dotted line, and continue to deliver recurrent after-tax income. The cycle begins anew each and every month for the rest of your life.

Reader challenge!

Have a go at explaining the two pathways to a fellow family member or friend based on your understanding of the diagrams overleaf.

Chapter highlights

- The path to prosperity is no barefoot stroll on the beach. The journey is strenuous. It requires planning and preparation and will require patience, skill and effort. Those who persevere are rewarded with a well-earned rest while they enjoy the view from the top of their wealth-creation mountain.
- You can fast-track your progress by adding an income accelerator. It might even take off and surpass the income you earn from your day job.
- Some reserves are prudent. Too many reserves act as a drag on your ability to attract wealth since they represent seed in the storehouse that would be better planted in the field.
- Beware of schemes that recommend leveraging your investment income to pay for living and lifestyle costs. They're a house of cards that could topple over and make a mess of your financial future.
- Are your investments sticks or boomerangs?
- You are financially free when your recurrent investment income (sometimes called your passive income) equals or exceeds your living expenses.

Pathway to Poverty

Pre-Retirement

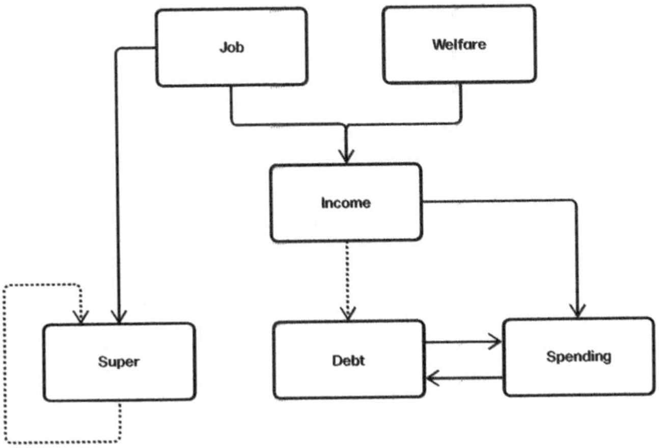

Post-Retirement

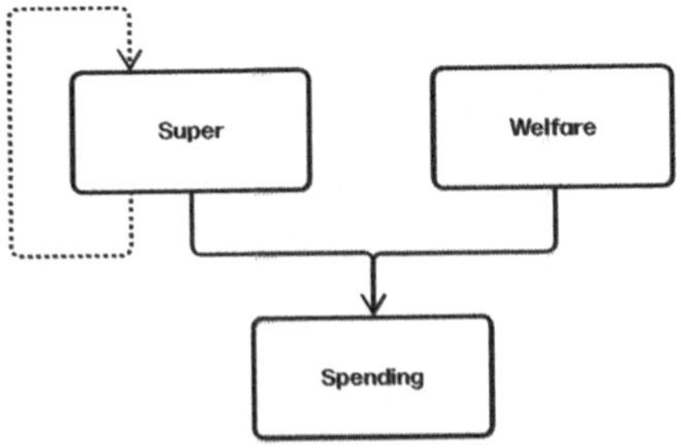

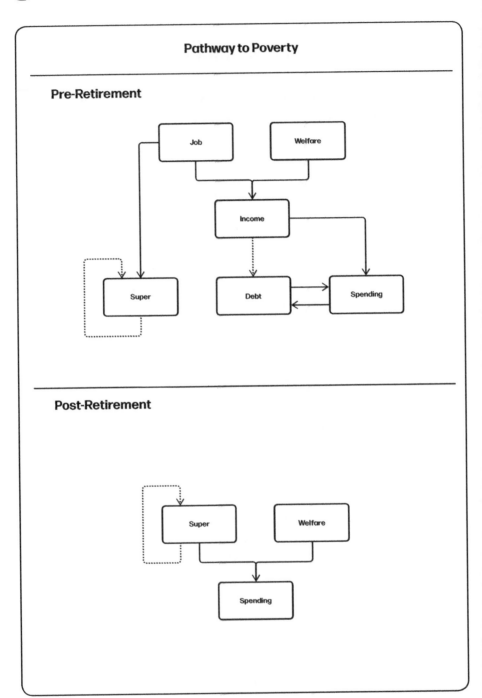

Pathway to Prosperity

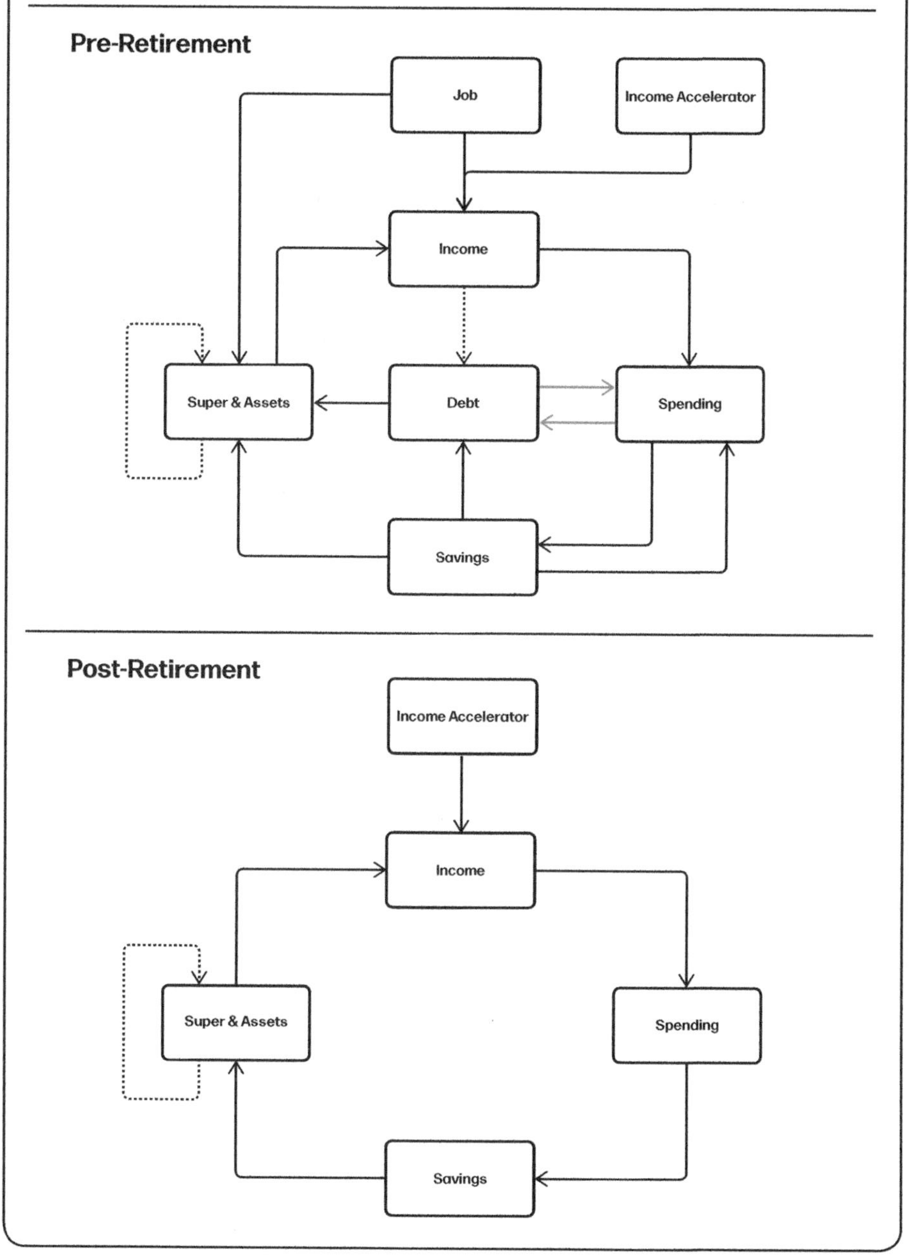

CHAPTER TWENTY-THREE

THE RECIPE FOR GETTING RICH

The antidote to risk is skill.

If there was a recipe you could follow that resulted in you becoming rich, would you want to know it?

It turns out there is a recipe, and even more amazingly, it's actually taught in high school. No, not in home economics, but rather in maths. You could easily have missed it because it was hidden among the 'time value of money formula calculations', and it wouldn't have been taught from the perspective of common-sense wealth building.

Let's ditch the word 'formula'—it can be intimidating unless you love maths or science—and replace it with the word 'recipe'. Everyone loves cooking, or at least eating.

The three ingredients

There are only three ingredients in the recipe for getting rich: savings, return and time.

1. *Savings:* the surplus of your income over your expenses that you use to buy investments. We've been over how this works in chapters 16, 17 and 18.
2. *Return:* also known as profit. This is the income and capital appreciation your investment provides.
3. *Time:* the amount of time you have to invest.

The simple recipe

Right then, here's how the three components combine into what I call 'the recipe for getting rich':

$$\text{Wealth} = \text{Savings} \times (1 + \text{Return})^{\text{Time}}$$

In words, here's how the recipe reads: the wealth you accumulate will be the outcome of your savings, multiplied by your return to the power of time.

The wealth you accumulate will be the outcome of your savings, multiplied by your return to the power of time.

The recipe's method is simple:

- The more savings, the more money you have to invest and the more wealth you'll accumulate.
- The higher the return, the more wealth you'll accumulate.
- The longer your investing time horizon, the more wealth you'll accumulate.

The relationship between savings, return and time

All three components are needed: if you didn't have any savings, you wouldn't have anything to invest with, and if you had no return or time, your savings would not multiply. That said, if you had to pick a 'super power', which would you choose: savings, return or time?

Before you answer, take a look at the following table. Three investors are listed: Alex, Allan and Ally. Each has an advantage over the others in that they have a different double of one of the ingredients:

- *Alex:* double the savings, but average return and average time
- *Allan:* double the return, but average savings and average time
- *Ally:* double the time, but average savings and average return.

Investor	Saving	Return	Time
Alex	$30,000	8%	10 years
Allan	$15,000	16%	10 years
Ally	$15,000	8%	20 years

Who do you think will accumulate the most wealth?

Here's the outcome:

Investor	Recipe	Result
Alex	$\$30,000 \times (1.08)^{10}$	$64,768
Allan	$\$15,000 \times (1.16)^{10}$	$66,172
Ally	$\$15,000 \times (1.08)^{20}$	$69,914

Ally is the winner, and by winning she demonstrates a very important principle: that the power of time trumps savings and return.

The power of time trumps savings and return.

The advanced recipe

The earlier recipe is fine if you deploy your savings once and reinvest the returns, as Allan did: invest $15 000 for 10 years and reinvest the 16 per cent per annum return. But what about when there's a series of recurring payments, like saving $5000 a year for 10 years? Is the simple recipe still suitable? Not quite. While the ingredients remain the same—savings, return and time—the method is a bit more complicated:

$$\text{Wealth} = \text{Savings}\left(\frac{(1+\text{Return})^{\text{Time}} - 1}{\text{Return}}\right)$$

The recipe works by multiplying the savings amount by an accumulation uplift, which is determined by the relationship between return and time. Let's see how it works by revisiting Alex, Allan and Ally and changing their situation so they all end up saving and deploying the same amount of money—$150 000—but at different savings rates, returns and time periods, as shown in the following table (i.e. Alex: $30 000 × 5 years, Allan $15 000 × 10 years, Ally $5000 × 30 years).

Investor	Annual saving	Return	Time
Alex	$30,000	8%	5 years
Allan	$15,000	16%	10 years
Ally	$5,000	8%	30 years

Who do you think would end up accumulating the most wealth now?

The following table reveals Ally is once again the winner, but now by an even bigger margin. 'But hang on,' you might say. 'What about inflation?'

Investor	Recipe	Result
Alex	$\$30,000 \times [(1.08)^{5} - 1) \div 0.08)]$	$175,998
Allan	$\$15,000 \times [(1.16)^{10} - 1) \div 0.16)]$	$319,822
Ally	$\$5,000 \times [(1.08)^{30} - 1) \div 0.08)]$	$566,419

Good question! Ally's longer time period means she will be more exposed to the effects of inflation, meaning her future money buys less. However, adjusting the returns for inflation at an average of 2 per cent per annum, Ally's wealth-building outcome is still significantly superior:

Investor	Result after inflation @ 2 per cent
Alex	$159,407
Allan	$262,365
Ally	$312,702

In order to take full advantage of the power of compounding returns, you must reinvest them, not eat them. It might be tempting to consume some (or all) of your investing profits. Try to avoid doing that because spending will be a drain on your wealth accumulation potential and your money will go to work for someone else, so you'll lose the compounding power of that capital.

• • •

The numbers aren't really important. They only serve to illustrate the key essential truth that time is the most powerful wealth-accumulation ingredient, and the less of it you have, the higher the savings and the greater the return needed to compensate.

Online calculators

If you'd like to play around with various recipe scenarios, then you'll find the online calculators at **www.moneymagnet.au** helpful.

More and less

The proportion of the three ingredients can be modified so less of one can be compensated by more of another. For example, if you had a low ability to save, you could offset that shortage by getting a higher return and/or investing for a longer period.

The proportion of the three ingredients can be modified so less of one can be compensated by more of another.

Now for some fun. Looking back at the results of the table on page 290, how much would Alex's savings need to be, or Allan's annual return need to be, in order to accumulate the same wealth as Ally? We can find out using the advanced recipe:

Investor	Ingredients needed to accumulate $566 419		
	Annual saving	Return	Time
Alex	$30,000 **$106,610**	8%	5 years
Allan	$15,000	16% **32%**	10 years
Ally	$5,000	8%	30 years

Wow! Alex would need to more than triple his savings, and Allan double his return, to arrive at the same outcome as 'slow and steady Ally'.

Most people have a reasonably fixed ability to save, and a reasonably fixed investing timeframe, and if so, the only ingredient they can vary is return. The following table provides a guide for what rate of return is needed for a given amount of savings and time.

Most people have a reasonably fixed ability to save, and a reasonably fixed investing timeframe, and if so, the only ingredient they can vary is return.

Time	Savings		
	A lot	Average	A little
A lot	Low	Low-medium	Low-medium
Average	Low-medium	Medium	Medium-high
A little	High	High	Very high

For instance, if you had an average amount of savings and an average amount of time, you would need to target a medium return on your investment. Alternatively, if you had a little amount of time, and a little ability to save, you would need to target a very high rate of return to compensate. Finally, a longer investing period compensates for less savings and lower returns, so if you had a lot of time but only a little savings, then you would only need a low-to-medium return.

A longer investing period compensates for less savings and lower returns.

How high is high, and how low is low? It's subjective: how much is a lot, and how much is a little? The takeaway is not a number, but rather an understanding of the compensatory relationship between time, savings and return.

Risk, return and skill

A universally accepted investing principle is, the higher an investment's risk, the higher its return must be to compensate for it.

The higher an investment's risk, the higher its return must be to compensate for it.

Investing risk is not something to be feared—something you run away from lest it bite you. Nor should it be favoured—something you embrace to add a little spice to life. Risk needs to be properly named, numbered and numbed. Unfortunately, explaining how I recommend doing this is beyond the scope of this book, except to share this Steveism: that the antidote to risk is skill.

Your best-returning investment opportunities will be where your financial IQ and financial EQ provide a risk-to-return competitive advantage.

For example, say a $5 000 000 commercial property was for sale offering a stabilised return of 15 per cent per annum. The only problem is that the building is presently vacant and so the in-place return is actually negative because there are ownership costs but no income. Furthermore, the seller has been trying to lease the building for two years with no luck.

Although the return is attractive, the high price, negative return and vacancy would be a risk many investors wouldn't want to tackle. However, if it were me, I'd be weighing up the merits of putting the property under contract with an appropriately worded due diligence clause that gave me 90 days to complete my pre-purchase review, which would include advertising for a tenant and showing the property. I'd then put my knowledge of finding tenants, and network of high-quality leasing agents, to work to solve the problem. If I was able to find a tenant, then the risk would have been tamed. I'd be purchasing a tenanted building at a vacant price, with the difference—probably hundreds of thousands of dollars—being my return. If not, the property wouldn't pass due diligence, I'd terminate the contract and my whole deposit would be refunded.

You know the saying: a fool and his money are soon parted. Being wise is the opposite of being foolish, so be sure to invest for knowledge before investing for return.

Efficient and inefficient markets

All investors would be wise to be aware of this investing mantra: expect the lowest returns from efficient assets in efficient markets, and the highest returns from inefficient assets in inefficient markets.

Expect the lowest returns from efficient assets in efficient markets, and the highest returns from inefficient assets in inefficient markets.

Understanding how financial markets operate can be confusing, so let's bring it back to basics: fruit and vegetables.

On one hand, you can buy your fruit and veg from large chain supermarkets such as Coles, Woolworths or Aldi. These vendors are very efficient and have highly effective supply and logistics arrangements that allow them to access product from local, national and international growers. There is extra convenience for shoppers as they can source other food and grocery items at the same time and complete the purchase in a single transaction.

On the other hand, you may decide to buy your fruit and veg from a local 'market': one or more independent vendors who source their produce from the wholesale fruit markets, usually earlier that morning. They may have less buying power, but as their operating overheads are lower, they can usually offer a cheaper price as well as fresher produce of what's in season since the lead time from grower to market to shop is shorter.

The principle is this: convenience comes at a cost. If you care to put in the extra time to shop in 'local' markets, then the range might be smaller but the pricing will usually be more competitive and the produce 'fresher', resulting in an upside to the downside of arguably less convenience.

Convenience comes at a cost.

Financial markets operate much the same way. Certain markets, like the stockmarket, are very efficient. Take the Australian Stock Exchange (ASX), for example. It's very cheap and easy to buy and sell listed shares, and there are strict rules about companies announcing information so everyone has access to the same knowledge to try and level the playing field. There is also a lot of data available on financial performance, past returns and so on.

Not all investment markets are as efficient. Take direct property, for instance. The costs to enter and exit are much higher, the time to sell will be longer, making the investment harder to convert back to cash (i.e. less liquid), and the disclosure requirements are much less robust than the ASX rules. That's why it is arguably easier for a skilled and astute investor to unearth price mismatch opportunities in inefficient markets where they can build wealth by purchasing at a discount, or manufacturing profit by value-adding.

The more efficient a market is, the lower the potential profits will be from transacting in it.

Here's a general rule: the more efficient a market is, the lower the potential profits will be from transacting in it. If that's the case, then why doesn't everyone invest in inefficient markets for higher returns? Because more time and skill is required to spot and evaluate opportunities, and many people are happy to sacrifice return for the sake of less effort and more convenience.

Is paying for convenience a bad thing? Not if the investor wouldn't otherwise have access to the investment opportunity (i.e. because they lack the time, skill or risk profile to purchase the asset directly). An ideal outcome would be if the cost of convenience was recouped by the extra return gained from the manager's skill and expertise.

Efficient and inefficient assets

As was the case with markets, assets can also be efficient and inefficient. I call efficient assets 'solutions', and inefficient assets 'problems'. From my experience, the most money can be made in the quickest time when you turn problems into solutions under a buy-solve-sell or a buy-solve-hold strategy. Your profit will be the excess of the perceived value you add over the actual cost you incur to fix or solve the problem.

The most money can be made in the quickest time when you purchase problems and solve them.

Once again, an inherent problem to overcome is that successfully buying and solving inefficiencies or problems requires a higher skill level and risk tolerance. Not every investor has the time, knowledge or risk appetite to 'shop' in that market and therefore many prefer to forego return for an 'easier' lower risk and low-aggravation asset.

Here's another rule to remember: it is almost impossible to achieve an inefficient return from an efficient investment. By its nature, an efficient asset in an efficient market must have an efficient price. Consider the following image. An asset's efficiency *at purchase* is being measured, with efficient assets (i.e. solutions) at the left of the horizontal line, and inefficient assets (i.e. problems) on the right.

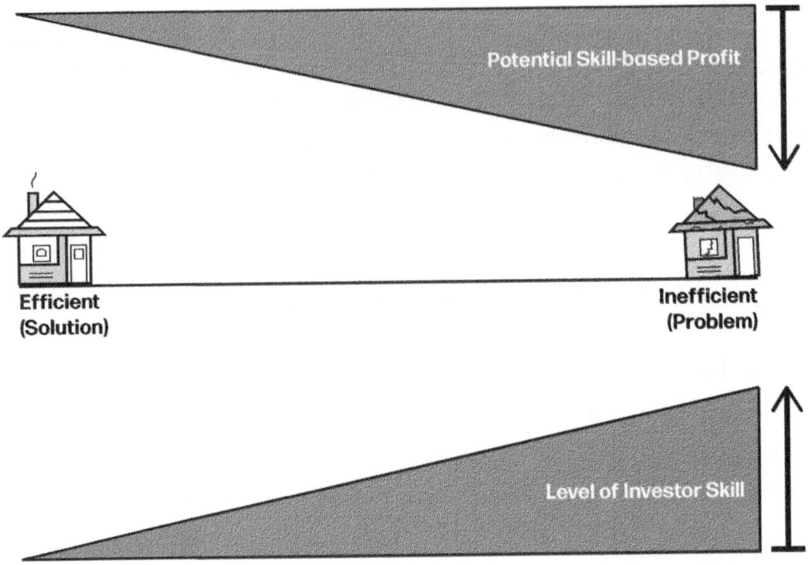

The potential profit an investor can make is being measured above the line, indicating that the more inefficient an asset is, the greater the potential profit that can be made by purchasing it and solving the problem. Below the line is the amount of skill required. More skill allows an investor to target a higher number of (or bigger) problems.

The image also explains that an investor with little skill will need to rely predominantly on what I call *generic* profits—that is, profits returned by the market as a whole rather than returns *manufactured by the investor*.

What do we learn? If you want to fast-track your wealth and achieve above 'market' returns then you'll need to learn how to 'manufacture' profit by leveraging your investing skill and looking to one or more of the following:

1. Exploit price-to-risk mismatches of efficient assets incorrectly classified as inefficient. For instance, a tricky problem for one investor could be an easy fix for another

2. Buy assets in inefficient markets, and sell them in efficient markets. For example, buying in doom-times and selling in boom-times

3. Value-add by converting inefficient assets into efficient assets. That is, buying problems and selling solutions.

If you're interested ...

At the time of writing, my investment team and I are scoping the possibility of starting a new managed investment fund. Our aim will be to open up opportunities not normally available to retail investors, while also leveraging our knowledge and skill to identify and solve inefficiencies to manufacture profits (i.e. the three points mentioned earlier). If you'd like to find out more, then follow the links at **www.moneymagnet.au**

The 'No-plan plan'

I wanted to conclude this part of the book by outlining what I call my 'No-plan plan'. This is a slow and steady, no-frills plan that takes into account everything I've outlined in Part 3, and most of all, the power of time.

The three rules of the No-plan plan are:

1. 10 per cent of your gross salary goes to compulsory superannuation

2. 10 per cent of your gross salary goes to non-super investments

3. 80 per cent is available to pay all other expenses and endeavours, including giving, income tax and living costs. Any surplus can be saved, or even used to make home-loan repayments.

GDR 70-20-10

The No-plan plan also aligns with the GDR 70–20–10 allowance model discussed in chapter 17. See the diagram on page 206. The compulsory superannuation is part of the Deductions, and the 10 per cent for non-super investments would be sourced from Savings.

Like any model, the No-plan plan is only as good as the assumptions behind it, which are:

No-plan plan assumptions	
Age and salary	**Returns and inflation**
• You start full-time work at age 25. • You finish working at age 65. • Your starting salary is $50 000. • Your salary increases by 2% p/a.	• The annual after-tax return on your superannuation is 9%, and 8% on non-superannuation investments. • All returns are re-invested. • Inflation averages 3% p/a.

Here's the outcome after each five-year period:

Year & age		Spending	Investments			
			Super	Non-super	Total	Inflation adjusted
5	30	$212,944	$31,674	$28,963	$60,637	$52,306
10	35	$447,940	$83,002	$73,074	$156,076	$116,135
15	40	$707,393	$165,544	$139,532	$305,076	$195,817
20	45	$993,849	$296,482	$238,331	$534,813	$296,113
25	50	$1,310,122	$502,295	$383,820	$886,115	$423,213
30	55	$1,659,313	$823,765	$596,589	$1,420,354	$585,167
35	60	$2,044,849	$1,323,687	$906,159	$2,229,846	$792,450
40	65	$2,470,516	$2,098,730	$1,354,861	$3,453,591	$1,058,722

Looking back over the numbers in the table, do you see how the power of savings, return and time compounds your 20 per cent into $3 453 591? That's more than $1 000 000 higher than the 80 per cent you've spent over the same time.

For those who like diagrams, here's what the No-plan plan looks like.

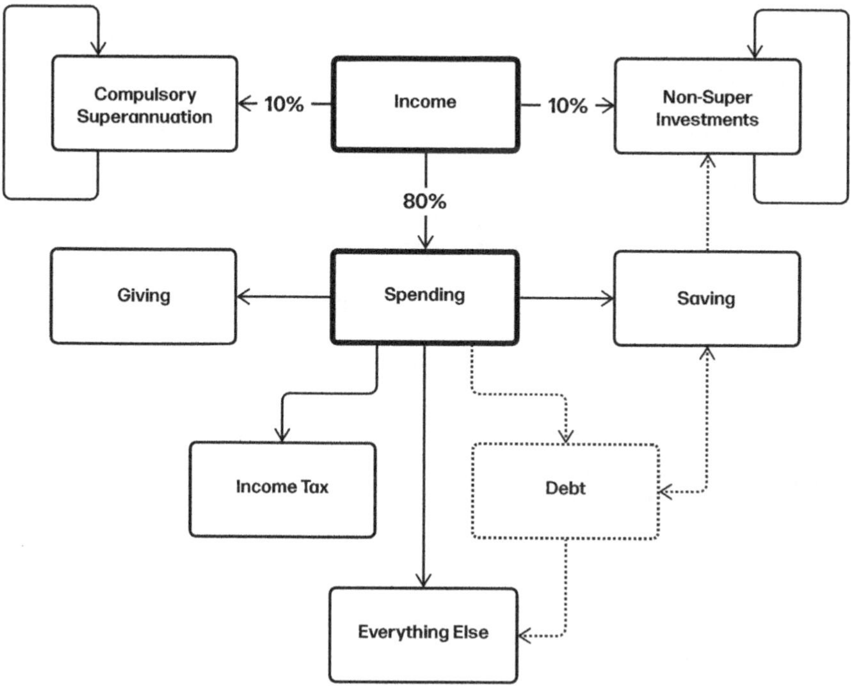

Once you retire, and assuming your capital earns an annual 8 per cent income return, your investments will deliver an annual self-funded pension of $276 287 (or inflation adjusted, $84 698) for the rest of your life, plus if you've managed your money well, you'll own your home outright too.

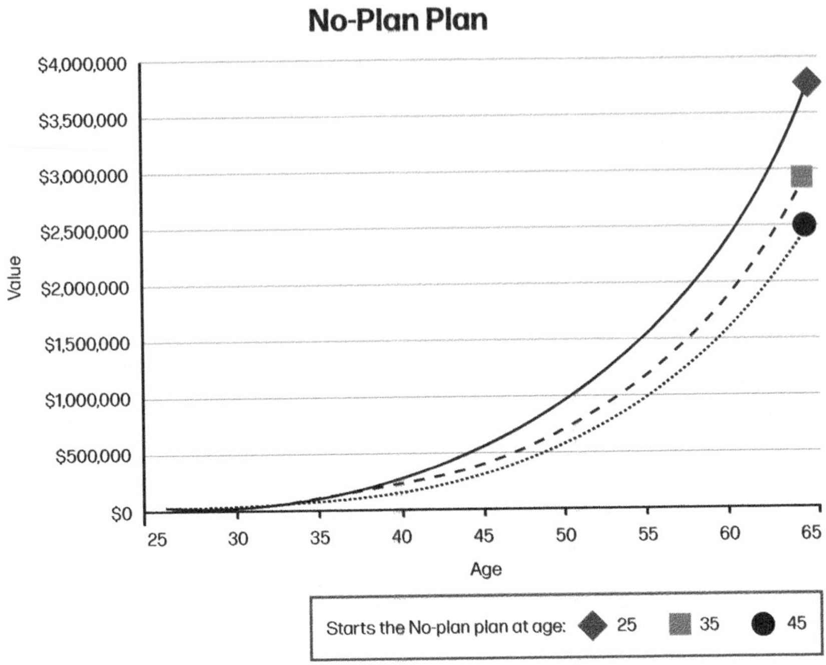

The impact of lost time

Take a look at the above graph. You'll notice three lines:

- The top line measures the wealth of someone who starts the No-plan plan at 25.
- The middle line measures the wealth of someone who starts the No-plan plan at 35. They still have compulsory superannuation accruing from age 25.
- The bottom line measures the wealth of someone who starts the No-plan plan at 45. They still have compulsory superannuation accruing from age 25.

Looking at the top line, do you notice how it is flattish at the start, before gently curving through to about age 50, then sharply bending thereafter? This illustrates two truths about the benefit of compounding returns:

1. The longer the time period, the better the results
2. The greatest gain is in the final third of the compounding period.

The longer you work compounding, the better compounding will work.

Looking at the top line in the graph again, you'll see that more wealth is made in the last 10 years than the previous 25.

The longer you work compounding, the better compounding will work.

The effect of a delay in starting to set aside extra money to invest is pushing out the beginning of the sharper bending curve to a later age.

The following table reveals that delaying starting to make your 10 per cent non-superannuation investment by 10 years would result in \$748 615 less wealth at age 65. Delaying 20 years releases an extra \$123 814 in spending money, but comes at the cost of nearly 10 times that amount in less retirement capital, with the flow-on effect of less retirement income.

Starting age	Wealth accumulated	Cost of delay	Extra spending
25	$3,763,623	N/A	N/A
35	$3,015,008	$805,309	$55,742
45	$2,740,581	$1,261,259	$123,814

Late to the party

Hang on a moment... what if you're only coming across this knowledge for the first time and you're already past your mid-20s? I think you know what I'll say... the less time you have to take advantage of compounding, the greater your savings and the higher the investment return you'll need to compensate for the lack of time.

Too little too late?

Wish you'd known about this when you were younger? If I had a dollar for every time someone said to me, 'I wish I knew what you're teaching 10 or 20 years ago', then I'd never have to worry about finding money for parking again.

If you're feeling like you might have left your run a bit late, then understand this: yesterday is a memory and tomorrow is a promise; you can only act now. Yes, delaying may have compromised how much wealth you could possibly have accumulated had you started earlier, but what you lack in time you can make up for with tenacity and wisdom. Just know this: every moment you keep procrastinating will result in less benefit you can draw from compounding, and less wealth you'll accumulate. Don't worry about missing out on what's gone. Worry about maximising what's left.

Chapter highlights

- Accumulating wealth shouldn't be a mystery but rather a mathematical fact.
- The three ingredients in the recipe for riches are savings, return and time. The most important ingredient to maximise is time.
- Foolish investors eat their profits. Wise investors re-invest them.
- You can compensate for less time with more savings and a higher investment return.
- Risk and return are related. Higher return = higher risk.
- The antidote to risk is skill. The more investing skill you have, the more safely you'll be able to tolerate high-risk investments.
- Inefficiencies rarely exist in efficient markets or efficient assets. If you want to manufacture your profit, buy problems and sell solutions.
- Procrastination leads to lost opportunity as there is less time to take advantage of the power of compounding returns.
- Don't worry about how much time has gone. Worry about maximising the wealth-building time you have left.
- All donations to my spare change for parking are gratefully received.

PART THREE SUMMARY

- Say 'Y–E=S' to accumulate wealth.
- Investing out of a financial crisis is extremely difficult because even if you make a profit, persistently living beyond your means will return you to a financially desperate situation.
- Adding an income accelerator that provides a money multiple of greater than one is a smarter option than working harder in a job where you swap time for money.
- When you get into debt, you reach into tomorrow, borrow money you have not yet earned and spend it today. Getting into debt means you need your job more, which makes it the antithesis of financial freedom.
- Debt is always dangerous and never good. Use it carefully, and only when it adds more wealth than it takes.
- Buying a home at the cost of saving and investing leads to an asset-rich, income-poor outcome later in life, and a reliance on welfare to keep food on the table. Those with enough financial IQ and financial EQ can walk a different path and arrive at a different destination: a family home and financial freedom.

- There's a recipe for getting rich. If you follow it and give the ingredients enough time to properly 'cook', you'll win the wealth game even if you go at a slow and steady pace.
- Accessing inefficient investments with higher returns will accelerate the rate at which you build wealth. However, higher returns attract higher risk. Skill up before investing in assets by acquiring the knowledge to manage and mitigate dangers.
- Time is your friend, until it is your enemy. Make the most of what you have left in order to benefit as much as possible from the power of compounding returns.

PART FOUR
MAKING YOUR MONEY COUNT

Imagine there's a 'coin' that represents how you make your money count.

On one side of that coin is your head. It symbolises the wealth you attract and accumulate to survive financially. On the other side of the coin is your heart, symbolising the way you use and utilise your wealth to give your life significance or meaning.

It's now time to stop talking about 'heads'—how to make your money count (i.e. multiply) for personal *survival* purposes—and start talking about 'hearts'—how to make your money count (i.e. matter) for personal *significance* purposes.

If you can master both, then it doesn't matter which side the coin lands on—you'll be a winner.

CHAPTER TWENTY-FOUR

DEFINING SIGNIFICANCE

Use your head to count money, and your heart to make money count.

Imagine that you're standing at the bottom of a mountain. You look up and see a peak in front of you. It's a long hike ahead, and after a considerable and steady effort, you reach the summit. Wiping the sweat from your brow you're surprised to see a second and even higher mountain before you. You couldn't see that second peak when you set off; the first mountain obscured it. If the view from the first peak is spectacular, imagine what the view from the second peak must be like. You have a decision to make: do you rest and proceed higher, or do you call it quits here?

This is what survival and significance look like. The first 'hike' is up the survival mountain — accumulating enough wealth to not have to worry about money. Some people spend their whole life hiking this mountain and never make it to the top. The second 'hike' is up the significance mountain — managing and using your money in a way to add meaning to your life.

Achieving financial freedom

My quest for financial freedom was seeded from purely selfish motives. I didn't want to have to work until my mid 60s in a job I didn't like just to pay the bills, only to end up without enough money to live the life I desired when I finally retired.

The motivation for change was strong. After five years of hard work, and using the power of positive cashflow property, my wife and I had accumulated enough investment income to pay our living costs. We had achieved financial freedom.

I don't remember the day it happened. There was no celebratory cake. No streamers fell from the sky. No songs were sung. What I do remember, or perhaps remember by reflecting upon it later on, is that achieving financial freedom didn't dramatically increase my happiness. If anything, the opposite was true. I had been so consumed with getting to the goal that, upon achieving it, I kind of felt, 'oh, is that it, is it?' Actually, it was a bit lonely. All my friends still had to work so I had time, but no-one to play with. Furthermore, there is only so much time Julie wanted me hanging around the house before she said, usually but not always nicely, 'Don't you have somewhere else to be?'

I've done a lot of soul-searching on this topic and here's what I've come up with. My quest for survival was also my source of significance. This was a very inward, somewhat selfish, perspective and one that defined who I was by what I did and had. It was ego enriching, but not soul nourishing. A new adventure beckoned: to use my newly freed-up time, and newly made money, to add meaning to my life.

Revisiting faith

Growing up, I used to get dragged off to church every Sunday morning. Oh Lord, how I hated it. It was so boring. Somehow Dad got off the hook and didn't have to go, and Mum would spend forever afterwards chatting with people. On about my 13th birthday, Mum said 'Okay Steve, you're old enough to make up your own mind now about whether or not you keep coming to church'. Amen to that! I promptly declared to never go again, save for perhaps special occasions as and when warranted.

Fast forward 20 or so years. Allan, a friend of a friend, was doing some graphic design work for me, turning my stick drawings into appealing illustrations. Allan knew I'd been very financially successful from investing in real estate, and one afternoon asked me an intriguing question: 'Steve, does all that wealth make you happy?'

'Surprisingly, not as much as I thought it would,' I replied.

It turns out that Allan used to be a pastor, and he mused, 'Maybe there's an answer in the Bible'.

'Pfffft,' I said. 'Unlikely.'

'I don't know,' Allan said. 'The Bible contains stories that span thousands of years, including how people were slaves to, and masters of, money. There might be something in there that you'll find relevant.'

'Really?' I silently wondered. My sketchy recollections of Sunday School Bible stories were more about fish (including some poor guy being eaten by one, and something about loaves and fishes) than finances.

'I've tried reading the Bible once or twice,' I said. 'Never got too far.'

'That's because, Steve,' Allan replied, 'you don't read the Bible like a novel—you study and discuss it. In fact, if you're interested, I'd be happy to study the Bible with you for a while'.

I was hooked.

The rollercoaster ride

What happened next has been a personal rollercoaster ride that could easily fill a book, or two. It turns out there is a lot in the Bible about money. It was even the topic that Jesus spoke most about.

Studying the Bible is best described as a journey, not a destination. Like an onion, it has layers, and it's your choice how deep you go. One of the constant themes is a warning about keeping a 'right attitude' about money. Nowhere does it say that being wealthy is bad, but in plenty of places it warns about the perils of trusting or falling in love with money, and money becoming your master, rather than you mastering it.

Jesus talked about storing up treasure in heaven that won't be destroyed, rather than on earth where thieves can steal it. The accountant in me imagines two bank accounts: one for 'Earthly Treasure', the other for 'Heavenly Treasure'. I imagine looking at the balances in both to see which is bigger, and as I do I hear Jesus' words: 'Where your treasure is, there your heart will be also'[21].

I prefer to keep my giving and generosity a matter between me and God. That said, there are two stories I am happy to share here for context, and two more in the chapters to come.

The first is the year I boasted to God that I would do my best to out-give his expectations by donating what I thought was an eye-watering sum of money. That same year I received an unexpected payment that was about 10 times the amount I gave away. I can just imagine God shaking his head. 'No, Steve. You can't out-give me.'

The second was a monetary gift that Julie and I made in an unusual circumstance. My family had the wonderful opportunity to live in the United States for a year from mid 2016 until mid 2017. While we were there, we went on a short vacation to Savannah, Georgia. We woke up one lazy Sunday morning and decided to do something very different: to visit

[21] Matthew 6:19

a predominantly African American church and experience their worship service. Yes, it was quite amazing—and long! It went for over three hours, and even had an intermission. But, oh, was it something to remember! The singing and the preaching were filled with love and heartfelt.

During the service, the pastor provided an update on a fundraising effort to raise $5000 to purchase a minibus that could be used to pick up kids and families who didn't have their own transport and bring them to church, and to be used during the week to transport older persons who couldn't drive to appointments. After the service, Julie and I talked about it, and we decided to give them all the money they needed. We wrote them a letter thanking them for their hospitality, and enclosed a cheque. Here's part of the message we received from the senior pastor:

> *My heart is overflowing with joy. I have been in ministry for over 25 years and cannot remember anyone being as generous as you and your family. Words cannot express our gratitude for the generous donation that you have given to our congregation.*

What a blessing it is to be a blessing! I'm not sharing these stories to impress you, but rather to impress upon you, that the significance you'll feel by investing your money in causes that matter will far exceed the happiness you glean from watching your money multiply.

The significance you'll feel by investing your money in causes that matter will far exceed the happiness you glean from watching your money multiply.

And here's the good news: you don't have to wait until after you've achieved survival to experience significance. You can top up your 'significance account' any time you choose, and when you do, the feeling that will fill your soul will be a portion of the love you gave others being reflected back upon you.

Chapter highlights

- You can make your money 'count' in the sense of multiplying it, and you can make your money 'count' in the sense of giving it a purposeful meaning.
- Don't put your money where your mouth is; put your money where your heart is, or where you want your heart to be.
- Be careful not to confuse survival with significance. One is more inward and has a somewhat selfish focus; the other is outward and selfless.
- How much treasure do you have in your survival account? How much in your significance account? What does that say about your priorities and where your heart is?
- The soul-enriching feeling you get from investing in significance is the love you show others reflected back upon you.

CHAPTER TWENTY-FIVE
THE THREE Cs OF SIGNIFICANCE

Don't be put off by what you can't do – be empowered by what you can.

With my quest for financial freedom complete, my fervour for real estate investing had dwindled in lockstep with my motivation to make more money for more money's sake. If I was going to continue 'paying the price' to accumulate more wealth—to sacrifice and delay gratification—I had to reignite my passion to find a new purpose.

It was around this time that my first book—*From 0 to 130 Properties in 3.5 Years*—was released, and it sold like hotcakes, resulting in significant royalties. Given my intention for writing the book was to share information rather than establish a new income stream, I approached my business partner, Dave Bradley, with the idea of doing something special with the royalty money.

In the course of buying loads of property, Dave and I completed heaps of property inspections. I remember one inspection we did together that had a profound impact upon us. The property up for sale was a rental. It was a mid-morning inspection, and as we walked through the front door we were confronted with an awful smell: one part dirty nappy, one part stale cigarette and one part vomit. The unemployed tenants were home. Dad was on the couch smoking, with a can of beer in hand. Mum was in the kitchen with bubs on her hip, cooking something. Another child was in a cot, screaming.

After completing the inspection, Dave and I looked at each other, not sure what to make of what we'd just seen. A few minutes passed before Dave remarked, 'There, but for the grace of God, go we'.

The McKnight Family Foundation

As we talked over what to do with the royalty money, Dave and I remembered that property inspection, and others similar to it. We wondered whether there was something we could do for families, and in particular children, who were experiencing financial hardship. There seemed something poetic and win-win about writing a book on the topic of financial empowerment, to earn royalties that could be used to empower people to overcome financial hardship.

So it was that the Bradley McKnight Foundation, later renamed the McKnight Family Foundation after Dave and I parted ways, was formed. Into it has been funnelled every last cent of all the royalties I've ever received. To date 'the Foundation', as I call it, has distributed more than $1.5 million to a wide variety of charities that help disadvantaged children and families. This really is one of those 'loaves and fishes' stories, where the fragments of my skills have been multiplied into something that has helped 'feed' a lot of people. The stories of the lives it has changed are beyond inspiring.

Once again, I don't share this story to win your favour or high opinion, but to demonstrate that when the three Cs of significance — care, cause and context — come together, the significance you feel by the blessing reflected back upon you is heart-warming and soul-nourishing.

Over the years, people have asked me from time to time how they can add significance to their wealth and meaning to their life. That's when I tell them about the three Cs of significance.

Care

I believe everyone has at least one care etched on their hearts at birth, or engraved on their hearts from life experience. You'll be able to identify what that care is if you shut out the 'busy-ness' of life and listen to the quiet voice of your soul, or engage your self-awareness by looking for issues that trigger an above-average or disproportionate emotional response.

You'll be able to identify what that care is if you shut out the 'busy-ness' of life and listen to the quiet voice of your soul.

Possibilities include social justice issues, animal welfare, the environment, politics, gender and social equality, faith, health, nutrition, sport… the list is just about endless. Furthermore, there are niches within niches. For instance, animal welfare might be your thing, and within that, you might be particularly concerned with the wellbeing of koalas, and more specifically again, orphaned koalas in south-east Queensland.

The 'thing' you care about may be a burning passion, or just a glowing ember. It may also change over time. For the moment, all that's important is that you identify something you care about. Does something come to mind?

Cause

Have you heard the story of the little girl walking along the beach tossing washed-up starfish back into the ocean? An old man walks past and asks, 'Why bother? Look at the thousands of starfish washed up. What difference will it make?' Picking up another starfish and tossing it back into the water, she replies, 'It made a difference to that one'.

The secret is to stop thinking 'me', and start thinking 'we'. Sometimes the things we care about seem too big, complex or challenging to do anything meaningful about, or our resources are insignificant compared to the scale of the problem. Being overwhelmed, the temptation is to feel defeated, conclude 'why bother', and use your time and energy to solve survival problems closer to home.

The secret is to stop thinking 'me', and start thinking 'we'.

If you're in this boat, then, as demonstrated by the young girl on the beach, don't be put off by what you can't do—be empowered by what you can. Many people giving small amounts is just as effective as a few people giving large amounts.

It's very unlikely you'll be the only person in the world who cares about the issue on your heart, and I'd be quite surprised if there wasn't an already established 'cause' you could partner with to be the change you hope to see.

Alternatively, you could pioneer a cause and become a conduit for others who want to partner with you. That's exactly what I'm doing with my efforts to re-plant a new permanent native forest on land that was once cleared and is now a weed-infested mess. More on that in the next chapter.

Time or money?

I'm sometimes asked whether it is better to give time or money. What I'd say is this: you can only give from what you have. If you have money, give money. If you have time (including expertise), give time. If you have both, give both.

What I do know is this: there's usually a lack of 'resourcers' over 'resources'; that is, people who can provide the financial resources to pay for the labour and material needed to resource the care. For instance, one cause I am supporting at the moment is promising groundbreaking medical research that if successful will save thousands and thousands of people from needing surgery. The people pursuing the cause don't need my time; they need me to use my time to make money, and to use my money to pay for the medical trial they need. Generous people feed their own needs by feeding the needs of others. Who are you feeding?

Generous people feed their own needs by feeding the needs of others.

Frequent or infrequent?

Recently, friends asked my advice about how they should structure their giving. They had made a substantial capital gain on an investment property, and wanted to generously donate $400 000 of their profit to causes that furthered things they cared about.

'From my experience,' I said, 'it's better to give less, more often, than more, less often'.

It's better to give less, more often, than more, less often.

What this means is that instead of giving large sums once, offer smaller sums over time. That is, most charitable organisations I know would rather have guaranteed financial supply over several years, rather than unreliable and infrequent one-off donations because they can then create and run programs they know they'll be able to resource and fund through to completion.

Returning to my friends and the large amount of money they had set aside, here's what I recommended:

1. Identify the things you care about.
2. Identify how many years you want to support those causes (x).
3. Identify how many charities or organisations you want to support (y).
4. [Sum available ÷ x ÷ y] is the annual amount you have available to give each charity, assuming you want to give an equal amount to each. For instance, if the time period was five years, and there were four charities, then each charity would receive $400 000 ÷ 5 ÷ 4 = $20 000 per annum for five years.
5. Ask each charity to provide you with a proposal for how they would use the money to specifically address the matters you care about.

One of my philanthropic rules is embodied by the words of Jesus, as recorded in Luke 12:48: 'to whom much is given, much will be required'. That is, as I'm accountable for the resourcing I'm given and giving, I expect others to be accountable for the resources they receive.

Capital and income

Finally, rather than giving capital, I much prefer to give from the recurrent income that invested capital generates. Giving capital is something you do once. Investing the capital and giving the income is something you can do forever.

Giving capital is something you do once. Investing the capital and giving the income is something you can do forever.

For instance, although my friends didn't want to do this given their age, they could have invested the $400 000, and assuming an after-tax return of 8 per cent per annum, donated $32 000 each year into perpetuity. After 12.5 years of giving, the total amount is the same, except the capital is preserved and can continue to generate income and support worthy causes forever—a magic giving pudding that never runs out!

Context

The cares you advance based on the causes you support will provide a context for your money that transcends dollars and cents. Your wealth gains meaning based on the means it provides for the causes you care about. Your life will count because your money counts, and the significance you generate will make you feel significant.

Chapter highlights

- Make your money count by giving it a significant purpose.
- The three Cs of significance are care, cause and context. Identifying a care and resourcing a cause that supports it will add a context to your money that transcends dollars and cents.
- If you're vocal about something, then put your money where your heart is. Be the change you want to see by supporting causes that do good work in fields you care about.
- You may not feel like you have much to contribute, but many people giving a little is just as effective as a few people giving a lot.
- From my experience, it's better to give less, more often, than more, less often. Aligned with that is my mantra of giving repeatedly from recurrent income, rather than once from capital.

CHAPTER TWENTY-SIX
LEAVING A LEGACY

Live according to how you want to be remembered.

How do you want to be remembered after you're gone?

If you don't care, then you can happily hike the survival mountain all the days of your life, and when you're gone, you'll be remembered for how well you survived.

If you do care, or want to care, then your life becomes what you do between two significant book-ends: vision for what you want to achieve, and legacy for what you have achieved.

Alfred Nobel

No doubt you've heard about the Nobel Peace Prize. But do you know the story of Alfred Nobel: the man behind the medal?

Alfred Bernhard Nobel was born in 1833. He died aged 63, and lived an extraordinary life.

Clearly a genius, Nobel was fluent in six languages and became an expert chemist, engineer and industrialist. He invented dynamite in 1867, gelignite in 1875 and Ballistite—a precursor to rocket propellant—in 1887.

Nobel was a controversial figure, and while his inventions improved the industrialised world, he was not universally loved. His work improving military explosives resulted in him being accused of high treason in France, causing him to move to Italy.

Upon his death, Nobel bequeathed 94 per cent of his estate—31 225 000 Swedish kondor (nearly US$200 million in today's money)—to be converted into a fund and invested in safe securities, with the income from those investments 'distributed annually in the form of prizes to those who during the preceding year have conferred the greatest benefit to humankind'.

(Notice how Nobel structured his giving: preserve the capital, donate the income?)

Why did Nobel perform such a generous act? No-one knows for sure, but one theory is that he was appalled at the thought of being remembered as 'the merchant of death' who 'became rich by finding ways to kill more people faster than ever before'—words used in an erroneous obituary published in a French newspaper that mistook his brother's death for his own (Magazine & Schultz, 2013).

Whether or not that was the precise trigger for making the bequest, what isn't in dispute is that Nobel was given the chance to reflect upon how he wanted to be remembered. Today, he is revered for his substantial and ongoing contribution to the promotion of peace—a legacy of significance funded by his significant wealth.

A one-word obituary

Maybe you've never thought about it, but what legacy do you want to leave and be remembered for?

We all have the opportunity to learn from Alfred Nobel and ask, 'Am I living congruently with how I want to be remembered?' and if not, 'What do I need to change while there's still time?'

For instance, when people ask me, 'How do I learn about leaving a legacy?' I say, 'What's one word that describes how you'd like to be remembered?' It might be loving, or honest, or faithful, or sincere or any number of things. Then I ask, 'And is that word congruent with how you're living now?' I wonder, what's your word?

A legacy framework

If you're interested in being organised and purposeful in leaving a legacy, here's a framework you can use.

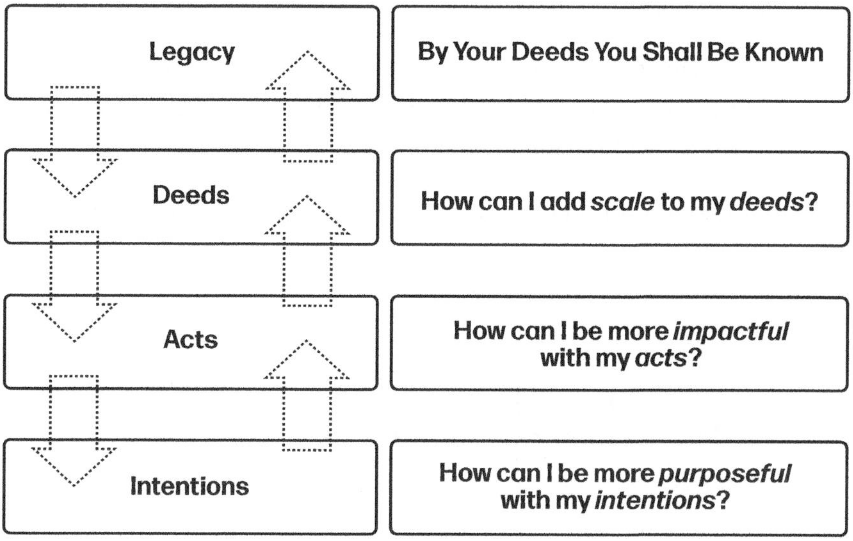

Working from the top down, your legacy:

- is the summary of your deeds, which
- is the summary of your acts, which
- is the summary of your intentions.

Do-Doing-Done

Back in my first mentoring program I came up with the following mantra for making continual progress:

Turn your dos into doings, and your doings into dones.

This later became known as Do-Doing-Done, and when mentorees became stuck it was usually because:

- they had nothing to do, either because they had ideas in their head but not on paper, or they hadn't actually cast a vision and so didn't have anything to purposefully achieve other than the pressing priorities of the day
- they weren't doing anything because their intentions weren't being acted upon, or else they had so much to do that they were lost in a sea of busy-ness
- not enough was getting done, or else everything had been done and there was nothing left to do.

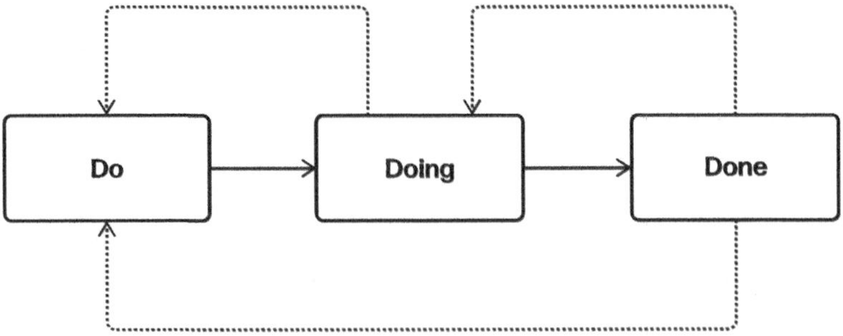

You can't be doing if you have nothing to do, and you can't be done if you're not doing.

Sometimes finished projects will need to be tweaked and sent back to 'doing', and sometimes doing tasks will need to be sent back to 'do'. When a task is done, it's back to the drawing board and planning the next task to 'do'. You can't be doing if you have nothing to do, and you can't be done if you're not doing.

Applying the Do-Doing-Done mantra and working from the bottom up, if you want to leave a lasting legacy:

1. *What do you need to DO?* Your intentions: get them out of your head and down 'on paper' so you can be purposeful about planning and implementing them.
2. *What are you DOING?* Your actions: the 'work in progress' to implement your intentions.
3. *What have you DONE?* Your deeds: the 'finished product'—an idea implemented to conclusion and fruition.

Doing is the difference between those who dream and those who get things done. How do you leave a lasting legacy? Get more things done, by doing more things, and by identifying more things to do.

Doing is the difference between those who dream and those who get things done.

Largesse

Your largesse is the way and extent to which you distribute money or gifts upon others. Largesse may be, but doesn't necessarily have to be, financial. To be significant, largesse must be predominantly selfless. Any contribution to humanity that results in a gift qualifies, which is why the largesse of the likes of Nelson Mandela, Mahatma Gandhi and Mother Teresa remain significant.

To be significant, largesse must be predominantly selfless.

Perhaps think of it this way: if your largesse was a stone dropped in a pond, how many ripples stem from it, with one ripple representing one generation impacted? What made Alfred Nobel's largesse so remarkable was:

- its size: it was considerable (a big stone)
- its structure: it was a gift that kept giving (new ripples are still being made)
- its significance: it was selfless for the good of others (there are many ripples).

A selfless act can't be called so if there are selfish ambitions behind it. Selfish largesse is rarely remembered beyond one generation, or is remembered for the wrong reasons, like the legacy of any historical tyrant you care to mention whose selfishness caused the death of countless innocent lives.

A selfless act can't be called so if there are selfish ambitions behind it.

Perhaps the ripples of the contribution you leave won't be as large or as wide as Alfred Nobel's. That doesn't make your effort any less important or worthy. As Isaac Newton—widely recognised as one of the most influential scientists of all time—wrote in 1675, 'If I have seen further it is by standing on the shoulders of giants'. Many small things done well are far better than a few great things done poorly.

Many small things done well are far better than a few great things done poorly.

Shady trees

A while ago I stumbled across this Greek proverb:

> *A society grows great*
> *when old men plant trees*
> *in whose shade they know*
> *they shall never sit.*

It's a beautiful vision: a gift for tomorrow seeded today. I wonder: what trees will you plant, and in years to come, who will be sitting in their shade?

Changing the world . . . one tree at a time

Well friend, the time has come to finish up, and I'd like to conclude with the story of a significant project I've started, and an invitation to partner with me and together leave an even bigger legacy.

I've taken that Greek proverb to heart and applied it figuratively, and literally. In 2018 I purchased approximately 600 hectares (1500 acres) of predominantly cleared land in north-east Victoria. It's steep territory and the soil nutrient load is low, so it cannot self-sustain cropping or grazing.

Etched on my heart is a vision to return the land back into a permanent multi-species native forest: a restored ecosystem providing a habitat—and hopefully the first of many such projects to restore what's been lost—under a program called 'TreeChange'.

If rehabilitating environments, restoring damaged ecosystems or renewing habitat for wildlife is something you care about, or if you'd just like to show your support and be a silent partner in this endeavour, then here's how you can leave a legacy. For a few dollars you can sponsor us to purchase and plant a tree (or trees) of your choosing, under whose shade another native plant, or native animal will one day sit. Or, for a few more dollars, you can sponsor the purchase and planting of lots of trees, and as they grow, cancel some or all of your annual carbon footprint. Alternatively, you can also lend your time and skills to the project — perhaps from afar, or even at one of our on-site working bees. The point is this: if you don't have your own legacy project on the go, you're welcome to 'graft' onto TreeChange and join with me, my family and others as we change the world one tree at a time.

TreeChange

To discover how you can get involved by sponsoring the purchase and planting of trees, cancelling your carbon, or volunteering please visit: **www.TreeChange.com**

Chapter highlights

- Your legacy determines how you'll be remembered. By what deeds will you be known?
- Do you want your legacy to be told from the perspective of how you used your money for survival, or how you used your money for significance?
- 'Doing' is the difference between those who dream and those who get things done.
- Doing many small things well is far better than doing a few great things poorly.
- What 'trees' have you planted, or will you plant, under whose shade others will sit?
- If you don't have your own specific legacy project in mind, then 'graft' onto someone else's. I'm sure your significant support will be very much appreciated.

PART FOUR
SUMMARY AND FINAL WORDS

How will you be recognised and remembered?

For some, the wealth they *accumulate* provides recognition — of their power and prowess. For others, the wealth they *distribute* provides recognition — of their largesse and legacy.

Both share in common that their net worth feeds their self-worth. The former are focused on counting their wealth for *survival*, and making their wealth count by multiplying it. The latter are focused on counting their wealth for *significance* and making their wealth count by using it altruistically.

By your deeds you shall be known. After you're gone, the way you counted your wealth and made your wealth count will be summarised by the legacy you leave. Be sure to live how you want to be remembered.

May God bless you, your family and your finances.

Yours in wealth,

Steve McKnight

READY TO DISCOVER NEW WAYS TO MAKE, MANAGE & MULTIPLY A FORTUNE THAT COUNTS?

Reading this book was just the beginning.

If you'd like to access more insights from Steve McKnight about how to make, manage and multiply your money so you can attract and keep a fortune that counts, visit **www.moneymagnet.au** and receive:

- Latest news and updates
- The official 'Money Magnet' podcast
- Calculators and online tools
- Video tutorials
- Bonus chapters
- Details of Steve's potential new managed fund
- And much, much more

REFERENCES

ACCC. (4 June 2021). Scammers capitalise on pandemic as Australians lose record $851 million to scams. Australian Competition and Consumer Commission. www.accc.gov.au/media-release/scammers-capitalise-on-pandemic-as-australians-lose-record-851-million-to-scams

Afterpay. (2022). How do payments work?–Afterpay. Afterpay. Accessed 29 August 2022. https://help.afterpay.com/hc/en-au/articles/360016052892-How-do-payments-work-

ASFA. (June 2022). ASFA Retirement Standard. www.superannuation.asn.au/resources/retirement-standard

ASIC. (2003). Financial literacy in schools. https://www.voced.edu.au/content/ngv:90079

Australian Bureau of Statistics. (30 October 2019). Life tables, 2018–2020. Table 6.1. www.abs.gov.au/statistics/people/population/life-tables/latest-release

Australian Government. (n.d.). Benefits of educational attainment income. Department of Education, and Department of Employment and Workplace Relations. www.dese.gov.au/zh-hant/node/8766

Australian Government Productivity Commission. (2018). Inquiry Report. *Superannuation: Assessing Efficiency and Competitiveness*

(p. 228). www.pc.gov.au/inquiries/completed/superannuation/assessment/report/superannuation-assessment.pdf

Canstar. (December 2021). Consumer Pulse Report 2021. www.canstar.com.au/consumer-pulse-report-2021

Department of Social Services. (n.d.). Age pension. Department of Social Services, Australian Government. www.dss.gov.au/seniors/benefits-payments/age-pension

Financial Rights Legal Centre. (30 November 2018). Buy now, pay later services. Financial Rights Legal Centre. https://financialrights.org.au/buy-now-pay-later-services-including-afterpay-humm-zip-klarna-openpay-2

Hayne, K. (2019). Final Report of the Royal Commission into Misconduct in the Banking, Superannuation and Financial Services Industry, Volume 1. https://treasury.gov.au/publication/p2019-fsrc-final-report

Kurt, D. (22 May 2022). Stock allocation rules. Investopedia. www.investopedia.com/articles/investing/062714/100-minus-your-age-outdated.asp

Loo, B. (21 July 2021). The complete guide to Flybuys rewards and earning points. Executive Traveller. www.executivetraveller.com/flybuys-rewards-guide

Macrotrends. (2021). Australia life expectancy 1950–2020. www.macrotrends.net/countries/AUS/australia/life-expectancy

Magazine, S. & Schultz, C. (9 November 2013). Blame sloppy journalism for the Nobel Prizes. *Smithsonian Magazine.* www.smithsonianmag.com/smart-news/blame-sloppy-journalism-for-the-nobel-prizes-1172688

Mandal, A. (2010). Cited in Wendy, S., Gu, Z., Meier, M. & Martin, N. Gambling addiction can be inherited equally by sons and daughters: Study. Archives of General Psychiatry. www.news-medical.net/news/20100610/Gambling-addiction-can-be-inherited-equally-by-sons-and-daughters-Study.aspx

Melbourne Institute: Applied Economic & Social Research. (2018). *The Household, Income and Labour Dynamics in Australia Survey: Selected Findings from Waves 1 to 16.* https://melbourneinstitute

.unimelb.edu.au/__data/assets/pdf_file/0009/2874177/HILDA-report_Low-Res_10.10.18.pdf

Melbourne Institute: Applied Economic & Social Research. (2021). *Poverty Lines: Australia.* https://melbourneinstitute.unimelb.edu.au/__data/assets/pdf_file/0007/3889393/Poverty-Lines-Australia-March-2021.pdf

NIH. (July 2010). Brain basics: Genes at work in the brain. National Institute of Neurological Disorders and Stroke. www.ninds.nih.gov/health-information/patient-caregiver-education/brain-basics-genes-work-brain

O'Neill, A. (10 March 2020). Life expectancy (from birth) in the United Kingdom from 1765 to 2020. Statista. www.statista.com/statistics/1040159/life-expectancy-united-kingdom-all-time

Olson, E. J. (2019). How many hours of sleep are enough for good health? Mayo Clinic. www.mayoclinic.org/healthy-lifestyle/adult-health/expert-answers/how-many-hours-of-sleep-are-enough/faq-20057898

Oz Lotteries. (8 June 2021). Exactly how much do Australians win on gambling? Oz Lotteries. www.ozlotteries.com/blog/how-much-do-australians-win-on-gambling

Parker, T. (29 October 2021). How much cash should I keep in the bank? Investopedia. www.investopedia.com/articles/personal-finance/040915/how-much-cash-should-i-keep-bank.asp

Parliament of Australia. (1 June 2010). Chronology of superannuation and retirement income in Australia. www.aph.gov.au/About_Parliament/Parliamentary_Departments/Parliamentary_Library/pubs/BN/0910/ChronSuperannuation

Price, M. (2008). 'Genes matter in addiction'. *American Psychological Association*, 39(6), 14.

Roy Morgan Research. (2003). ANZ survey of adult financial literacy in Australia: Final Report. www.anz.com.au/content/dam/anzcomau/documents/pdf/aboutus/2003-adult-financial-literacy-survey-full-results.pdf

Services Australia. (19 April 2022). How much you can get. www.servicesaustralia.gov.au/how-much-age-pension-you-can-get?context=22526

Shepard, D. & Huang, P. (2022, April 18). 42% of BNPL Users Have Made a Late Payment. *LendingTree*. https://www.lendingtree.com/personal/bnpl-survey/

Stanley, T. J. & Danko, W. D. (2010). *The millionaire next door: The surprising secrets of America's wealthy*. Taylor Trade Publishing.

Super Consumers Australia. (n.d.). *How much do you need to save for your retirement?*. Retrieved September 16, 2022. https://www.superconsumers.com.au/retirement-targets

The Treasury—Australian Government. (20 November 2020). Retirement income review—Final report. https://treasury.gov.au/publication/p2020-100554

US Bureau of Labor Statistics. (22 July 2021). Time spent in primary activities and percent of the civilian population engaging in each activity, averages per day by sex, 2019 annual averages. Table 1. www.bls.gov/news.release/atus.t01.htm

Vanguard. (2021). *The Power of Perspective*. https://intl.assets.vgdynamic.info/intl/australia/documents/resources/index_chart2021.pdf

Wallis, S. (29 June 2021). Australian household spending statistics. www.finder.com.au/australian-household-spending-statistics

Wilkins, R., Lab, I., Butterworth, P. & Vera-Toscano, E. (2019). *The Household, Income and Labour Dynamics in Australia (HILDA) Survey: Selected Findings from Waves 1 to 17*. Melbourne Institute. https://melbourneinstitute.unimelb.edu.au/HILDA-Statistical-Report-2019.pdf

APPENDIX 1

ESTIMATE OF ANNUAL SPENDING (SAVINGS APPROACH)

	Bank Balance Now $
−	Bank Balance Six Months Ago $
=	Movement in Bank Balance $
+/−	Adjustments for Non-Living Expenses $
=	Savings $

× 2

Annual Income Now		Annual Savings Now		Annual Spending Now
$	−	$	=	$

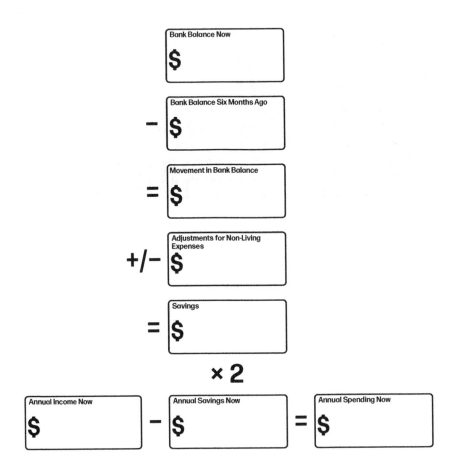

APPENDIX 2

ANSWERS TO FINANCIAL LITERACY QUESTIONS

Question 1
Suppose you put \$100 into a no-fee savings account with a guaranteed interest rate of 2 per cent per year. You don't make any further payments into this account and you don't withdraw any money. How much would be in the account at the end of the first year, once the interest payment is made?

Answer:
\$100 + (\$100 × 0.02) = \$102

Question 2
Imagine now that the interest rate on your savings account was 1 per cent per year and inflation was 2 per cent per year. After one year, would you be able to buy more than today, exactly the same as today or less than today with the money in this account?

Answer:
LESS. The price of goods are going up faster than the interest on your savings.

For instance, if you had \$100 in savings, then adding one year's interest would give a total of \$100 + (\$100 × 0.01) = \$101. However, with inflation at 2 per cent, the cost of something that was \$100 will be (\$100 × 0.02) = \$102 a year later. As \$101 is less than \$102, you would have less buying power.

Question 3
Do you think that the following statement is true or false? 'Buying shares in a single company usually provides a safer return than buying shares in a number of different companies.'

Answer:
FALSE. Owning one share is generally seen as riskier as you are not diversifying your investments, so if that single investment fails, then all your capital is at risk.

Question 4
Again, please tell me whether you think the following statement is true or false: 'An investment with a high return is likely to be high risk.'

Answer:
TRUE. An accepted investing principle is that risk and return are usually related.

Question 5*
Suppose that in four years' time your income has doubled, but the prices of all of the things you buy have also doubled. At that time, will you be able to buy more than today, exactly the same as today or less than today with your income?

* A slight modification was made to the wording of this question to remove the original time context, which is now redundant.

Answer:
SAME. Your income and prices are inflating at the same rate, so your buying power would be the same too.

APPENDIX 3
ANSWER TO SONJA'S SITUATION

Here is the solution to Sonja's situation as posed in Chapter 19.

Sonja

Sonja's payslip reveals she earns $42.23 in net pay per hour. She has $3000 in credit card debt, owes $12 000 on her car loan, has $1250 of buy-now-pay-later debt, and a home loan with $350 000 outstanding. She works a standard 8-hour day. How many work hours and work days does she owe? Assuming she works 260 days a year, how many years of future pay has Sonja already consumed?

Sonja owes $3000 + $12 000 + $1250 + $350 000 = $366 250

Non-Investment Debt		Hourly Net Pay		Hours Owed		Days Owed
$366,250	÷	$42.23	=	8,673 hrs	÷ 8 =	1,085 hrs

÷ 260 =

Years Owed
4.17 yrs

Note: hours and days have been rounded up to the nearest unit.

INDEX

Printed and bound by CPI Group (UK) Ltd, Croydon, CR0 4YY
05/10/2022
03152225-0001